FINANCIAL INSTITUTIONS AND SERVICES



# THE RECENT TREND OF HEDGE FUND STRATEGIES

# FINANCIAL INSTITUTIONS AND SERVICES

Additional books in this series can be found on Nova's website under the Series tab.

Additional E-books in this series can be found on Nova's website under the E-book tab.

FINANCIAL INSTITUTIONS AND SERVICES

# THE RECENT TREND OF HEDGE FUND STRATEGIES

YASUAKI WATANABE
EDITOR

Nova Science Publishers, Inc.
*New York*

For permission to use material from this book please contact us:
Telephone 631-231-7269; Fax 631-231-8175
Web Site: http://www.novapublishers.com



**LIBRARY OF CONGRESS CATALOGING-IN-PUBLICATION DATA**

The recent trend of hedge fund strategies /Editor, Yasuaki Watanabe.
ix, 207 p. : ill. ; 23 cm.
Includes bibliographical references and index.
ISBN 978-1-61668-338-2 (softcover)
1. Hedge funds. 2. Hedge funds --Management. I. Watanabe, Yasuaki.
(OCoLC)ocn587143154

2011282947

*Published by Nova Science Publishers, Inc. † New York*

# CONTENTS

# PREFACE

Hedge funds were used to “hedge” or protect against loss due to market uncertainties. The roots of hedge funds seem to be in the 1930s, but they formally broke ground with A.W. Jones in the late 1940s. The growth of hedge funds industry was slow, but steadily going well through the 1950s. The business of hedge funds began to bear fruits in the mid-1960s. Although they encountered some troubles with treacherous markets in the late 1960s and early 1970s, the business of hedge funds again enjoyed real growth and development in the 1980s. Recently, hedge funds encompass almost every financial product and tangible asset and follow both conservative and aggressive investing approaches.

This book presents the recent trend of hedge fund strategies from various points of views. We are now facing once a centennial event of financial crises around the glove. In a sense, the publication of this book will be timely. Because many hedge fund strategies were more or less involved in these financial crises. Thus, the authors introduce how each hedge fund performances were affected during past twelve months (January2008 – December 2008) on a monthly basis (Source: Hedge Fund Net.). For example, Market Neutral Equity: -3.37%, Macro: -1.75%, Multi-Strategy: -16.34%, Fixed Income (non-arbitrage): -13.60%, Long/Short Equity: -20.42%, Fund of Funds - Multi-Strategy: -20.24%, Convertible Arbitrage: -24.32%, Fixed Income Arbitrage: -10.55%, Event Driven: -20.65%, Distressed: -26.77%, Fund of Funds-Single Strategy: -16.75%, Emerging Markets: -39.61%, and CTA/Managed Futures: 10.93%. Judging from the performances, the strategy of CTA/Managed Futures is the only strategy which shows positive double-digit performance. Because enormous amount of funds flew in commodities markets after the subprime loan problems. The clue of Hedge Fund Industry’s revival lies in the factors, namely, transparency, efficiency, and liquidity. It is desirable that Hedge Fund Industry recovers smoothly by observing the regulations and providing with cutting edge topics.

Chapter 1 – This paper proposes a non-parametric portfolio selection criterion for the static asset allocation problem in TL-moments space. Using the shortage function approach of Luenberger (1995) and Trimmed version of the L-moments of Hosking (1989), the authors generalize the multi-objective optimization approaches of Briec et al. (2004 and 2007) and Jurczenko et al. (2006 and 2008) in the four trimmed L-moments space to deal with the poor sampling properties of conventional higher-order moments. After a theoretical presentation of the univariate L-moments and of their multivariate extensions (see, for instance, Elamir and Seheult, 2003, and Ser.ing and Xiao,2007), the authors derive a four-dimensional representation of the TL-mean-TL-variance-TL -skewness-TL-kurtosis primal efficient portfolio set, using a universe of 162 off-shore hedge funds. The empirical application serves to illustrate the typical non-linear trade-offs that can be found in the hedge fund industry and the computational tractabilty of the approach.

Chapter 2 – This chapter provides a comprehensive explanation of hedge fund replication. This chapter first reviews the characteristics of hedge fund returns. Then, the emergence of hedge fund replication products is discussed. Hedge fund replication methods are classified into three categories: Rule-based, Factor-based, and Distribution replicating approaches. These approaches attempt to capture different aspects of hedge fund returns. This chapter explains the three methods.

Chapter 3 – This paper proposes a new approach to investment style analysis by classifying the hedge fund universe with the Tibshirani, Walther and Hastie (2001) Gap Statistic. This study finds the statistical presence of only three broad hedge fund investment styles for the period 1994 to 2001. The investment styles can be best described as: quasi-long-equity; non-directional; and, global-directional. The authors validate the findings of the Gap Statistic by passively replicating the systematic returns of these three investment styles with traditional asset classes.

Chapter 4 – Although hedge fund managers are considered capable of generating positive returns regardless of market conditions, they are actually affected by the market to some extent. However, it is difficult to isolate the market effect, or beta, because hedge fund managers' beta has not been clearly defined yet. In addition, traditional methods, such as multi-regression analysis, are also not satisfactory due to hedge funds' dynamic strategy changes. In this analysis, the author attempt to apply a seven-factor Markov-Switching Model to the Fung and Hsieh approach (2004) to enhance the coefficient of determination by taking into consideration the unique characteristics of hedge fund managers—specifically their tendencies to switch their allocations to different strategies.

Chapter 5 – This paper examines the Lipper/TASS hedge fund database for the period 1994-2006 and the authors calculate hedge fund attrition, biases and the survivor premium. The authors estimate an attrition rate of between 9 to 10.5 per cent per year which is twice the rate reported in mutual fund studies. The authors measure the various hedge fund biases and we find that database returns in this sample are inflated by as much as 45 per cent. The authors find that the common characteristic of non-survival is chronic poor performance. Finally, the authors estimate the survivor premium which is the return investors receive if they are skilled or lucky enough to invest exclusively in surviving hedge funds only. After controlling for data biases the authors calculate a hedge fund survivor premium of nearly 600 basis points per year, which is twice the size of those reported in mutual fund studies. Finally, the authors reveal that the survivor premium increases to 821, 728 and 621 basis points per year when examining funds in the Managed Futures, Global Macro and Long/Short Equity Hedge investment categories, respectively.

Chapter 6 – The authors select the top four hedge fund strategies as desirable ones based on the Prospect Ratio in this paper, and the authors examine the risk factors of each hedge fund strategy to specify the source of return in the past ten years. The authors use multifactor models based on GMM analysis. And the authors use AIC (Akaike Information Criterion) and SIC (Schwarz Information Criterion) to resolve the problem to specify the valid exogenous variables in each strategy. The result shows that the selected model contains only significant exogenous variables in each strategy.

Yasuaki Watanabe, Ph.D., CMA, CIIA
Professor of Finance at Kochi University of Technology
Massachusetts Institute of Technology, Economics Department, Visiting Scholar (Former Stanford University Graduate School of Business, Visiting Scholar)

Summer 2009 at MIT in Boston, U.S.A.

In: The Recent Trend of Hedge Fund Strategies ISBN: 978-1-61668-338-2
Editor: Yasuaki Watanabe, pp. 1-19 

*Expert Commentary*

# THE 2008-2009 FINANCIAL CRISIS: RISK MODEL TRANSPARENCY AND INCENTIVES

***Terry Marsh and Paul Pfleiderer***[1]

## 1. Introduction

In this paper, we offer some analysis of the 2008-2009 financial crisis and its implications for financial industry reform and research. We primarily focus on issues relating to transparency and the measurement of risk and how these are affected by management incentives that are often misaligned with the incentives of those who are exposed in various ways to the risk being measured. In the aftermath of the crisis many have called for increased transparency, but as we will suggest below, while transparency is no doubt a desirable goal in many ways, increasing it in some contexts will be quite difficult.

Before considering issues related to transparency of the risk and valuation models used by financial institutions, we need to set the stage by very briefly summarizing our thinking on what caused the "financial crisis" and how it led to what has become known as the Great Recession. Unlike the stock market crash of 1987, for which there is still no consensus concerning what caused the sharp drop in stock prices, nearly everyone agrees that the current problems started to unfold after housing prices began to fall in late 2006 and early 2007 with a concomitant drop in sub-prime mortgage values. The problem spread beyond mortgage markets to a near breakdown in short-term funding markets in September and October 2008, while U.S. and global markets for longer-term corporate credit and equity securities continued to function relatively well.

Reinhardt and Rogoff (2008) point out that the 2007-2008 U.S. financial crisis has "stunning qualitative and quantitative parallels to 18 earlier post-war banking crises in industrialized countries," and they observe that the majority of these historical crises were preceded by financial liberalization. These stylized facts seem to implicate the financial liberalization that occurred over the prior decade or so, which allowed the spectacular growth in the "parallel" or "non-bank banking" system. Among other things this parallel banking system helped meet the need to "recycle" the accumulating global capital imbalances with the U.S. At the beginning of 1980, securities funded roughly 33% of U.S. household, nonfinancial corporate and nonfarm business debt; by the third quarter of 2008, that percentage had risen to around 64%. In reality though, the traditional commercial and investment banking institutions, along with some insurance companies and money market mutual funds, themselves became significant players in the non-bank banking system, via lines of credit, off-balance sheet special purpose vehicles, short-term commercial paper and repos, senior CDO tranche insurance, etc.[2]

While financial liberalization undoubtedly played a role as an "enabling factor" in the financial crisis,[3] no consensus has emerged concerning the precise

[1] Author bios follow the References.

[2] As Geithner (2008) describes: "Banks could not fully absorb and offset the effects of the pullback in investor participation – or the "run" – on this non-bank system, in part because they themselves had sponsored many of these off-balance-sheet vehicles. They had written very large contingent commitments to provide liquidity support to many of the funding vehicles that were under pressure. They had retained substantial economic exposure to the risk of a deterioration in house prices and to a broader economic downturn, and as a result, many suffered a sharp increase in their cost of borrowing.

" The funding and balance sheet pressures on banks were intensified by the rapid breakdown of securitization and structured finance markets. Banks lost the capacity to move riskier assets off their balance sheets, at the same time they had to fund, or to prepare to fund, a range of contingent commitments over an uncertain time horizon.

The combined effect of these factors was a financial system vulnerable to self-reinforcing asset price and credit cycles. The system appeared to be more stable across a broader range of circumstances and better able to withstand the effects of moderate stress, but it had become more vulnerable to more extreme events. And the change in the structure of the system made the crisis more difficult to manage with the traditional mix of instruments available to central banks and governments" ( p. 2).

[3] There was much less growth in non-banking activity in countries like Japan, China, and Canada over the same period. Since there was (broadly) less financial liberalization in these countries and they experienced much less or zero direct financial crisis, we could add that as a priori evidence of an association between financial liberalization and financial crisis. At the same time, not all else was equal: Japan's banks were still in recovery and merger mode; China was

channels through which the financial crisis in turn affected "Main Street" and the markets for real assets. On the one hand there is the distinct possibility that the additional risk-taking permitted in the liberal financial regime led in various ways to real assets being overvalued. After the financial crisis occurred these asset valuations were "corrected," which of course meant a decline in value. On the other hand, the financial crisis and associated credit freeze almost certainly helped precipitate the recession, which of course resulted in a downward revision of cash flow projections and valuations. Determining how much of the fall in real assets values can be attributed to the first effect and how much to the second is a challenge that has yet to be met. What is clear is that the lively discussion five years ago about the extent to which financial liberalization contributed to global economic growth has now been replaced by the equally lively one of "how mistaken ideas helped to bring the economy down." Numerous candidates for these mistaken ideas and potential feedback loops have been proposed, including Calvin Trillin's humor-tinged suggestion[4] that "the financial system nearly collapsed because smart guys had started working on Wall Street." Here, we focus on risk-taking incentives and the financial system – if those incentives have an ultimately negative impact on the real economy, then the taxpayer potentially "pays" twice, once in any bail-out subsidies and once in the direct damage to the real economy.

Clearly the large investment losses that in part defined "the crisis" are not *per se* evidence that "economists got it so wrong"; nor are the losses necessarily evidence of problems either in the management of financial institutions or the quality of the financial models that they use. For example, an accurate risk model – accurate in the sense that it misses none of the "knowable unknowns" – permits financial managers to take well-calculated bets, but these are not sure bets. Pure arbitrage aside, fund managers and investors must decide which risks to insure against, and which risks are priced attractively enough to warrant the costs of exposure. For all but the most conservative strategies there will be some risk of a large loss. An accurate risk model simply means that, *ex post*, managers and investors are not blind-sided by risk exposures that should have been known.

As established economics tells us, and as we are reminded almost daily by the financial media, incentives to take on risk are magnified in "heads I win and tails someone else loses" situations. In particular, implicit government insurance (e.g., too-big-to-fail insurance) potentially leads financial institutions to take on socially undesirable levels of risk, unless the government can somehow magically and

on the flip side of the U.S. capital inflows and its banks are still majority-owned by the State, which itself makes "free insurance" for banks from the Government somewhat moot.

[4] Calvin Trillin, "Wall Street Smarts," New York Times, October 15, 2009.

instantly adjust for the level of risk taken and perfectly price and charge upfront for the implicit insurance it provides. Financial liberalization permitted the financial sector to take on more leverage and more risk, and the incentives of managers and others all but guaranteed that would happen. There is certainly supporting anecdotal evidence of "risk-be-damned" behavior by large financial players prior to the crisis, e.g.: "[A former senior Lehman banker] recalls vividly the days in early 2007 at Lehman when his financial models began to throw up more warnings showing delinquencies and defaults, and he remembers colleagues on his desk raising questions about loan quality. But he said the firm's ranking as the top loan originator on Wall Street, not to mention the pressures put on the desk by Lehman's growth-obsessed leadership, made it difficult for even the most senior executives to raise questions" (New York Times, September 13, 2008 p. 7). Of course, different financial institutions have different cultures and compensation plans. All that economics can say is that implicit government insurance, among other things, creates incentives that can lead to more-than-otherwise prudent risk-taking. Management hubris or over-confidence undoubtedly played a role – the bail-out insurance simply lowers the downside costs of that behavior. The stunning magnitude of the bail-outs that did occur make it plausible that they played a major role in prior decision-making: Alessandri and Haldane (2009) calculate that "the scale of intervention to support the banks in the UK, US, and the euro-area during the current crisis…totals over $14 trillion or almost a quarter of global GDP. It dwarfs any previous state support of the banking system" (p. 2).

## 2. Incentives and Risk Models

The "heads-I-win, tails-the-Government-or-investor-loses" moral hazard incentives in turn have an impact on the quality of risk and valuation models. To explain how, we must clarify who is developing the risk models and how they are being used. Assume that there are two parties to a transaction (or ongoing economic relationship) and assume Party A has incentives to increase risk at the expense of Party B. In the case of implicit government insurance, the financial institution or bank is obviously Party A, and the government is Party B.[5] Now if Party B protects itself by using a risk model that it develops and controls, there is no obvious problem. However, to the extent that Party B relies on a risk model

[5] Alessandri and Haldane (2009) subdivide government insurance into deposit insurance (payouts to retail depositors), liquidity insurance (support to wholesale funders), and capital insurance (equity injections from the government). We lump these different insurance subsidies together in our discussion here.

developed and maintained by Party A, potential conflicts can arise. An obvious example is the case where capital requirements imposed by the government (Party B) are based on risk measures that are produced by risk models developed and maintained by the regulated financial institution (Party A). In those situations where the full cost of downside risk is not borne by Party A, then all else equal Party A would opt for a less-than-state-of-the-art risk model that underestimates risk. Among other things this means that Party A has an incentive to have fewer rather than more known unknowns in its models, since fewer known unknowns generally translates into lower risk measures like c-VaR. Moreover, the less transparent the risk model being used, the harder it is for Party B to detect the model's shortcomings, particularly when the risk model is applied in new areas and to complex new products. Since exploiting risk-shifting opportunities that benefit equity at the expense of others is in the interests of a financial entity's shareholders and its Board as well as management's, standard corporate governance can't be relied upon as a corrective. Lacking such a corrective, it seems particularly likely that the problems of model transparency for the more complex structured products will bedevil regulatory reforms involving capital requirements and leverage.

In the next section, we look more closely at the meaning of transparency. In Section 4, we look briefly at evidence on how the crisis unfolded and how transparency of risk and valuation models looked to be a potential issue. In Section 5, we discuss various solutions to the problems of ensuring model fidelity when the models are not completely transparent; in particular, we note that it doesn't follow that it would be optimal to require complete transparency, even if that were somehow counterfactually feasible.

## 3. Meaning of Transparency

Transparency has a variety of meanings. From the post-crisis perspective of both retail and institutional investors, more transparency typically means getting a better grasp on what their investment advisors / wealth managers / structured product sales and trading desks are delivering to them; these investors now find that the crisis has laid bare – made transparent – the emperor's state of undress.[6]

[6] "The economic crisis has presented client relationship managers with challenges that they have neither the experience nor the skills to deal with...[A] recent PricewaterhouseCoopers survey of 238 private banks and wealth management firms [found]. What is disturbing in the study's findings is that only now, after the crash, have wealth management firms realized they need to train advisers to do a better job" (New York Times, Friday, July 31, 2009).

The demand for what is essentially better stewardship is at its simplest a demand for better documentation and attribution. Such documentation transparency goes hand-in-hand with mandatory compliance procedures. The extent of documentation and compliance in the investment process had generally already been improving before the crisis, thanks in part to decreasing IT costs and the additional records needed to support public trading of all the newly-created credit instruments. However, documentation (and regulation and hence compliance) is always a catch-up game when financial innovation is rapid. [7] There are at least three general cases where investors were vulnerable due to transparency and documentation problems. First and most obvious, lack of audit and trade verification was a necessary condition for the Ponzi schemes exposed by the "receding tide" in the crisis. Brown, Goetzman, Liang, and Schwartz (2009) examined a sample of due diligence reports on asset managers and found substantial misrepresentation of documentable facts by the managers, e.g. 10% of the time the AUM data was incorrect and 4.5% of the time measured performance disagreed between the fund and the administrator or the auditor. Second, Zimmerman (2007) and Rajan, Seru, and Vig (2008) suggest that default models for securitized subprime mortgage claims failed in large part because "...the models relied entirely on hard information variables such as borrower scores, and ignored changes in the incentives of lenders to collect soft information about borrowers." Soft information "such as time since last bankruptcy, time on the job, length of time at same residence etc. are all important elements in mortgage credit, but these secondary attributes are not disclosed on a term sheet, and dealers, rating agencies, and investors seldom have access to that information" (Zimmerman, p. 12). These documentation transparency problems were complicated in the case of CDOs that held tranches of many different pools of mortgages, or CDOs that held tranches of CDOs that held various tranches of the mortgage pools, etc. Third, stewardship accounting is perhaps the most instrumental for documentation transparency. Yet during the financial crisis, pressured regulators relaxed accounting rules for consolidating special purpose vehicles onto balance sheets, for documentation of the "fair value" of positions in turbulent markets, and for loss provisioning and thus measurement of stated capital, arguably all of which decreased transparency. The bottom line is as important as it is obvious: transparency in a documentation sense is a *sine qua*

[7] The current failure rate in settlements is a good illustration of catch-up problems in documentation in the trade process – 29% for OTC derivatives, 16% across all instruments (Source: Smartstream Technologies) – that can contribute to market breakdown in crisis conditions, though we don't have evidence that about the mechanics of clearing and settlement was per se a major factor in September-October 2008.

*non* for high quality risk assessment, valuation, and enforcement of capital/leverage rules. Insofar as future research is concerned, issues concerning the most appropriate rules for "fair value" accounting that also provide an optimal level of transparency seem as pressing now as they ever were.

The term "transparency" as used in the introduction has to do with one's understanding of the important drivers of investment returns and risk. Documentation transparency is an obvious pre-requisite for determining these "drivers." One might think that complexity leads to reduced transparency in identifying these drivers of returns. But that is not necessarily the case. For example, a plan sponsor could enter into an agreement with an asset manager whereby the latter will run, as an agent, a very complex strategy for the sponsor. So long as the sponsor is able to verify that the manager is performing every step in the agreed-upon, complex algorithm, the drivers of the investment return will be fully transparent to the sponsor. Indeed, if the asset management contract can specify all the steps in the process and these steps can be audited for compliance, the principal-agent problem has again been reduced to a "check the boxes" task, consistent with what we've just termed documentation transparency. Consider now the case where the manager's investment process is not given by mechanical rules that can be audited, but instead has many elements that are subject to the discretion of the manager. When decisions are delegated to the manager, the sponsor is not expecting complete transparency. How can the investor be assured that the manager is delivering a product that has the expected risk and return characteristics? In the case of everyday consumer products that involve complex technology, we typically see Underwriters' Laboratories certification and expert guides. In the financial management industry, due diligence consulting firms like Albourne, and perhaps ratings firms such as Moody's, SandP, and Fitch, are very rough analogs to UL certification. The more severe the model (and documentation) transparency problem, the more due diligence that we'd expect to see, and the more critical become the fund consultants, ratings agencies or their successors. While our examples concern asset management, the point easily generalizes to large financial institutions carrying on a broad cross-section of complex activities.

If non-transparent risk models help managers exploit risk-taking incentives, then all things considered, are the best models those that maximize transparency? One example of transparent risk modeling is the Basel Committee's first set of "risk bucketing" rules for minimum capital requirements. These rules essentially reduced the transparency-of-models problem to one of documentation transparency, i.e. verify that an asset is in category X, and if so it gets weight Y%. Alas, the buckets were so broadly defined that the same bucket could potentially contain assets with quite different risks, e.g., a bucket containing all first-lien residential mortgages or a bucket containing all OECD countries lumped together. As is well-known, Basel I also missed altogether anything other than default risk, including, most critically, the market risk[8] of securities on a financial institution's balance sheet. Misclassification of assets by risk creates obvious opportunities for "regulatory arbitrage." The unregulated parallel banking system seems to have exploited many such opportunities to arbitrage institutional rigidities, inappropriate risk weights, and inaccurate ratings.[9]

The type of problems encountered with the risk bucketing approach would logically lead us toward a more "functional" approach to risk and valuation, and indeed that is the direction that Basel II took. In that functional approach, the objective is to define assets as having similar risk when their payoff profiles are similar.[10] The wrinkle, however, is that the functional approach typically involves a concomitant shift away from a check-list-like transparency-in-documentation to the generally lower transparency involved in identifying and assessing the quality of risk models.

## 4. Transparency and Market Stress

In the previous section, we suggested that one of the ways in which financial entities can take on more-than-prudent risk when they don't fully bear their downside losses is to have poorer quality risk models. We have been using too-big-to-fail banks as examples of such financial entities, but the skewed incentives would also be present for say hedge funds with nonlinear performance fees on one side and less sophisticated investors on the other. Because of a lack of transparency into these institutions, it is difficult to gather systematic evidence across them concerning the quality of their risk models going into the crisis. Of course, as we have repeatedly argued above, it is precisely this lack transparency along with potentially misaligned incentives that creates the possibility that low quality models may have been used.

---

[8] The BIS defines market risk factors as: "the market rates and prices that affect the value of the trading positions" (July 2009).

[9] This is hardly an "Anglo-Saxon business model" problem, as some European critics have argued. Witness the Credit Lyonnais problems over a decade ago that are eerily reminiscent of Fannie Mae, but where the pressures were to make poor decisions about credit risk for political ends, while the push on Fannie Mae appears to have been for explicit monetary ends. At the end of the day, these were in many ways differences without distinction.

[10] That is, the assets are "functionally similar" in the same sense that Robert Merton classifies financial institutions as similar if they perform the same function.

Lapses in risk control have certainly been implicated in some of the major "blow-ups" in Q4 2008. For example, former AIG CEO Hank Greenberg testified to Congress that: "There is no question that management took their eye off the ball and that risk management was not getting the right instructions, and that's what led to the downfall" (Teitelbaum and Son (2009, p. 36). Of course, this testimony is anecdotal evidence of a failure of risk management, not necessarily of a failure of the models. However, AIG had been writing insurance on the senior securitized CDO tranches at 15 bps, and at the same time a senior AIGFP official famously contended in an August 2007 conference call that "it is hard for us…to even see a scenario within any kind of realm of reason that would see us losing a dollar in any of those transactions." [11] It was widely claimed at the time that AIG was effectively "arbitraging" the fact that it was an insurance company and not subject to Federal Reserve, FDIC, or SEC rules and supervision. Note that a case could be made that the clients of AIGFP and the senior management of AIGFP and AIG were all acting quite rationally, if they anticipated there was a good chance that Government assistance would be provided in those negative fat tail scenarios evidently "ignored" by AIGFP.

One scenario that should have been within the "realm of reason" of AIG's risk models is a stress scenario in which so-called contagion or "network" effects cause reverberations across institutions. The worry is that these network effects amplify the transparency issues that we discuss here. Note that the entities that are most likely to explicitly or implicitly consider themselves too-big-to-fail are the ones that have the largest number of network connections. Of course, if systemic risk is an important factor that can result in losses for some or all the interconnected institutions, each of those firms would ideally have an incentive to take the systemic network effects into account in each one of their in-house models. However our point is that if those same too-big-to-fail institutions want to downplay known unknowns in their risk controls, the network effects are certainly not transparent and *ipso facto* they are easy to ignore.

The less transparent the asset values and risk models of counter-parties in "the network," the more the collateral that will be demanded, and the shorter the term will be funding against that collateral. As is well known, when transparency problems become too substantial, even short-term funding breaks down and without complete certainty of Government bail-outs in the bad scenario, we have

[11] "What brought the company down, [wind-up head Gerry] Pasciucco says, was its exposure to fewer than 200 insurance contracts that were sensitive to AIG's credit ratings and the value of the underlying CDOs" (p. 29). Presumably this would be the place to start with forensics; we don't have the information to assess the relative importance of these 200 contracts, but the

a classic bank run. Up to September 2008, AIG had been providing the CDS insurance on senior tranches of securitized debt, and this insurance was a key feature in having those tranche bonds play the wholesale funding AAA "equivalent" of demand deposits, albeit with AIG's backing rather than the FDIC's.

Liquidity or market network effects are more likely to occur when a financial entity's balance sheet is more complex and risk and valuation models less transparent, all else equal. One reason for this became clear in the thick of the financial crisis, when institutions by-and-large tried to sell off assets rather than deleverage by substituting equity for debt. Structured mortgage credit instruments, like the swaps on CDO bonds that AIGFP was writing, trade in an OTC dealer market, so "selling off" those assets is difficult. We think that this illiquidity and the contagion it engendered should have been a "knowable unknown" factor in risk and valuation models; even in normal times, that OTC market was relatively narrow, with around ten serious dealers and further specialization among them. Trading was relatively opaque, e.g. only the counter-parties to trades, one of whom was typically the dealer, knew prices. Moreover, in the case of CDOs with their complicated hierarchical structuring,[12] the dealers arguably not only possessed better price information, they were also better informed about deal structures than most counter-parties; many of these counter-parties post-2004 were relatively new to the market and were inexperienced, in some cases lacking good information about how much sub-prime exposure was even in the underlying the CDO tranche bonds (which itself would be consistent with our thesis that parties didn't particularly want to know these risks given their downside loss protection and, in the case of entities subject to BIS, didn't want to in any way jeopardize the zero risk weight applied to these securities.)

Within the mortgage-backed securities markets, network or liquidity risk turned out to be less severe for the ABX Index market than it was for the individual CDO constituents of that Index. The ABX Indices, introduced at the beginning of 2006, consisted of a series of equally weighted, static portfolios of CDSs referencing twenty subprime MBS transactions. As Gorton (2008) suggested, these ABX Indices were already important pre-crisis in aggregating and revealing market information about subprime values and risks. In Figure 1,

evidence seems to be that they were substantial, e.g. AIG reportedly needed $40 billion in cash as of the weekend before the Lehman bankruptcy filing (Stewart (2009, p. 66)).

[12] Most CDOs had some structured product tranches as collateral, but it was not easy to even figure out where the sub-prime exposure was.

we show the spreads on the ABX.HE Index AAA tranche and non-AAA tranche from June 30, 2008 through June 30, 2009.

The spread on the junior (non-AAA) tranche begins to increase in the second half of 2008 around mid-September, the time of the Lehman bankruptcy and AIG bailout (the spread had already increased substantially in 2007 and H1 2008).

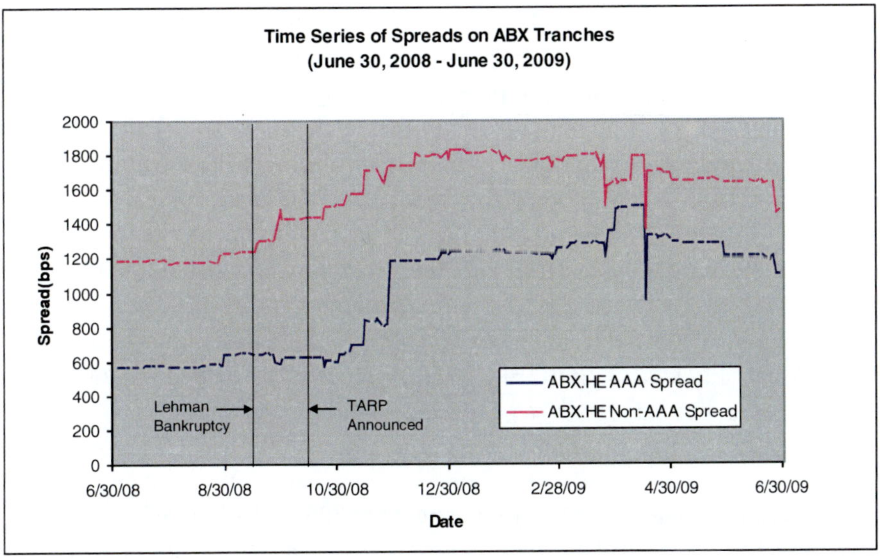


Figure 1. Time Series of Spreads on ABX-AAA and ABX-non AAA Tranche Bonds (June 30, 2008 – June 30, 2009).

This increasing spread is consistent with the deterioration in the value of the junior claims. Notice, however, that the senior tranche spread doesn't itself start to increase until mid-November, well after the TARP announcement. In mid-November, the VIX index for equities peaked out at 88.86%. This VIX index is often used by traders as a gauge for the correlation of the values of the assets (here, mortgages and mortgage derivatives) in the underlying pool. The thinking appears to be that the higher the VIX, the higher the correlation within the pool – another item for more research. Granting for the moment that the assumption about correlation is correct, we would *expect* to see spreads on the senior tranches rise relative to those on junior tranches as the VIX peaks, since it is only with many simultaneous defaults that loss rates would "reach up" to the senior and super-senior levels. This is by no means a complete analysis of these spreads, but it does suggest that they were in step with fundamentals.

If we broaden our scope of analysis still further from the MBS Indices to the markets for longer-term corporate credit instruments and equities, the evidence is still stronger that price behavior there was dominated by fundamentals. In the corporate bond and equity markets, there were more data available that could be used to calibrate risk and valuation models,[13] and thus our thesis would say there was less scope for opportunistically tweaking the specification and parameters for those models. Broker-dealers and banks also hold only a small fraction of (cash market) U.S. corporate bonds and equities, e.g. less than two percent of equities outstanding are held directly by broker-dealers and banks, reducing even further the likelihood that misaligned incentives would have an impact there. Consistent with our reasoning, the market for longer-term corporate credit risk appeared to have continued functioning relatively normally during the crisis, insofar as corporate credit spreads moved roughly in line with the predictions of structural models for credit risk. Our evidence for the normal functioning of the corporate credit market is partly anecdotal, based on discussions with traders, and partly drawn from Coval, Jurek, and Stafford (2009), who present evidence showing that "...changes in fundamentals, as reflected in the equity market, account for a large portion of the re-pricing of [corporate] credit that...occurred." Three comments are warranted: (i) The shifts in the variance-covariance of the values of assets of companies that have issued debt results in "multivariate fat tails" in default risk for pooled debt securities, but these are picked up in models like Quantal's and in the procedure used in Coval, Jurek, and Stafford (2009), if not in the notorious Gaussian copula modeling; (ii) it is true that the basis difference between corporate credit spreads and their respective CDS spreads did generally widen through much of the last quarter of 2008, but we would expect to see this given the increase in perceived counter-party risk; and (iii) short-term corporate commercial paper demand dried up, not surprisingly given the quasi-bank-run in other parallel banking short-term funding.

Finally, while equity prices fell sharply and volatility increased sharply, the price discovery process for equities also continued to function, albeit with controversial restrictions on the shorting of financial stocks in 2008. In particular, there was no repetition of the problems of October 1987 where it is seems that market transparency problems may have contributed to the 22% drop in the Dow Jones Index on October 19th, e.g. Grossman (1988), Gennotte and Leland (1990)

[13] The National Association of Securities Dealers (NASD) has required, since July 1, 2002, that dealers report all OTC corporate bond transactions in the U.S. (with a phase-in through February 2004 for BBB-rated bonds). This is done through the NASD TRACE (Trade Reporting and Compliance Engine) bond price reporting system.

and Jacklin, Kleidon and Pfleiderer (1992) who hypothesize that investors may not have been able to differentiate portfolio-insurance-generated trading from information-motivated equity trading. Moreover, not only did equity markets not freeze up, but also volume remained roughly constant in the U.S. during the crisis, and fell off only slightly in Europe and Asia; activity in after-hours trading in SandP cash and futures markets seems to have remained at its normal level during the crisis (Avramonic (2009) – we didn't see panicked after-hours activity like the large "unusual" EFP trades after-hours in October 1987.

## 5. Discussion

The 2008-2009 financial crisis has focused concern on the risk-taking incentives of financial entities. This is especially true for the too-big-to-fail institutions where the "heads I win, tails the Government loses" problem looms large. Investors in privately managed funds are also concerned that their contracts with managers containing performance fees might contain the same misaligned management incentives. In the case of the funds, investors sometimes try to ameliorate the potential misalignment by including contractual terms like high-water-marks, and by limiting their investments to managers who have a substantial fraction of their own capital at risk. If a financial institution has virtually complete transparency so that the principals – the regulator or the sophisticated investors – can effectively monitor and control their investment risk from the outside, then the misaligned incentives have limited consequences. The necessary level of transparency would require, at a minimum, a high level of documentation transparency. It would also presumably require that the financial entity's investment book and strategies be quite straightforward. In the case of a large financial institution, these two conditions might at best be fulfilled for a version of "utility" banks" that take in deposits and carry out a conventional loan business[14] – we say "might" here because it is hard to claim that the conventional loan business was itself ever very transparent. For funds, a "utility" strategy that closely tracks an index, or is designed to closely replicate

[14] We are borrowing this "utility bank" terminology from a September 29 Financial Times column by Martin Wolf, "Why Narrow Banking is Not the Finance Solution." In one rendition, the term "utility" bank refers to a deposit-taking institution with 100% of its liabilities backed by "genuinely safe liquid assets", i.e. essentially a money market mutual fund. We are using the term in a slightly broader and arguably more practical sense. The "casino" consists of all other financial activities, for which we speculate that the pressures for implicit guarantee would be as strong as we see today for the financial sector.

a basket of hedge fund returns using a prescribed set of rules, could be transparent.

However, if may be impractical to split off the "utility" operations of large banks from the decidedly non-transparent "casino operations." In the case of hedge funds, if they run sophisticated strategies, it will generally not be feasible for an outsider – regulator or investor – to perfectly observe risk-taking, or observe the quality and internal usage of risk models. As discussed earlier, there is ample evidence from the financial crisis to suggest that the risk models for complex securitized products turned out to be an example par excellence. Moreover, even if transparency into the quality of models being used were feasible at a point in time, the models themselves need to evolve over time as conditions change, as an entity's business and products change, and as the most important stress scenarios change. Indeed, even documentation transparency needs to be in real-time if positions change quickly. This transparency of the banks' or funds' risk and valuation models is where the "rubber hits the road" in terms of potential problems of alignment of incentives. There may be perfectly legitimate reasons for the principal to not want to make the internal risk and valuation models completely transparent – after all, these models are part and parcel of the entity's charter to identify risks and keep those that have the best reward-to-(accurately measured) risk ratio, and insure against other known unknowns by efficiently hedging them; indeed, it is the improved reward-to-accurate risk ratio that provides the incentive to develop and deploy state-of-the-art models from both the manager's and investor's point of view. This is similarly true for process-driven trading where both the risk and also the perceived proprietary information involve knowing the "reservoirs of liquidity."

More stringent capital and margin requirements can in principle dampen some of the incentives of large financial institutions to increase risk, since reductions in leverage generally reduce opportunities for risk shifting gains. But modest changes in capital requirements cannot make the problem go away. Further, if managers are in part focused on achieving target levels of ROE (return on equity), enforced reductions in leverage can create additional incentives for managers to seek out higher return–higher risk activities, cloaking the latter in ultimately misleading risk models, parameterized to include fewer known unknowns.

The new Basel II set of rules, which in the U.S. require large financial institutions to use internal ratings based models as a part of determining capital requirements, can be expected to correct the problems of crude (credit) risk bucketing in the Basel I calculation of risk-weighted capital discussed earlier:

presumably these internal models are better customized to the institution's products and strategies. But, as pointed out earlier, that same customization is likely to "up the ante" with respect to ensuring the adequacy of these internal models when transparency is an issue. Schwarcz (2009) also reminds us that agency conflicts between top management and middle-level management within a large institution are especially severe for financial firms where products and models are complex. In the Basel II rules, these middle-management conflicts in incentives are largely rolled into operational risk, and problems of transparency into the models used by middle managers become a part of operational risk.

One concern with monitoring the internal ratings based systems is that it is virtually impossible to do it properly without transactions and holdings data, especially when stress-testing an entity's risk. Rather than have the regulatory body periodically review systems and models, it seems worth investigating whether securities clearing and settlement corporations could be enlisted to do real-time auditing and risk assessment. These clearing corporations already have market and holdings and transactions data; they also have a good deal of experience in netting counter-claims and in using a portfolio approach to risk; and they could in principle monitor risk on at the same frequency as the entities' risks can change. Of course, in those cases in which the financial entities' balance sheets include non-traded credit lines, loans, etc. outstanding, the relevant databases would have to be separately loaded.

There are many subtle underlying questions. For example, would a "clearing corporation as auditor" or similar solution require all OTC contracts to be standardized and possibly exchange-traded and cleared by the same clearing corporation? Presumably not, but any monitoring system (be it operated by a clearing house or, say, a Federal regulator) will presumably be cheaper to operate with some level of standardization that facilitates documentation transparency. Moreover, the marginal cost of auditing risk measurement is low if the transactions are already being cleared through the system. Presumably entities that trade both standardized exchange-traded-and-cleared instruments and OTC traded contracts could be audited by the clearinghouse; the audit would simply be more expensive for the non-standardized and non-exchange-traded contracts.

One obvious caveat is that all these potential solutions for monitoring the risk and valuation models of financial entities are potentially costly. Whilst one might reply that "so is another financial crisis," we need to be persuaded that the reforms would indeed help prevent another crisis, when they haven't necessarily done so in the past. Indeed, some well-intentioned reforms may have even helped exacerbate problems when they engendered large scale regulatory arbitrage. If risk-taking incentives remain, as we think they almost surely will, then the details of trying to ensure risk and valuation model transparency matter crucially – improving transparency in some areas but not in others runs the danger of leaving things worse off, not better off. Moreover, unintended incentive problems aside, disclosing more data obviously does not necessarily mean better transparency. Lessig (2009) has recently claimed that all-out transparency in the political arena that involves simply providing "lots of data" won't be optimal if users of data don't have the bandwidth or skill to put the data in context and interpret it correctly. [15] The same point would undoubtedly be true here if lots of data about risk and valuation models is just shoveled over to regulators or investors without carefully thinking about how it is useful in evaluating the models. Risk models, which as abstractions necessarily contain assumptions and parameters, can't simply be "crash tested" to evaluate the parameterization, even in a market crash scenario, since the models involve the probabilities of gains and losses on portfolios of assets.

For the dwindling few who haven't lost faith in the markets (or at least haven't found a better alternative), a possible alternative to outside audits of risk systems would be shift to more reliance on market pricing of financial entity risk. Indeed, Basel II previously suggested that market calibration supplement its system of capital guidelines. For example, CDS contracts on a financial institution reflect the market's evaluation of the risk of that CDS insurance. Of course, market pricing of any risk is only as good as the information available to the parties to the contracts being priced, so in the case of these CDS contracts, the market participants would presumably need a basis on which to adjust for misaligned incentives that potentially lead to biased usage of risk and valuation models within the respective entities. Moreover, there is a potential problem in looking at the pricing of CDS insurance on, say, Citigroup. CDS traders would logically account for the probability of government bailout in their expectations of default losses. This will make it more difficult for the government to use market pricing to infer the risk that it (the government) faces.

A final measure, one that undoubtedly deserves as much consideration as anything else that has been proposed, is to appoint more women to the Boards of financial institutions: "Far from focusing on traditionally 'soft' areas, boards with

[15] Lessig's discussion largely concerns data on the political process, but he points out that Justice Brandeis' famous 1914 statement on transparency, that "sunlight is the best disinfectant", was published in a book entitled "Other People's Money" that was highly critical of bankers' limited disclosures.

more women surpass all-male boards in their attention to audit and risk oversight and control" (Brown, Brown, and Anastasopoulos, Conference Board of Canada Report, 2002)!

## References

Acharya, Viral V., Stephen Schaefer, and Yili Zhang, 2007, "Liquidity Risk and Correlation Risk: A Clinical Study of the General Motors and Ford Downgrade of May 2005," Manuscript, London Business School, November.

Alessandri, Peirgiorgio and Andrew G. Haldane, 2009, "Banking on the State," Manuscript, Bank of England, November.

Avramonic, Ana, 2009, "Who Says Markets aren't Efficient," Credit Suisse Portfolio Strategy, September 22.

Bank for International Settlements, 2009, "Revisions to the Basel II Market Risk Framework," July: http://www.bis.org/publ/bcbs158.pdf?noframes=1

Brown, David A.H., Debra L. Brown and Vanessa Anastasopoulos, 2003, "Women on Boards: Not Just the Right Thing...But the 'Bright' Thing," *The Conference Board of Canada*, Report, May.

Brown, Stephen, William Goetzman, Bing Liang, and Christopher Schwartz, 2009, "Trust and Delegation," June 16: http://business.rutgers.edu/files /trustanddelegationpaperbystephenbrown2.pdf

Chako, George, 2008, "Liquidity Risk in Financial Markets," Chapter 7 in: Innovations in Investment Management, edited by H. Gifford Fong, Bloomberg Press.

Coval, Joshua, Jakub Jurek, and Erik Stafford, 2009, "The Pricing of Investment Grade Credit Risk during the Financial Crisis," Working Paper, Harvard Business School, March 30.

Crystal, Graef, 2009, "Obama's $500,000 Cap Feels Great, Does Nothing," Bloomberg News, February 9, 2009. Text available at: http://graefcrystal.com.

Geithner, Timothy F., 2008, "Reducing systemic risk in a dynamic financial system," Remarks at the Economic Club of New York, NY, June 9.

Gennotte, Gerard, and Hayne Leland, 1990, "Market Liquidity, Hedging, and Crashes," 1990, American Economic Review, 80, 999-1021.

Gorton, Gary B., 2008, "The Subprime Panic," NBER Working Paper 14398, October.

Grossman, Sanford J., 1988, "An Analysis of the Implications for Stock and Futures Price Volatility of Program Trading and Dynamic Hedging Strategies," *Journal of Business*, **61**, July, 275-298.

Jacklin, Charles J., Allan W. Kleidon, and Paul Pfleiderer, 1992, "Underestimation of Portfolio Insurance and the Crash of October 1987," *Review of Financial Studies*, **5**(1), 35-83.

Lessig, Lawrence, 2009, "Against Transparency: The perils of openness in government," *The New Republic*, October 9: http://www.tnr.com /article/books-and-arts/against-transparency?page=0,10

King, Mervyn, Enrique Sentana, and Sushil Wadhwani, 1994, "Volatility and Links between National Stock Markets," *Econometrica*, **62**(4), July, 901-933.

Marsh, Terry A., 2008, "Correelation in Daily Equity and Fixed-Income Returns: Implications for a Cross-Asset Factor Model," in H. Gifford Fong, ed, *Innovations in Investment Management*, Bloomberg Press.

Phelps, Edmund, 2009, "A fruitless clash of economic opposites," *Financial Times*, November 3, 2009.

Rajan, Uday, Amit Seru, and Vikrant Vig, 2008, "The Failure of Models that Predict Failure: Distance, Incentives, and Defaults," Stephen M. Ross School of Business, University of Michigan, *Research Paper* No. **1122**.

Reinhart, Carmen M., and Kenneth S. Rogoff, 2008, "Is the 2007 Sub-prime Financial Crisis So Different? An International Historical Comparison, National Bureau of Economic Research Working Paper 13761, January.

Samuelson, Paul A., 1976, "Optimality of Sluggish Predictors under Ergodic Probabilities," *International Economic Review*, **17**(1), February.

Steven L. Schwarcz, 2009, "Conflicts and Financial Collapse: The Problem of Secondary-Management Agency Costs," *Yale Journal on Regulation*: http://ssrn.com/abstract=1322536.

Stewart, James B., 2009, "Eight Days," The New Yorker, September 21, 58-81.

Teitelbaum, Richard, and Hugh Son, 2009, "The Man taking apart AIG," Bloomberg Markets, August, pp. 27-38.

# *Author Bios:

*Terry Marsh* is President and C.E.O. of Quantal International Inc., and an Emeritus Professor of Finance at U.C. Berkeley's Haas School of Business. He received his MBA and Ph.D. degrees from the University of Chicago. Terry served on the finance faculty at UC Berkeley until 2005, and is a former chairman of the Haas Finance Group. Before joining Berkeley, Terry was an Associate Professor of Finance at MIT. He is a recipient of the Batterymarch Fellowship, was a National Fellow at Stanford's Hoover Institution, and is a CPA Fellow of the Australian Society of Accountants. He has consulted for the New York Stock Exchange, the Options Clearing Corporation, the Industrial Bank of Japan, New Japan Securities, and Banamex, and was a member of the Presidential Task Force on Market Mechanisms which investigated the 1987 stock market crash. Terry was a Yamaichi Fellow and Visiting Professor of Economics at the University of Tokyo in 1993.

*Paul Pfleiderer* has M.A. and Ph.D. degrees from Yale University. He is the C.O.G. Miller Distinguished Professor of Finance at the Graduate School of Business, Stanford University, Co-Director of the Financial Management Program, and served as Head of the finance group from 1995 to 2007. Paul's research interests are in market microstructure and the design of financial markets, disclosure regulation, corporate finance and venture capital, and portfolio theory and portfolio optimization. He was awarded a Batterymarch Fellowship in 1987. Paul teaches in Stanford's Executive Program, and has consulted for a number of financial institutions.

In: The Recent Trend of Hedge Fund Strategies ISBN 978-1-61668-338-2
Editor: Yasuaki Watanabe, pp. 21-56 

*Chapter 1*

# FUND OF HEDGE FUNDS PORTFOLIO SELECTION: A ROBUST NON-PARAMETRIC MULTI-MOMENT APPROACH

***Emmanuel Jurczenko***[1*] ***and Ghislain Yanou***[2†]
[1] ESCP EUROPE, 79 avenue de la République
75543 Paris Cedex 11 - Office 2509
[2] University of Paris-1 (Finance/CES/CNRS)

**Abstract**

This paper proposes a non-parametric portfolio selection for the static portfolio selection problem in a robust multi-moment setting. Using the shortage function approach of Luenberger (1995) and the Trimmed L-moments of Elamir and Seheult (2003), we generalize in this article the multi-objective optimization approaches of Briec *et al.* (2004 and 2007) and Jurczenko *et al.* (2008) in the four TL-moment space to deal with the poor sampling properties of the algebraic moments and ordinary L-moments (see Sillitto, 1969). After a theoretical presentation of the univariate Trimmed L-moments and of their multivariate extensions, we derive a four-dimensional representation of the TL-mean-variance-skewness-*kurtosis* primal efficient portfolio set, using a universe of 94 hedge funds coming from 11 different strategies.

**J.E.L. Classification:** G.110, G.120.

**Keywords:** Shortage Function, Efficient Frontier, TL-Moments, TL-coskewness and TL-*cokurtosis*.

*E-mail addresses: ejurczenko@escpeurope.eu
†E-mail address: ghislain.yanou@univ-paris1.fr

# 1. Introduction

The mean-variance decision criterion is inadequate for allocating wealth when dealing with alternative investments. Not only are hedge fund return distributions asymmetric and leptokurtic; but investors tend to display also preference for positively skewed and light-tailed asset return distributions (see for instance, Beedles and Simkowitz, 1978, Dittmar, 2002, Jurczenko and Maillet, 2006-a, and Jondeau and Rockinger, 2009).

While several approaches have been proposed to incorporate higher-order risk preferences into decision criterion[1], no single conclusive method seems to have emerged yet, due to the theoretical and numerical challenges of portfolio optimization with higher-order statistics.

Indeed, the modifications and simplifications that have been proposed in the financial literature limit the scope and the practical interests of the existing multi-moment asset allocation models. For instance, Moment-based primal approaches are partial, since they generally focus only on one particular objective of the multi-moment program at the cost of the others (see Lai, 1991, Athayde and Flores, 2002 and 2003, Sun and Yan, 2003, Mencia and Sentana, 2009, and Davies and Kat, 2009); while Utility-based dual approaches are arbitrary, since they aggregate investor's objectives in a global weighted target function (see Jurczenko and Maillet, 2006, Guidolin and Timmermann, 2008, and Jondeau and Rockinger, 2003-b, 2006 and 2009). Moreover, the previous methods can only guarantee local optimal portfolio solutions, not global ones (see Kerstens *et al.*, 2009). They inevitably require to convexify some part of the non-convex multi-moment efficient frontiers, by using either *ad-hoc* moment or risk preference restrictions. Moreover, most of the existing multi-moment approaches suffer from the traditional drawbacks of algebraic moments. First, higher-order moments do not always exist (see Lux, 2000 and 2001, and Jondeau and Rockinger, 2003-a and 2003-b); and even when they do, such moments do not always uniquely define a probability distribution function (see Heyde, 1963). Secondly, conventional moments[2] tend to be very sensitive to few extreme observations (see

[1]See Athayde and Flôres (2002, 2004 and 2006), Briec *et al.* (2007), Jurczenko and Maillet (2006-b), Jurczenko *et al.* (2006-c and 2008) and Mencia and Sentana (2009) for the primal approaches of the mean-variance-skewness-*kurtosis* portfolio decision problems; and Jurczenko and Maillet (2001 and 2006-a), Jondeau and Rockinger (2003-b, 2006, and 2009), and Guidolin and Timmermann (2005 and 2008) for the dual approaches of the higher-order moment asset allocation problems.

[2]Denoted C-moments hereafter (see Ulrych *et al.*, 2000).

Hampel *et al.*, 2005). The asymptotic efficiency of the empirical moments is also rather poor, especially for distributions with fat tails [3].

The aim of this paper is to overcome the limits of the multi-moment allocation models by combining a non-parametric multi-objective optimization approach, called the shortage function, with a new set of robust statistics, namely the Trimmed L-moments. Indeed, the shortage function is a Goal Programming Method that can guarantee global optimal solutions for non-linear Multi-objective Optimization Programs. Basically, the shortage function is a directional distance that rates the performance of any portfolio by measuring a distance between its moment coordinates and those of its radial projection onto the (weakly) efficient frontier. It has been first introduced in production theory by Luenberger (1995), then applied to portfolio performance appraisals in the Two-moment space by Morey and Morey (1999), and recently extended to higher-order moments by Briec *et al.* (2007) and Kerstens *et al.* (2009). Concerning the shape descriptors, Trimmed L-moments represent an alternative set of statistics that offer a number of advantages over traditional population moments and L-moments[4]. Indeed, TL-moments exist under less restrictive moment conditions than conventional (L)-moments. Their sample estimates are also less prone to the influence of outliers and more stable than their traditional moment counterparts. Moreover, TL-moments constitute more coherent risk measures[5], since they are translation and scale invariants (see Pérez *et al.*, 2003, and Serfling and Xiao, 2007).

Thanks to the global optimality of the shortage function and the sampling superiority of the TL-moments, we generalize in this article the traditional multi-moment portfolio approaches in the four TL-moment space and provide various geometrical representations of the efficient frontier for 94 hedge funds. To the best of our knowledge, this contribution constitutes the first asset allocation application of Trimmed L-moments [6].

The reminder of the paper is organised as follows. In section 2, we recall

[3]In the context of hedge funds, the addition of higher-order moments in portfolio analysis exacerbates estimation risk, since small datasets are responsible for the large confidence intervals observed for sample skewness and *kurtosis*.

[4]Introduced by Sillitto (1969) as alternatives to conventional population moments, L-moments can be obtained as particular case of TL-moments (see Elamir and Seheult, 2003, Hosking 1987, and below).

[5]In the sense of Artzner *et al.* (1999).

[6]There exist only a limited number of financial applications of TL-moments (see Karkaven, 2006, and Darolles *et al.*, 2009).

the theoretical definition of the Trimmed L-moments and establish some of their main properties. In section 3, we describe the optimal portfolio asset allocation within the four TL-moment framework. Section 4 presents the data and the results of the various optimal fund of hedge fund allocations. Section 5 concludes. Proofs are left in the appendixes.

## 2. Trimmed L-Moments Definitions

Introduced by Elamir and Seheult (2003), as an extension of the L-moments of Silitto (1969), the Trimmed L-moments offer a number of advantages over ordinary L-moments and product moments as shape descriptor measures. First, population TL-moments exist and determine uniquely a probability distribution under less restrictive conditions than for population (L)-moments. Indeed, for a symmetric trimming parameter $r$ and a real valued random variable $X$, all the TL-moments exist if $E\left[|X|\right]^{-(1+r)} < \infty$. (see Hosking, 2007, theorem 1). That is, a distribution may be specified by its TL-moments, even if some of its L-moments and C-moments do not exist[7]. Furthermore, this specification is unique. Second, Trimmed L-moments are more robust to data outliers and less sensitive to sample size, since they are linear combinations of order statitics, that assign zero weight to a predetermined number of extreme sample values. They also provide a large class of reliable estimators for extreme value densities, that encompass most of the robust statistics that have been used in regional frequency analysis, where large deviations matter (see Hosking, 1990).[8]

After recalling the different definitions of the univariate population Trimmed L-moments, we present in the following sub-section their sample unbiased estimator counterparts and discuss their interpretations in terms of quantile distorsion function.

[7]For instance, a distribution may be specified by the TL-moments, even if the distribution does not have a finite first order (L)-moment as for the Cauchy distribution.

[8]The main area of application of Trimmed L-moments is the analysis of catastrophic events, such as extreme floods (see Hosking and Wallis, 2007, Wang, 1997, Bayazit and Onoz, 2002, Moisello, 2007); rainfall extremes (see Guttman *et al.*, 1993, Lee and Maeng, 2003); extreme wind speeds (see Whalen, 2004), or extreme traffic volumes in computer networks (see Hosking, 2007).

## 2.1. Population Trimmed L-Moments

Population TL-moments are defined as particular weighted sums of expectations of remaining order statistics, after trimming (a)symmetrically some extreme observations in the conceptual samples of the underlying random variable[9].

More formally, let $\{X_j\}$, with $j = [1, \ldots, k+2r]$ and $(k \times r) \in (IN_+^* \times IR_+)$, be a conceptual random sample of size $(k+2r)$, drawn from a continuous probability distribution $F(.)$ of a real-valued random variable $X$, with $E\left[\|X\|\right]^{-(1+r)} < \infty$; $Q\left(u\right) = F^{-1}\left(u\right)$, for $u = ]0,1[$, a quantile function, and $X_{[1:k+2r]} \leq X_{[2:k+2r]} \leq \cdots \leq X_{[k:k+2r]}$ denoting the corresponding order statistics[10]. Then, the $k$-th population univariate TL-moment is defined $\forall\left(k \times r\right) \in \left(IN_+^* \times IR_+\right)$ as (see, Elamir and Seheult, 2003, and Hosking, 2007):

$$\begin{aligned} \lambda_k^{(r)}\left(X\right) &= \sum_{j=0}^{k-1} \left(-1\right)^j \left\{\frac{\left[(k-1)!\right]}{\left[k\left(k-j-1\right)!j!\right]}\right\} E\left(X_{[k+r-j:k+2r]}\right) \\ &= \int_0^1 Q\left(u\right) H_{k-1}^{(r)}\left(u\right) du \end{aligned} \tag{1}$$

with:

$$\left\{\begin{aligned} E\left(X_{[n:k]}\right) &= \left\{\left[(n-1)!\left(k-n\right)!\right]^{-1}\left(k!\right)\right\} \\ &\quad \times \int_0^1 Q\left(u\right) u^{n-1}\left(1-u\right)^{k-n} du \\ H_k^{(r)}\left(u\right) &= \left\{\left[\left(k+1\right)\left[\left(k+r\right)!\right]^2\right]^{-1}\left[\left(k\right)!\left(k+1+2r\right)!\right]\right\} \\ &\quad \times u^r\left(1-u\right)^r P_k^{*(r)}\left(u\right) \end{aligned}\right.$$

where $\lambda_k^{(r)}\left(.\right)$ is the TL-moment of order $k$ with (symmetric) trimming degree $r$, $n = \left[0, \ldots, \left(k-1\right)\right]$, $E\left(.\right)$ is the expectation operator, $H_k^{(r)}\left(.\right)$ is the weighting polynomial of degree $k$ and $P_k^{*(r)}\left(.\right)$ is the shifted orthogonal Jacobi polynomial

[9]Following the approach of Elamir and Seheult (2003), we focus in this article on the symmetrical trimming case only.

[10]$X_{[j:k]}$ corresponds to the $j$-th smallest observation from a sample of size $k$.

of degree $k$, defined such as:

$$\begin{cases} P_k^{*(r)}(u) = \sum_{j=0}^{k} p_{k,,j}^{*(r)} \times \left[u^j (1-u)^{k-j}\right] \\ p_{k,,j}^{*(r)} = (-1)^{k-j} \left[(k+r-j)!j!\,(r+j)!(k-j)!\right]^{-1} \times \left[(k+r)!\right]^2 \end{cases}$$

where $p_{k,,j}^{*(r)}$ correspond to the $j$-$th$ coefficient of the shifthed Jacobi polynomial $P_k^{*(r)}(.)$[11].

The shifted Jacobi polynomials are orthogonal on the interval $[0,1]$, with weight function $u^r(1-u)^r$, so that $\forall\,(k,l,r) \in \left(IN_+^{*2} \times IR_+\right)$:

$$\begin{cases} P_0^{*(r)}(u) = 1 \\ \int_0^1 u^r(1-u)^r P_k^*(u) P_l^*(u) du = \begin{cases} 0 & \text{if } k \neq l \\ \frac{[\Gamma(k+r)]^2}{(2k+2r-1)[(k-1)!\Gamma(k+2r)]} & \text{if } k = l \end{cases} \end{cases} \quad (2)$$

where $\Gamma(.)$ is the complete Gamma function.

By the orthogonality of the Jacobi polynomials, the TL-moments $\lambda_k^{(r)}(.)$ capture differing informations about the distribution function of the underlying variable. In particular, the first four population Trimmed L-moments satisfy, for trimming level $r \geq 0$:

$$\begin{cases} \lambda_1^{(r)}(X) = E\left(X_{[1+r:1+2r]}\right) \\ \lambda_2^{(r)}(X) = (2)^{-1} E\left(X_{[2+r:2+2r]} - X_{[1+r:2+2r]}\right) \\ \lambda_3^{(r)}(X) = (3)^{-1} E\left[\left(X_{[3+r:3+2r]} - X_{[2+r:3+2r]}\right)\right. \\ \qquad \left. - \left(X_{[2+r:3+2r]} - X_{[1+r:3+2r]}\right)\right] \\ \lambda_4^{(r)}(X) = (4)^{-1} E\left[\left(X_{[4+r:4+2r]} - X_{[1+r:4+2r]}\right)\right. \\ \qquad \left. -3\left(X_{[3+r:4+2r]} - X_{[2+r:4+2r]}\right)\right] \end{cases} \quad (3)$$

Using relation $(1)$, they also satisfy the following equalities:

$$\begin{cases} \lambda_1^{(r)}(X) = \int_0^1 Q(u)\, H_0^{(r)}(u)\, du \\ \lambda_2^{(r)}(X) = \int_0^1 Q(u)\, H_1^{(r)}(u)\, du \\ \lambda_3^{(r)}(X) = \int_0^1 Q(u)\, H_2^{(r)}(u)\, du \\ \lambda_4^{(r)}(X) = \int_0^1 Q(u)\, H_3^{(r)}(u)\, du \end{cases} \quad (4)$$

[11]Note that $P_k^{*(r)}(u) = P_k^{(r)}(2u-1)$, where $P_k^{(r)}(.)$ is the traditional (unshifted) Jacobi polynomial of degree $k$ (see Abramowitz and Stegun, 1972, equation 22.3.1, p. 775).

where $H_k^{(r)}(.)$ is the weighting polynomial of degree $k$, defined as in $(1)$, with $k = [0, \ldots, 3]$[12].

Clearly, when $r = 0$, the population TL-moments reduce to the ordinary population L-moments. For $r = 1$, the first four theoretical TL-moments are then given by[13]:

$$\begin{cases} \lambda_1^{(1)}(X) = E\left(X_{[2:3]}\right) = \int_0^1 Q(u)\, H_0^{(1)}(u)\, du \\ \lambda_2^{(1)}(X) = (2)^{-1} E\left(X_{[3:4]} - X_{[2:4]}\right) = \int_0^1 Q(u)\, H_1^{(1)}(u)\, du \\ \lambda_3^{(1)}(X) = (3)^{-1} E\left[\left(X_{[4:5]} - X_{[3:5]}\right) - \left(X_{[3:5]} - X_{[2:5]}\right)\right] \\ \qquad = \int_0^1 Q(u)\, H_2^{(1)}(u)\, du \\ \lambda_4^{(1)}(X) = (4)^{-1} E\left[\left(X_{[5:6]} - X_{[2:6]}\right) - 3\left(X_{[4:6]} - X_{[3:6]}\right)\right] \\ \qquad = \int_0^1 Q(u)\, H_3^{(1)}(u)\, du \end{cases} \tag{5}$$

with:

$$\begin{cases} H_0^{(1)}(u) = (3!) \times \left(u - u^2\right) \\ H_1^{(1)}(u) = (3!) \times \left(-2u^3 + 3u^2 - u\right) \\ H_2^{(1)}(u) = (3)^{-1} \times 20 \times \left(-5\,u^4 + 10\,u^3 - 6\,u^2 + u\right) \\ H_3^{(1)}(u) = (2)^{-1} \times 15 \times \left(-14\,u^5 + 35u^4 - 30\,u^3 + 10\,u^2 - u\right) \end{cases}$$

Notice that $\lambda_1^{(r)}(.)$, $\lambda_2^{(r)}(.)$, $\lambda_3^{(r)}(.)$ and $\lambda_4^{(r)}(.)$, are respectively population measures of location, scale and shape, analogous to the corresponding ordinary

---

[12] That is, $\forall\,(k \times r) \in ([1, \ldots, 4] \times IR_+)$:

$$\begin{cases} H_0^{(r)}(u) = [(1+2r)!] \times [u^r\ (1-u)^r] \\ H_1^{(r)}(u) = \frac{[(2+2r)!]\left[u^{r+1}(1-u)^r - u^r(1-u)^{r+1}\right]}{[2\,(r!)(1+r)!]} \\ H_2^{(r)}(u) = \frac{\left\{u^{r+2}(1-u)^r - 2[(r+1)!]^{-2}[r!(r+2)!]\,u^{r+1}(1-u)^{r+1} + u^r(1-u)^{r+2}\right\}}{\{[(3+2r)!]\}^{-1}\,[3\,(r!)(2+r)!]} \\ H_3^{(r)}(u) = \frac{\left\{u^{r+3}(1-u)^r - 3\left[(r+1)^{-1}\right](r+3)\,u^{r+2}(1-u)^{r+1}\right.}{\left\{[(4+2r)!]^{-1}\right\}[4\,(r!)(3+r)!]} \\ \qquad + \frac{\left\{3\left[(r+1)^{-1}\right](r+3)u^{r+1}(1-u)^{r+2} - u^r(1-u)^{r+3}\right\}}{\left\{[(4+2r)!]^{-1}\right\}[4\,(r!)(3+r)!]} \end{cases}$$

[13] Elamir and Seheult (2003) derive explicitly the first four TL-moments, with a symmetric trimming degree $r = 1$, for a Gaussian distribution with parameters $(\mu, \sigma)$, such as: $\lambda_1^{(1)} = \mu$, $\lambda_2^{(1)} = 0.297\,\sigma$, $\lambda_3^{(1)} = 0$ and $\lambda_4^{(1)} = 0.18\ \sigma$; for a Logistic distribution with parameters $(\mu, \sigma)$, such as: $\lambda_1^{(1)} = \mu$, $\lambda_2^{(1)} = 0.5\ \sigma$, $\lambda_3^{(1)} = 0$ and $\lambda_4^{(1)} = 0.042\ \sigma$; for a Cauchy distribution with parameters $(\mu, \sigma)$, such as: $\lambda_1^{(1)} = \mu$, $\lambda_2^{(1)} = 0.698\,\sigma$, $\lambda_3^{(1)} = 0$ and $\lambda_4^{(1)} = 0.239\,\sigma$; and for an Exponential distribution with parameter $\alpha$, such as: $\lambda_1^{(1)} = (6)^{-1}\,5\,\alpha$, $\lambda_2^{(1)} = (4)^{-1}\,\alpha$, $\lambda_3^{(1)} = (36)^{-1}\,2\,\alpha$ and $\lambda_4^{(1)} = (48)^{-1}\ \alpha$.

(L)-moments. The first order TL-moment, for $r \geq 0$, is the expectation of the median of a conceptual random sample of size $(1 + 2r)$, and the second TL-moment is a measure of the expected range of a conceptual random sample of size $(2 + 2r)$, after deleting the $r$-*th* smallest and $r$-*th* largest conceptual observations. In short, the third TL-moment simply represents the expected difference between the upper tail and the lower tail from a conceptual sample of size $(3 + 2r)$, and measures the skewness of the population distribution from which the random sample has been drawn. Similarly, the fourth L-moment measures the *kurtosis* of the probability distribution function, since it can be expressed, for a conceptual sample of size $(4 + 2r)$, as a (rescaled) difference between the spread in the tails and the spread in the center[14].

The patterns of the first four weighting polynomials $H_k^{(r)}(.)$ are displayed in figure 1 for varying degree of trimming parameter $r$. This figure shows how the population TL-moments give less weights than the population L-moments $(r = 0)$ to the extreme observations, which are generally outliers, and eventually more weights to the median. Indeed, the polynomials $H_k^{(r)}(.)$ introduce shrinkages in the neighboroods of quantile values $u = 0; 1$ and eventually $0.5$. These shrinkages are controlled by the amount of trimming and the order of the TL-moment.[15]

While equation $(1)$ is the classical L-functional's definition for the population TL-moments, there exist several other definitions for $\lambda_k^{(r)}(.)$ that prove to be useful for financial applications (see below). For example, using the definition of the Probability Weighted Moments, we can express equation $(1)$ as a

[14]It is also possible to define scale-free versions of population TL-moments, by dividing higher-order TL-moments by the second TL-moment, that is, $\forall (k \times r) \in ([IN_+^* - \{1,2\}] \times IR_+)$ (see Elamir and Seheult, 2003):

$$\tau_k^{(r)}(X) = \left[\lambda_2^{(r)}(X)\right]^{-1} \times \left[\lambda_k^{(r)}(X)\right]$$

with:

$$\left|\tau_k^{(r)}(X)\right| \leq \frac{2(r+1)!(k+2r)!}{k(k+r+1)!(2r+2)!}$$

where $\tau_k^{(r)}(.)$ is the population TL-moment ratio of order $k$, and $\lambda_2^{(r)}(.)$ and $\lambda_k^{(r)}(.)$ are respectively the second and the $k$-*th* population TL-moment, for trimming level $r$, as defined in $(4)$. Contrary to the L-moment ratios, population TL-moments ratios are not bounded by 1 in absolute value (see Hosking, 2007).

[15]The weighting polynomials $H_1^{(r)}(.)$ define for instance distorsion risk measures (see Wang 2000-a, 2000-b, and Gourieroux and Liu, 2006).

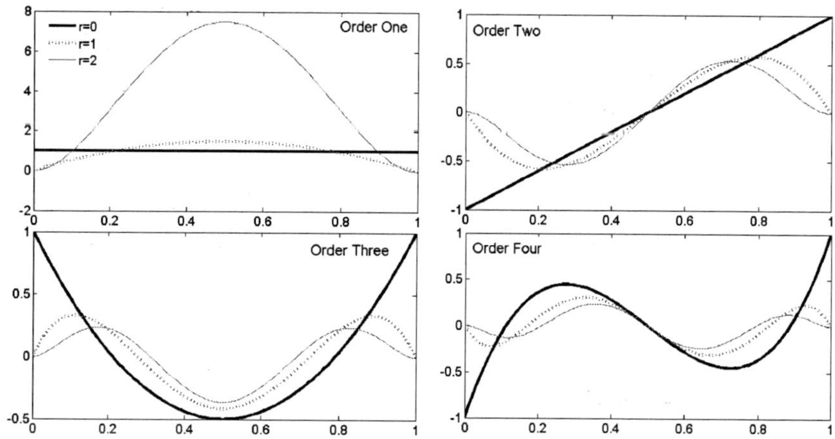


Figure 1. Polynomial weights for first four-order Trimmed L-moments with different degree of trimming parameter *r*.

linear function of Probability Weigthed Moments, that is (see Greenwood *et al.*, 1979, and Hosking, 2007):

$$\lambda_k^{(r)}(X) = \sum_{i=r}^{(k-1+2r)} z_{k-1,i}^{(r)} \beta_i(X) \tag{6}$$

with:

$$\begin{cases} \beta_i(X) = E\left\{X\ [F(X)]^i\right\} = \int_0^1 Q(u)\ u^i\, du \\ z_{k,i}^{(r)} = (-1)^{k+r-i}\left[(k+1+2r)!\,(k+i)!\right] \\ \qquad \times\left[(k+1)\,(k+r)!(k+2r-i)!(i-r)!i!\right]^{-1} \end{cases}$$

where $z_{k,i}^{(r)}$ is the coefficient of $u^i$ in $P_k^{*(r)}(u)$, the shifted Jacobi polynomial of degree $k$, as defined previously in $(1)$, with $(k \times r) \in (IN_+^* \times IR_+)$; and $\beta_i(X)$ is the Probability Weighted Moment of order $i$, with $i = [r, \ldots, (k-1+2r)]$.

Using the definition and orthogonal property of the shifted Jacobi polynomials, the *k-th* population TL-moment can also be represented alternatively, for $r \geq 0$, as the covariance between the random variable $X$ and a particular function of its (centered) rank, denoted $F(X)$, that is (see Serfling and Xiao, 2007):

$$\lambda_k^{(r)}(X) = Cov\left\{X,\, H_{k-1}^{(r)}[F(X)]\right\} \tag{7}$$

with:

$$\begin{cases} E\left\{H_{k-1}^{(r)}\left[F\left(X\right)\right]\right\} = \int_0^1 1 \times H_{k-1}^{(r)}\left(u\right) du = 0 \\ H_k^{(r)}\left(u\right) = \left\{\left[\left(k+1\right)\left[\left(k+r\right)!\right]^2\right]^{-1}\left[\left(k\right)!\left(k+1+2r\right)!\right]\right\} \\ \qquad \times u^r\left(1-u\right)^r P_k^{*(r)}\left(u\right) \\ P_0^{*(r)}\left(u\right) = 1 \end{cases}$$

where $Cov(.,.)$ is the covariance operator, $H_k^{(r)}(.)$ and $P_k^{*(r)}(.)$ are respectively the weighting polynomial and the shifted Jacobi polynomial of degree $k$, defined as in $(1)$, with $(k \times r) \in \left(IN_+^* \times IR_+\right)$.

Since $E\left[F\left(X\right)\right] = 1/2$, the first four population TL-moments in $(5)$ can then be reexpress as:

$$\begin{cases} \lambda_1^{(1)}\left(X\right) = -\left(3!\right) E\left\{\left[X - E\left(X\right)\right]\left[F\left(X\right) - E\left[F\left(X\right)\right]\right]^2\right\} \\ \lambda_2^{(1)}\left(X\right) = -\left(3!\right)\left[2E\left\{\left[X - E\left(X\right)\right]\left[F\left(X\right) - E\left[F\left(X\right)\right]\right]^3\right\}\right. \\ \qquad \left. -\left(4\right)^{-1}\lambda_2\left(X\right)\right] \\ \lambda_3^{(1)}\left(X\right) = -\left(3\right)^{-1} 20\left[5E\left\{\left[X - E\left(X\right)\right]\left[F\left(X\right) - E\left[F\left(X\right)\right]\right]^4\right\}\right. \\ \qquad \left. +\left(4\right)^{-1}\lambda_1^{(1)}\left(X\right)\right] \\ \lambda_4^{(1)}\left(X\right) = -\left(2\right)^{-1} 15\left[14E\left\{\left[X - E\left(X\right)\right]\left[F\left(X\right) - E\left[F\left(X\right)\right]\right]^5\right\}\right. \\ \qquad \left. +\left(12\right)^{-1} 5\,\lambda_2^{(1)}\left(X\right) - \left(16\right)^{-1} 7\,\lambda_2\left(X\right)\right] \end{cases} \tag{8}$$

with:

$$\begin{cases} E\left[F\left(X\right)\right] = 1/2 \\ \lambda_2\left(X\right) = 2E\left\{\left[X - E\left(X\right)\right]\left[F\left(X\right) - E\left[F\left(X\right)\right]\right]\right\} \end{cases}$$

where $\lambda_1^{(1)}(.)$ and $\lambda_2^{(1)}(.)$ correspond respectively to the TL-mean and the TL-variance, with $r = 1$, $\lambda_2(.)$ is the L-variance, and $\lambda_3^{(1)}(.)$ and $\lambda_4^{(1)}(.)$ represent respectively the unscaled versions of the TL-skewness and TL-*kurtosis* of the population distribution $F(.)$.

The population TL-moments, presented in $(1)$ or $(5)$, are defined for a given probability distribution, but in practice, they are directly estimated with some uncertainty from a finite sample, corresponding to an unknown probability distribution. The following sub-subsection is devoted to a brief presentation of the sample counterparts of the population TL-moments.

## 2.2. Sample Trimmed L-Moments

Following Hosking (1989), the sample TL-moments can be estimated in a straigthforward manner, by estimating the empirical quantile function in conjunction with the L-statistic representation (4).

Indeed, let $X_{[1:T]} \leq X_{[2:T]} \leq \cdots \leq X_{[T:T]}$ be the order statistics of $T$ identically and independently distributed observations $\{X_{t,}\}$, drawn from a continuous probability distribution, with a cumulative distribution function $F(.)$, and $Q(u) = F^{-1}(u)$, for $u = ]0,1[$, a quantile function with $t = [1, \ldots, T]$ and $T \in IN_{+}^{*}$. The sample quantile function estimator is then given by:

$$\widehat{Q}_T(u) = \inf\left\{X \colon (T)^{-1} \sum_{t=1}^{T} \mathbf{1}_{(X_t \leq x)} \geq u\right\} \tag{9}$$

where $\widehat{Q}_T(.)$ is the empirical quantile function estimator.

For a sample of size $T$, the $k$-th univariate TL-moment can be consistently estimated by (see Serfling and Xiao, 2006):

$$\widehat{\lambda}_k^{(r)}(X) = \int_0^1 \widehat{Q}_T(u)\, H_{k-1}^{(r)}(u)\, du \tag{10}$$

where $\widehat{\lambda}_k^{(r)}(.)$ is the sample counterpart of the corresponding *k-th* population TL-moment $\lambda_k^{(r)}(.)$, $(r \times k \times T) = IR_{+} \times \left(IN_{+}^{*}\right)^2$, with $r < k < T$; $H_{k-1}^{(r)}(.)$ is the weighting quantile polynomial of degree $(k-1)$, defined as in equation (1), and $t = [1, \ldots, T]$.

This TL-moment estimator is also equivalent to[16]:

$$\begin{aligned}
\widehat{\lambda}_k^{(r)}(X) &= (T)^{-1} \sum_{t=1}^{T} \left[\int_{(t-1)/T}^{t/T} H_{k-1}^{(r)}(u)\,(du)\right] \times X_{[t:T]} \\
&= (T)^{-1} \sum_{t=1}^{T} H_{k-1}^{(r)}(t/T) \times X_{[t:T]} + o_{H_{k-1}^{(r)}}(1)
\end{aligned} \tag{11}$$

where $o_{H_{k-1}^{(r)}}(.)$ correspond to the Landau symbol[17]. In particular, the first four

[16] The asymptotic properties of the estimated TL-moments follow from the asymptotic properties of the quantile function estimator.

[17] From Landau's notation, $o\left[f(x)\right]$ means that:

$$\lim_{x \longrightarrow 0} \left\{f(x)^{-1} o\left[f(x)\right]\right\} = 0$$

sample Trimmed L-moments are given, with $r = 1$, by (with previous notations):[18]

$$\begin{cases} \widehat{\lambda}_1^{(r)}(X) \simeq (T)^{-1} \sum_{t=1}^{T} [(1+2r)!] \{(t/T)^r [1-(t/T)]^r\} X_{t:T} \\ \widehat{\lambda}_2^{(r)}(X) \simeq (T)^{-1} \sum_{t=1}^{T} \frac{\{(t/T)^{r+1}[1-(t/T)]^r - (t/T)^r[1-(t/T)]^{r+1}\}}{\{[(2+2r)!]^{-1}\}[2(r!)(1+r)!]} X_{t:T} \\ \widehat{\lambda}_3^{(r)}(X) \simeq (T)^{-1} \\ \times \sum_{t=1}^{T} \frac{\{(t/T)^{r+2}[1-(t/T)]^r - 2[(r+1)!]^{-2}[r!(r+2)!](t/T)^{r+1}[1-(t/T)]^{r+1}}{\{[(3+2r)!]\}^{-1}[3(r!)(2+r)!]} \\ + \frac{(t/T)^r[1-(t/T)]^{r+2}\}}{\{[(3+2r)!]\}^{-1}[3(r!)(2+r)!]} X_{t:T} \\ \widehat{\lambda}_4^{(r)}(X) \simeq (T)^{-1} \\ \times \sum_{t=1}^{T} \left[ \frac{\{(t/T)^{r+3}[1-(t/T)]^r - 3[(r+1)^{-1}](r+3)(t/T)^{r+2}[1-(t/T)]^{r+1}}{\{[(4+2r)!]^{-1}\}} \right. \\ \left. + \frac{3[(r+1)^{-1}](r+3)(t/T)^{r+1}\}}{\{[(4+2r)!]^{-1}\}} \right] \frac{\times[1-(t/T)]^{r+2} - (t/T)^r[1-(t/T)]^{r+3}\}}{[4(r!)(3+r)!]} X_{t:T} \end{cases} \quad (12)$$

Figure 2 illustrates the time-evolutions of the (rescaled) recursive sample TL-moment against their corresponding L-moment and C-moment estimates, calculated on a long history of daily quotes of the S&P500 stock index, from 1950 to 2009. As expected, this figure confirms that the sample TL-moments are less prone to the influence of outliers and more stable than their traditional L-moment and C-moment counterparts.

The main properties of the population TL-moments and their corresponding sample quantities now stated, we generalize in the next section, by using the shortage function approach of Briec *et al.* (2004), the mean-variance efficient frontier in the first four TL-moment space.

---

[18]Analogously to (11), sample TL-moment ratios are defined, $\forall k \in IN^* - \{1\}$, as:

$$\widehat{\tau}_k^{(r)}(X) = \left[\widehat{\lambda}_2^{(r)}(X)\right]^{-1} \times \left[\widehat{\lambda}_k^{(r)}(X)\right]$$

where $\widehat{\tau}_k^{(r)}(.)$ is the sample TL-moment ratio of order $k$; and $\widehat{\lambda}_2^{(r)}(.)$ and $\widehat{\lambda}_k^{(r)}$ are respectively the second and *k-th* sample TL-moment defined in (11).

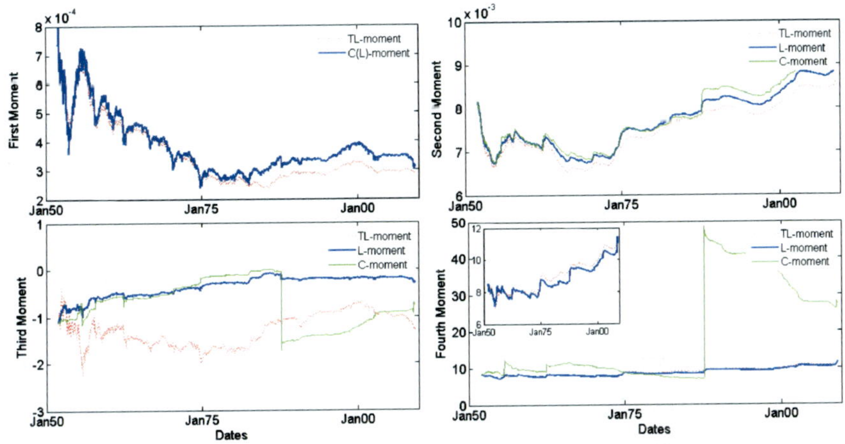


**Source**: Bloomberg, daily net asset values (1950-2009); computations by the authors. The y-axis corresponds to the level of the recursive classical moments (in blue line); the corresponding recursive ordinary L-moments (in blue line) and TL-moments (in red line). The TL-moments are rescaled in order to get the same means as their relative conventional counterparts.

Figure 2. Comparison of ordinary moments and L-moments versus TL-moments.

# 3. Portfolio Selection with Higher-order Trimmed L-Moments

In this section, we lay out the foundations for the multi-objective portfolio optimization program used to derive the four TL-moment efficient frontier. Basically, we follow the non-parametric portfolio performance gauging method initiated by Briec *et al.* (2004) in the mean-variance plane, and generalized into higher-order moment spaces by Jurczenko *et al.* (2006 and 2008) and Briec *et al.* (2007)[19]. By analogy with production theory (see Luenberger, 1995), these authors have defined a shortage function that measures the distance between the portfolios (assets) under evaluation and their moment-based radial projections onto the Pareto efficient frontier. Starting from a selected portfolio, this method looks simultaneoulsy for the maximum possible contraction in the even

[19]See also Kerstens *et al.* (2009) and Bacmann and Benedetti (2009).

moment space and the maximum possible expansion in the odd moment dimensions. Moreover the shortage function ensures that the final optimal solutions ly on the non-convex efficient frontier, since it respects the sufficient conditions for global optimality (see Briec *et al.*, 2007). This section essentially summarizes the theoretical framework developped in Jurczenko *et al.* (2008), except that we now extend the L-moment portfolio selection framework to allow for trimming outlier observations.

## 3.1. Notations and Hypotheses

We consider the problem of an investor selecting a portfolio from $N$ risky assets (with $N \geq 4$) in the TL-mean-variance-skewness-*kurtosis* space. We assume that the investor does not have access to a riskless asset, implying that portfolio weights must sum to one. In addition we impose a no short-sale portfolio constraint, so that asset positions must be non-negative. Let $\mathbf{w}_p$, $\mathbf{R}$, $\mathbf{E}$ and $\epsilon$ denote respectively the $(N \times 1)$ vectors of weight, rate of returns, expected returns and centered returns for the risky assets in the portfolio $p$; and $\mathbf{\Sigma}_{p,1}^{(TL)}$, $\mathbf{\Gamma}_{p,1}^{(TL)}$, $\mathbf{\Phi}_{p,1}^{(TL)}$ and $\mathbf{\Psi}_{p,1}^{(TL)}$ represent respectively the $(N \times 1)$ vectors of the first four TL-comoments, defined as (with previous notations):

$$\begin{cases} \mathbf{\Sigma}_{p,1}^{(TL)} = Cov\left[\mathbf{R}, H_0^{(1)}\left[F\left(R_p\right)\right]\mathbf{1}\right] = -\ (3!)\ E\left[\epsilon \times \left(\eta_p\right)^2 \mathbf{1}\right] \\ \mathbf{\Gamma}_{p,1}^{(TL)} = Cov\left[\mathbf{R}, H_1^{(1)}\left[F\left(R_p\right)\right]\mathbf{1}\right] \\ \qquad = -\,12\,E\left[\epsilon \times \left(\eta_p\right)^3 \mathbf{1}\right] + 3\,E\left(\epsilon \times \eta_p\,\mathbf{1}\right) \\ \mathbf{\Phi}_{p,1}^{(TL)} = Cov\left[\mathbf{R}, H_2^{(1)}\left[F\left(R_p\right)\right]\mathbf{1}\right] \\ \qquad = -\ (3)^{-1}\,100\,E\left[\epsilon \times \left(\eta_p\right)^4 \mathbf{1}\right] + 10\,E\left[\epsilon \times \left(\eta_p\right)^2 \mathbf{1}\right] \\ \mathbf{\Psi}_{p,1}^{(TL)} = Cov\left[\mathbf{R}, H_3^{(1)}\left[F\left(R_p\right)\right]\mathbf{1}\right] = -\,105\,E\left[\epsilon \times \left(\eta_p\right)^5 \mathbf{1}\right] \\ \qquad + (2)^{-1}\,75\,E\left[\epsilon \times \left(\eta_p\right)^3 \mathbf{1}\right] + (4)^{-1}\,5\,E\left[\epsilon \times \left(\eta_p\right)\mathbf{1}\right] \end{cases} \tag{13}$$

with:

$$\begin{cases} \epsilon = (\mathbf{R} - \mathbf{E}) \\ \eta_p = \left\{F\left(R_p\right) - E\left[F\left(R_p\right)\right]\right\} \\ E\left[F\left(R_p\right)\right] = 1/2 \end{cases}$$

where $H_k^{(1)}(.)$ is the weighting polynomial of order $k$, defined as in (1), with $k = [0, \ldots, 3]$; $\epsilon$ is the vector of centered returns of the risky assets, and $\eta_p$ is the centered distribution of the portfolio rate of return $F\left(R_p\right)$.

The set of the feasible portfolio weights $\mathfrak{F}_p$ can then be expressed as follows:

$$\mathfrak{F}_p = \left\{ \mathbf{w}_p \in IR^N \,\middle|\, \mathbf{w}_p^{'} \mathbf{1} = 1 \text{ and } \mathbf{w}_p \geq \mathbf{0} \right\} \tag{14}$$

where $\mathbf{w}_p^{'}$ is the $(1 \times N)$ transposed vector of the investor's holdings in the various risky assets, $\mathbf{1}$ is the $(N \times 1)$ unitary vector, and $\mathbf{0}$ is the $(N \times 1)$ null vector.

Using the covariance definition of the TL-moments $(7)$ and the bi-linear property of the covariance operator, the TL-mean, TL-variance, TL-skewness and TL-*kurtosis* of the return on any feasible portfolio $p$ are respectively given, for $r = 1$, by:

$$\begin{cases} \lambda_1^{(1)}(R_p) = \sum_{i=1}^{N} w_{pi}\, Cov\left\{R_i,\, H_0^{(1)}[F(R_p)]\right\} \\ \lambda_2^{(1)}(R_p) = \sum_{i=1}^{N} w_{pi}\, Cov\left\{R_i,\, H_1^{(1)}[F(R_p)]\right\} \\ \lambda_3^{(1)}(R_p) = \sum_{i=1}^{N} w_{pi}\, Cov\left\{R_i,\, H_2^{(1)}[F(R_p)]\right\} \\ \lambda_4^{(1)}(R_p) = \sum_{i=1}^{N} w_{pi}\, Cov\left\{R_i,\, H_3^{(1)}[F(R_p)]\right\} \end{cases} \tag{15}$$

with, $\forall i \in [1, \ldots, N]$:

$$\begin{cases} Cov\left\{R_i,\, H_0^{(1)}[F(R_p)]\right\} = -\,(3!)\, E\left[\epsilon_i \times (\eta_p)^2\right] \\ Cov\left\{R_i,\, H_1^{(1)}[F(R_p)]\right\} = -\,12\, E\left[\epsilon_i \times (\eta_p)^3\right] + 3\, E\left[\epsilon_i \times \eta_p\right] \\ Cov\left\{R_i,\, H_2^{(1)}[F(R_p)]\right\} = -\,(3)^{-1}\, 100\, E\left[\epsilon_i \times (\eta_p)^4\right] \\ \qquad\qquad + 10\, E\left[\epsilon_i \times (\eta_p)^2\right] \\ Cov\left\{R_i, H_3^{(1)}[F(R_p)]\right\} = -\,105\, E\left[\epsilon_i \times (\eta_p)^5\right] \\ \qquad + (2)^{-1}\, 75\, E\left[\epsilon_i \times (\eta_p)^3\right] + (4)^{-1}\, 5\, E\left[\epsilon_i \times (\eta_p)\right] \end{cases}$$

and:

$$\begin{cases} R_p = \sum_{i=1}^{N} w_{pi}\, R_i \\ E[F(R_p)] = 1/2 \end{cases}$$

where $w_{pi}$, $R_i$ and $\epsilon_i$ correspond, respectively, to the security's $i$ weight, performance and centered retun; and $Cov\left\{R_i,\, H_{k-1}^{(1)}[F(R_p)]\right\}$ is the TL-co-moment of order $(k-1)$ between the security $i$ return and the portfolio $p$ return, with $k = [1, \ldots, 4]$ . That is:

$$\begin{cases} \lambda_1^{(1)}(R_p) = \mathbf{w}_p' \, \mathbf{\Sigma}_{p,1}^{(TL)} \\ \lambda_2^{(1)}(R_p) = \mathbf{w}_p' \, \mathbf{\Gamma}_{p,1}^{(TL)} \\ \lambda_3^{(1)}(R_p) = \mathbf{w}_p' \, \mathbf{\Phi}_{p,1}^{(TL)} \\ \lambda_4^{(1)}(R_p) = \mathbf{w}_p' \, \mathbf{\Psi}_{p,1}^{(TL)} \end{cases} \tag{16}$$

where $\mathbf{\Sigma}_{p,1}^{(TL)}$, $\mathbf{\Gamma}_{p,1}^{(TL)}$, $\mathbf{\Phi}_{p,1}^{(TL)}$ and $\mathbf{\Psi}_{p,1}^{(TL)}$are defined in (14).

As in Markowitz (1952), the set of the feasible portfolio weights can be represented in the first four TL-moment space as:

$$\Lambda(\mathfrak{F}_p) = \left\{ \lambda_p^{(1)} \mid \mathbf{w}_p \in \mathfrak{F}_p \right\} \tag{17}$$

with:

$$\lambda_p^{(1)} = \left[ \lambda_1^{(1)}(R_p) \; ; \lambda_2^{(1)}(R_p) \; ; \; \lambda_3^{(1)}(R_p) \; ; \; \lambda_4^{(1)}(R_p) \right]'$$

where $\Lambda(.) : IR^N \longrightarrow IR^4$, is the function that maps the portfolio weight space into the four-dimensional TL-moment portfolio space, and $\lambda_p^{(1)}$ is the $(4 \times 1)$ vector of the first four TL-moments of a given portfolio $p$.

The investment opportunity set $\Lambda(\mathfrak{F}_p)$ can then be extended by defining a disposal representation set, denoted $\mathfrak{D}_p$, such as (see Briec *et al.,* 2004, and 2007):

$$\mathfrak{D}_p = \Lambda(\mathfrak{F}_p) + [(IR_-) \times (IR_+) \times (IR_-) \times (IR_+)] \tag{18}$$

This disposal representation is necessary to ensure the convexity of the feasible portfolio set in the four dimensional TL-moment space[20].

With respect to the four TL-moment portfolio coordinate space, we define a preorder on $IR^4$, denoted by $\succeq$, such that, $\forall \left(\lambda_p^{(1)}, \lambda_q^{(1)}\right) \in \left(IR^4\right)^2$ :

$$\lambda_p^{(1)} \succeq \lambda_q^{(1)} \Longleftrightarrow \left[ \lambda_{1,p}^{(1)} \geq \lambda_{1,q}^{(1)}, \lambda_{2,p}^{(1)} \leq \lambda_{2,q}^{(1)}, \lambda_{3,p}^{(1)} \geq \lambda_{3,q}^{(1)}, \lambda_{4,p}^{(1)} \leq \lambda_{4,q}^{(1)} \right] \tag{19}$$

altogether with a strict preference relation, denoted by $\succ$, as such:

$$\lambda_p^{(1)} \succ \lambda_q^{(1)} \Longleftrightarrow \left[ \lambda_{1,p}^{(1)} > \lambda_{1,q}^{(1)}, \lambda_{2,p}^{(1)} < \lambda_{2,q}^{(1)}, \lambda_{3,p}^{(1)} > \lambda_{3,q}^{(1)}, \lambda_{4,p}^{(1)} < \lambda_{4,q}^{(1)} \right] \tag{20}$$

[20]For the consequences of the non-convexity of the feasible set on the efficient portfolio frontier, see for instance, Zhang (2008) and Kerstens *et al.* (2009).

The weakly efficient portfolio frontier $\mathfrak{L}_p$ is then defined as follows:

$$\mathfrak{L}_p = \left\{ \lambda_p^{(1)} \in \mathfrak{D}_p \middle| \forall\, \lambda_q^{(1)} \in \left(IR^4\right),\, \lambda_q^{(1)} \succ \lambda_p^{(1)} \Rightarrow \lambda_q^{(1)} \notin \mathfrak{D}_p \right\} \tag{21}$$

while the strictly efficient frontier $\mathfrak{L}_p^*$ is defined as:

$$\mathfrak{L}_p^* = \Big\{ \lambda_p^{(1)} \in \mathfrak{D}_p \Big| \forall\, \lambda_q^{(1)} \in \left(IR^4\right),\, \lambda_q^{(1)} \succeq \lambda_p^{(1)} \text{ and } \lambda_q^{(1)} \neq \lambda_p^{(1)} \Rightarrow \lambda_q^{(1)} \notin \mathfrak{D}_p \Big\} \tag{22}$$

In brief, the strictly Pareto optimal frontier is the set of all the TL-mean, TL-variance, TL-skewness, TL-*kurtosis* portfolio quadruplets that are not strictly dominated in the investment opportunity set $\mathfrak{D}_p$. It is given in the simplex as:

$$\mathfrak{W}_p^* = \left\{ \mathbf{w}_p \in \mathfrak{F}_p \middle| \lambda_p^{(1)} \in \mathfrak{L}_p^* \right\} \tag{23}$$

The next section introduces the shortage function as an indicator of a portfolio TL (in)-efficiency and presents the non-convex portfolio optimization program in the first four TL-moment space. The solution of the resulting program will be called the four TL-moment efficient frontier.

## 3.2. The Shortage Function and the TL-Mean-Variance-Skewness-*Kurtosis* Efficient Frontier

Introduced by Luenberger (1995) in production theory, the shortage function is a directional distance function that offers a perfect representation of multidimensional choice sets and can position any feasible point relative to the efficient frontier. In particular, starting from a given portfolio, the shortage function is an efficiency measure that looks for the maximum potential improvements in the performance and risk dimensions. Thus, a given portfolio can either turn out to be efficient, or it may be inefficient, and then the shortage function bridges the distance to the Pareto frontier and provides an indication about its degree of inefficiency. It is this characteristic that makes the shortage function a perfect tool for solving Multi-objective Optimization Programs and representing portfolios and their projections in multidimensional spaces. The basic properties of the investment opportunity set $\mathfrak{D}_p$ on which the shortage function is defined have already been discussed in the higher moment space by Briec *et al.* (2004 and

2007) and Jurczenko *et al.* (2006 and 2008). Their definitions can now be extended in the context of portfolio selection with Trimmed L-moments to derive the four TL-moment efficient frontier.

The shortage function associated to a feasible portfolio $p$, with reference to the direction vector g in the TL-mean-variance-skewness-*kurtosis* space, is the real-valued function $\mathcal{S}_{\mathbf{g}}(.) : IR^4 \longrightarrow IR_+ \cup \{-\infty, +\infty\}$, defined as:

$$\mathcal{S}_{\mathbf{g}}\left[\Lambda\left(\mathbf{w}_p\right)\right] = \underset{\delta \in IR_+}{\text{Sup}} \left\{ \delta \,\middle|\, \lambda_p^{(1)} + \delta\, \mathbf{g} \in \mathfrak{D}_p \right\} \tag{24}$$

with:

$$\begin{cases} \lambda_p^{(1)} = \left[\lambda_1^{(1)}\left(R_p\right) ; \lambda_2^{(1)}\left(R_p\right) ; \lambda_3^{(1)}\left(R_p\right) ; \lambda_4^{(1)}\left(R_p\right)\right]' \\ \mathbf{g} = \left(g_1 ; g_2 ; g_3 ; g_4\right)' \end{cases}$$

where $\mathbf{g} \in IR_+ \times IR_- \times IR_+ \times IR_- \backslash \{0\}$ is the direction vector in the four TL-moment space.

The disposal representation of the investment opportunity set can now be used for deriving the lower bound of the true, but unknown, TL-moment efficient frontier, through the computation of the associated portfolio shortage function. Let us consider for instance a specific portfolio $q$ generated from a sample of $N$ assets - or portfolios - whose relative (in)-efficiency needs to be accessed in the first four TL-moment dimensions. Using the Goal Attainment method approach (see Gembicki and Haimes, 1975), the shortage function for this portfolio, in the four TL-moment space and in the direction vector $\mathbf{g}$, is computed by solving the following non-linear optimization program:

$$\begin{aligned} \mathbf{w}_p^* &= \underset{(\mathbf{w}_p, \delta) \in (\mathfrak{F}_p \times IR_+)}{Arg\,Max} \{\delta\} \\ & s.t. \begin{cases} \lambda_1^{(1)}\left(R_p\right) \geq \lambda_1^{(1)}\left(R_q\right) + \delta\, g_1 \\ \lambda_2^{(1)}\left(R_p\right) \leq \lambda_2^{(1)}\left(R_q\right) + \delta\, g_2 \\ \lambda_3^{(1)}\left(R_p\right) \geq \lambda_3^{(1)}\left(R_q\right) + \delta\, g_3 \\ \lambda_4^{(1)}\left(R_p\right) \leq \lambda_4^{(1)}\left(R_q\right) + \delta\, g_4 \end{cases} \end{aligned} \tag{25}$$

where $\mathbf{w}_{p^*}$ is the $(N \times 1)$ weakly efficient portfolio weight vector that maximizes the relative improvements over the evaluated portfolio TL-moment coordinates $\lambda_q^{(1)}$ in the direction vector $\mathbf{g} = \left(g_1 ; g_2 ; g_3 ; g_4\right)'$.

Using the vectorial notations of the portfolio Trimmed L-moments in (17) and the absolute values for the first four TL-moments of the specific portfolio $q$ in the expression of the direction vector g, the multi-objective portfolio optimization program (25) can be restated such as (with previous notations):

$$\mathbf{w}_p^* = \underset{(\mathbf{w}_p,\delta)\in(\mathfrak{F}_p\times IR_+)}{Arg\,Max} \{\delta\}$$
$$s.t. \begin{cases} \mathbf{w}_p^{'}\,\mathbf{\Sigma}_{p,1}^{(TL)} \geq \lambda_1^{(1)}(R_q) + \delta\left|\lambda_1^{(1)}(R_q)\right| \\ \mathbf{w}_p^{'}\,\mathbf{\Gamma}_{p,1}^{(TL)} \leq \lambda_2^{(1)}(R_q) - \delta\left|\lambda_2^{(1)}(R_q)\right| \\ \mathbf{w}_p^{'}\,\mathbf{\Phi}_{p,1}^{(TL)} \geq \lambda_3^{(2)}(R_q) + \delta\left|\lambda_3^{(1)}(R_q)\right| \\ \mathbf{w}_p^{'}\,\mathbf{\Psi}_{p,1}^{(TL)} \leq \lambda_4(R_q) - \delta\left|\lambda_4^{(1)}(R_q)\right| \end{cases} \tag{26}$$

with:

$$\mathbf{g} = \left[\left|\lambda_1^{(1)}(R_q)\right| ;\ -\left|\lambda_2^{(1)}(R_q)\right| ; \left|\lambda_3^{(1)}(R_q)\right| ;\ -\left|\lambda_4^{(1)}(R_q)\right|\right]^{'}$$

This particular choice of the direction vector turns the shortage function (25) into a proportional distance function, where the TL-mean and TL-skewness are proportionaly increased; while the TL-variance and TL-*kurtosis* are decreased in the same proportions[21].

Of key importance, is that the shortage function approach (24) respects sufficient conditions for a global optimum on the non-convex Trade-off surface (see Briec *et al.*, 2007, or Appendix 1 below). This makes the shortage function technique superior to the other primal and dual approaches, since the latter may only reach local optimal solutions. However the shortage function can only guarantee theoretically the weak efficiency for a portfolio, since it does not exclude projections on the vertical and horizontal parts of the investment opportunity set, allowing for additional improvements. To ensure that the radial projections of the four TL-moment points are part of the strongly efficient frontier, we then

[21] It is also necessary to use absolute values for the direction vector coordinates in the optimization program (26), since negative values cannot be precluded in practice for the TL-mean and the TL-skewness.

consider the following iterative version for (26):[22]

$$\mathbf{w}_p^{(j)*} = \underset{\left(\mathbf{w}_p^{(j)},\delta^{(j)}\right)\in(\mathfrak{F}_p\times IR_+)}{ArgMax} \left\{\delta^{(j)}\right\}$$
$$s.t. \begin{cases} s_{1,q}\left(\mathbf{w}_p^{(j)},\delta^{(j)},\mathbf{g}^{(j)}\right)\leq 0 \\ s_{2,q}\left(\mathbf{w}_p^{(j)},\delta^{(j)},\mathbf{g}^{(j)}\right)\geq 0 \\ s_{3,q}\left(\mathbf{w}_p^{(j)},\delta^{(j)},\mathbf{g}^{(j)}\right)\leq 0 \\ s_{4,q}\left(\mathbf{w}_p^{(j)},\delta^{(j)},\mathbf{g}^{(j)}\right)\geq 0 \end{cases} \tag{27}$$

with $s_{k,q}\left(\mathbf{w}_p^{(j)},\delta^{(j)},\mathbf{g}^{(j)}\right)$ the value of the $k$-*th* slack or surplus variable at step $j$, that is:

$$\begin{cases} s_{1,q}\left(\mathbf{w}_p^{(j)},\delta^{(j)},\mathbf{g}^{(j)}\right) = \lambda_1^{(1)}(R_q)+\delta^{(j)}g_1^{(j)}-\mathbf{w}_p^{(j)'}\boldsymbol{\Sigma}_{p,1}^{(j)(TL)} \\ s_{2,q}\left(\mathbf{w}_p^{(j)},\delta^{(j)},\mathbf{g}^{(j)}\right) = \lambda_2^{(1)}(R_q)+\delta^{(j)}g_2^{(j)}-\mathbf{w}_p^{(j)'}\boldsymbol{\Gamma}_{p,1}^{(j)(TL)} \\ s_{3,q}\left(\mathbf{w}_p^{(j)},\delta^{(j)},\mathbf{g}^{(j)}\right) = \lambda_3^{(1)}(R_q)+\delta^{(j)}g_3^{(j)}-\mathbf{w}_p^{(j)'}\boldsymbol{\Phi}_{p,1}^{(j)(TL)} \\ s_{4,q}\left(\mathbf{w}_p^{(j)},\delta^{(j)},\mathbf{g}^{(j)}\right) = \lambda_4^{(1)}(R_q)+\delta^{(j)}g_4^{(j)}-\mathbf{w}_p^{(j)'}\boldsymbol{\Psi}_{p,1}^{(j)(TL)} \end{cases}$$

and:

$$\begin{cases} \mathbf{g}^{(1)'}\in(IR_+\times IR_-\times IR_+\times IR_-)\setminus\{0\} \\ g_k^{(j)} = g_k^{(j-1)}\times \mathbf{1I}_{k\notin K^{(j-1)}} \\ K^{(j)} = \left\{k\in[1,\ldots,4]\,\middle|\, s_{k,q}\left(\mathbf{w}_p^{*(j)},\delta^{*(j)},\mathbf{g}^{(j)}\right)=0\right\} \end{cases}$$

where $\delta^{(j)}$ and $g_k^{(j)}$ correspond respectively to the shortage function of the evaluated portfolio and the $k$-*th* entry of the direction vector $\mathbf{g}^{(j)}$ at step $j$; $\mathbf{g}^{(1)}$ is the initial search direction vector; $\mathbf{1I}$ and $K^{(j)}$ represent respectively the indicator function and the set of indexes of saturated constraints in the multi-objective optimization program (27) at step $j$; and $(j\times k)=(IN^*\times[1,\ldots,4])$.

The intuition of this evolutionary method is to saturate at each step $j$, at least one of the four Trimmed L-moment inequality constraints in the optimization

[22]To ensure strict efficiency, one can also use an alternative directional efficiency measures in the multi-objective optimization program, such as the Färe-Lovell function, or consider additional restrictions on the marginal rates of subsitution (see, for instance, Wierzbicki, 1986, and Kerstens *et al.*, 2009).

program (27), while keeping saturated the already saturated ones. The starting point at each optimization step is then the weakly Pareto optimal portfolio characteristic vector in the four TL-moment space obtained at the previous step, and the direction function is modified in order to let the optimization process follow a path along the weakly efficient frontier. Because of its additional flexibility in choosing the direction vector, the evolutionary model (27) will always lead to zero-slack solutions on the strongly efficient frontier. For this model, the set of the non-dominated solutions always coincides with the Trade-off surface.

For illustrative purpose, we solve (27), starting with a specific portfolio $q$ and an initial direction vector $\mathbf{g}^{(1)} = (1, -1, 1, -1)^{'}$. Let $\left(\mathbf{w}_p^{1*}, \delta^{1*}\right)$ be the optimal solution obtained, and let $K^{(1)}$ be the set of indexes of saturated constraints at step one. If not all the inequality constraints are saturated at the optimum, *i.e.* $K^{(1)} \neq \{1, \ldots, 4\}$, we consider a second optimization step, where all the entries of the new direction vector $\mathbf{g}^{(2)}$ are defined such as $g_k^{(2)} = g_k^{(1)}$ if $k \notin K^{(1)}$, and $g_k^{(2)} = 0$ otherwise. If the slack or surplus variables are zero at the optimum, *i.e.* $K^{(1)} = \{1, \ldots, 4\}$, the portfolio solution then belongs to the strongly efficient portfolio frontier set, and the optimization process is stopped. If not, the optimization process will continue, until all constraints are saturated.

While the whole efficient frontier can be generated by using a simple fixed direction vector with different starting points, in the following application, we consider, as in Jurczenko *et al.* (2008), different initializing direction vectors in $(]0, \alpha] \times [-\beta, 0[ \times ]0, \gamma] \times [-\delta, 0[)$ to speed-up the convergence of the iterative optimization process (27). The intensity values are set in realistic ranges of potential improvements and take into account the scaling differences betwen the first four TL-moments[23].

# 4. Empirical Application to Hedge Funds

In this section, we compute and represent geometrically, for a universe of hedge funds, the strong efficient portfolio frontier resulting from the TL-moment non-parametric optimization framework.

Our dataset consists of monthly US denominated returns of 94 off-shore hedge funds, provided by *Bloomberg*, for the period December 31th, 1998 -

[23]The scalars $\alpha, \beta, \gamma$ and $\delta$ correspond in our empirical application to the absolute maximum estimated values of the first four TL-moments for the hedge funds (see below).

March, 1st 2008 (9212 observations). We select funds that come from 11 different strategies, among which "Equity Market Neutral", "Event Driven", "Fixed Income Arbitrage", "Funds of Hedge Funds", "Global Macro", "Managed Futures", "Merger Arbitrage", "Fixed Income Relative Value", "North America and Western Europe Long Short" and "North America and Western Europe Short Bias". Unless for the "Short Bias" style that contains only 4 hedge funds, each hedge fund category is comprised of nine funds. The estimation method used for the efficient frontier is based on the evolutionary Goal Programming Method presented in the previous section, where we start the iterative optimization process by generating randomly thirty arbitrary funds of hedge funds, and then project each one onto the theoretical efficient frontier, using our distance function in 9,637 ($11^4$) TL-moment directions[24].

The Figures 3 to 7 represent geometrically the five Trimmed L-moment efficient frontiers from four different viewpoints. Figures 3 and 4 show the three-dimensional shape of the efficient frontier, respectively in the mean-TL-variance-TL-skewness and mean-TL-skewness-TL-*kurtosis* sub-spaces. In addition, we also illustrate in Figures 5 to 7 the orthogonal projections of the empirical efficient frontier into three of its natural two-dimensional sub-spaces: namely, the mean-TL-variance, TL-skewness-TL-variance and the TL-skewness-TL-*kurtosis* planes. In each of these figures, colour shadings are added to represent one of the missing dimension. Note, that all the projection points obtained here, belong to the theoretical Pareto efficient frontier, since they correspond to the optimal solutions with all zero slacks in the multi-objective optimization program (27).[25]

We focus first on the three-dimensional representations of the TL-moment portfolio efficient set, adding colours onto the surfaces so that we can recover all the optimal moment trade-offs. As can be seen from Figures 3 and 4, while increasing the (TL)-mean implies, at optimum an increase of the TL-variance, as in the traditional Markowitz paradigm, the maximisation (minimization) of the expected return (TL-variance) implies, for hedge funds, also an increase of the TL-skewness (TL-*kurtosis*). That is, while the higher-order individual risk preferences cause high TL-*kurtosis* and TL-variance to be traded for higher (TL)-mean and TL-skewness, hedge funds do not seem to exhibit the same type of

[24]This number corresponds to the combinations of 11 possible intensity values - ranging from 0 to 1, with 0.1 step size - for each TL-moment direction.

[25]Then, it is not possible for an efficient projected point to improve one of its moment-dimension without simultaneously detoriating at least another.

trade-offs between odd L-moments that are typically observed in the underlying stock markets (see Krauss and Litzenberger, 1976, and Harvey and Siddique, 2000).

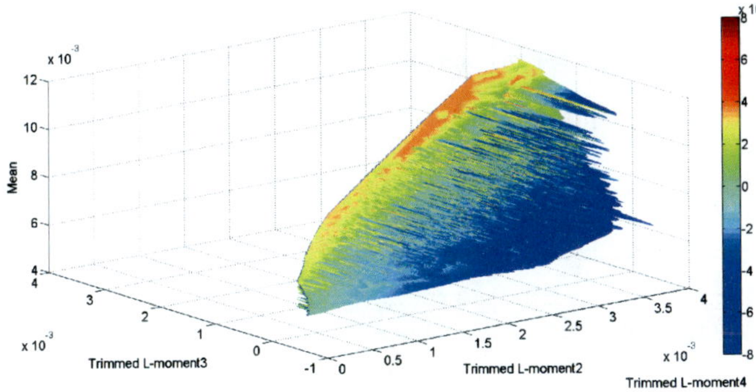


**Source**: Bloomberg, monthly net asset values (31/1998-03/2008) in USD of 94 hedge funds coming from 11 strategies; computations by the authors. The efficient frontier is obtained after optimization of 30 random funds of hedge funds in 9,637 directions. Colour shading represents the level of the TL-Kurtosis.

Figure 3. First Four TL-moment Efficient Frontier in the Mean-TL-Variance-TL-Skewness space.

These findings are confirmed by Figures 6 to 8 that represent the projections of the four TL-moment efficient portfolios in two specific moment dimensions. When projected into the mean-L-variance plane, the hull of the projected frontier is identical to the traditional Markowitz efficient frontier. That is, all portfolios that are efficient in the (TL)-mean-TL-variance space are characterized by a nonlinear positive relation between their first and second TL-moments. However, when looking at the other moment characteristics of the projected points, we see that optimizing with respect to the first two TL-moments can lead to highly undesirable effects in presence of higher-order moments. Indeed, optimal portfolios in the two-moment robust framework are not necessarily efficient in terms of TL-skewness and TL-*kurtosis*. For instance, in Figure 5, one can observe that for a given level of expected return, it is possible to obtain at optimum a higher third-order TL-moment if the TL-variance is increased. Likewise, it is possible to decrease the fourth-order TL–moment when controlling for the TL-mean. As high TL-skewness or low TL-*kurtosis* are associated with

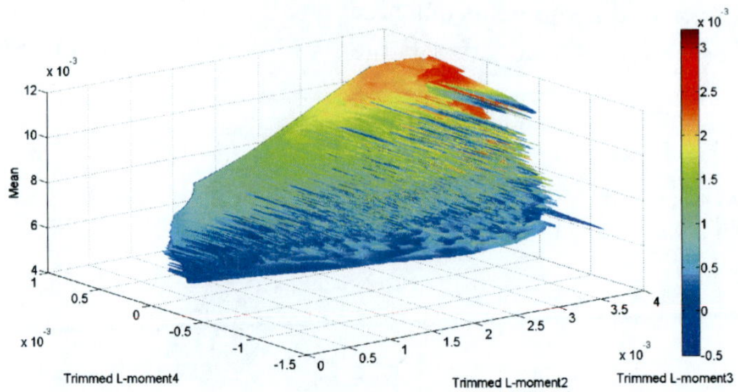


**Source**: Bloomberg, monthly net asset values (31/1998-03/2008) in USD of 94 hedge funds coming from 11 strategies; computations by the authors. The efficient frontier is obtained after optimization of 30 random funds of hedge funds in 9,637 directions. Colour shading represents the level of the TL-Skewness.

Figure 4. First Four TL-moment Efficient Frontier in the Mean-TL-Variance-TL-Kurtosis space.

high TL-variance, it becomes apparent that mixed-risk averse decision makers (see Caballé and Pomansky, 1996), *i.e.* prudent and temperant investors, will not necessarily choose low volatility portfolios, as they also tend to exhibit a higher likehood of extreme (negative) events. Which of the portfolios on the surface the agents should choose will depend on their specific risk preferences and utility functions. When controlling now for the TL-variance, it seems neither possible to increase at the optimum the TL-skewness or to decrease the TL-*kurtosis* at the cost of the first TL-moment. These observations generalize the point raised by Malevergne and Sornette (2005) and Davies *et al.* (2009) into the TL-moment space, namely that mean-variance portfolio optimizers may be nothing more than skewness minimisers and *kurtosis* maximisers.

Three additional comments should be adressed here. First, one can remark that almost any optimal four-moment combinations are here accessible with the shortage function, except low TL-mean returns associated with low TL-skewness and high second and fourth TL-moments (see the right bottom parts of Figure 5 and 7). Secondly, our work confirms the dangers of using dual utility-based approaches to portfolio selection with higher-order moments, due to the numerous discontinuities present in the strongly portfolio efficient set

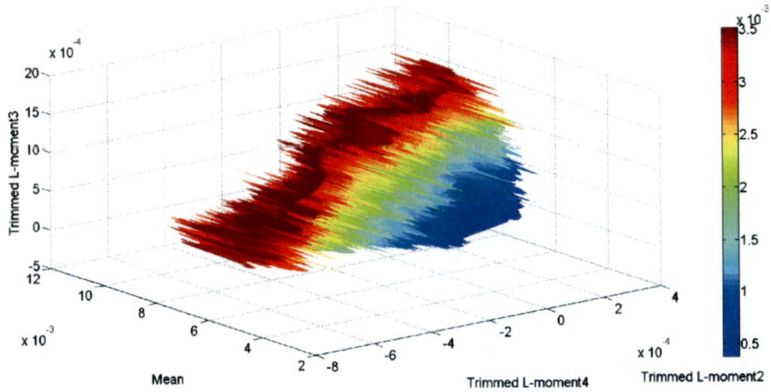


**Source**: Bloomberg, monthly net asset values (31/1998-03/2008) in USD of 94 hedge funds coming from 11 strategies; computations by the authors. The efficient frontier is obtained after optimization of 30 random funds of hedge funds in 9,637 directions. Colour shading represents the level of the TL-Variance.

Figure 5. First Four TL-moment Efficient Frontier in the Mean-TL-Skewness-TL-Kurtosis space.

(see Kerstens *et al.*, 2009). Furthermore, the figures shown in this empirical work reveal that contrary to the two-moment case, there does seem to be such a thing as a typical shape for the efficient frontier in the presence of higher-order TL-moments[26].

# 5. Conclusion

In this article, we have introduced a general method for deriving the surface of the Pareto optimal portfolios in the non-convex four-moment space, using the shortage optimization tool and a set of robust statistics called the Trimmed L-moments (see Briec *et al.*, 2004, and Elamir and Seheult, 2003). The portfolio efficiency is simply evaluated by looking simultaneously for TL-variance and TL-*kurtosis* reductions and TL-mean and TL-skewness augmentations. An empirical application on a universe of 94 hedge funds provides a four-dimensional vizualisation of the non-convex four TL-moments efficient portfolio frontier and

[26]See Jurczenko *et al.* (2006) and Kerstens *et al.* (2009) for a similar result in the conventional multi-moment framework and Jurczenko *et al.* (2008) in the ordinary L-moment setting.

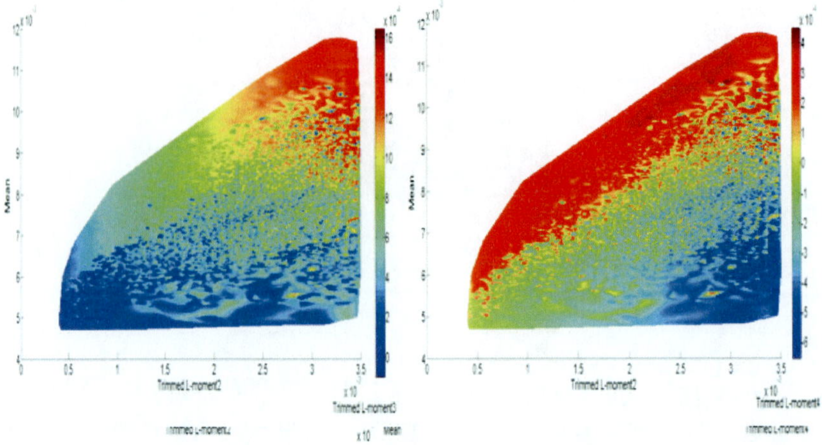


**Source**: Bloomberg, monthly net asset values (31/1998-03/2008) in USD of 94 hedge funds coming from 11 strategies; computations by the authors. The efficient frontier is obtained after optimization of 30 random funds of hedge funds in 9,637 directions. Colour shadings represent (respectively) the level of the TL-Skewness (TL-Kurtosis) on the left (right) figure.

Figure 6. First Four TL-moment Efficient Frontier in the Mean-TL-Variance plane.

illustrates the computational tractabilty and relative robustness of the approach.

The proposed framework approximates non-parametrically the true but unknown four TL-moment efficient frontier via a non-parametric efficiency measurement that guarantees a global optimality in a four-dimensional space. Furthermore, the shortage optimization function approach has the advantage to be comptabible with any particular version of the multi-moment asset allocation model that focus on one, two or three parameters at the cost of the other dimension(s), such as the (TL)-return maximization model, the (TL)-variance minimization model, the (TL)-skewness maximization model and (TL)-*kurtosis* minimization model (see Konno and Suzuki, 1995, Athayde and Flôres, 2004, and Joro and Na, 2006).

A first natural extension of this study will be to apply the proposed methodology to gauge the performance of mutual and hedge funds (see Briec *et al.*, 2004, Brandouy *et al.*, 2008, and Darolles *et al.*, 2009). A second possible

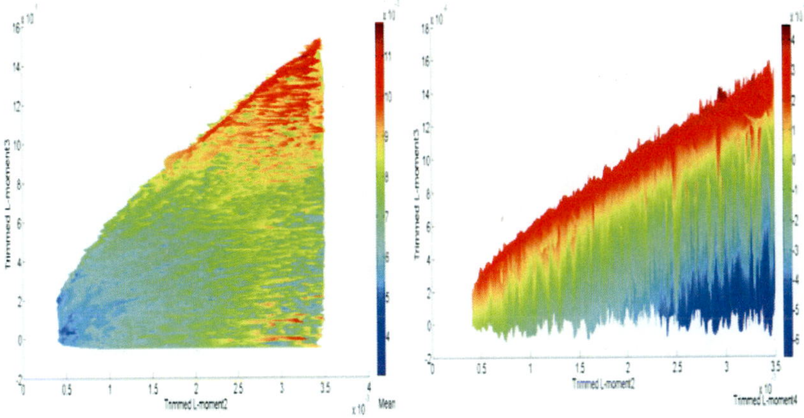

**Source**: Bloomberg, monthly net asset values (31/1998-03/2008) in USD of 94 hedge funds coming from 11 strategies;computations by the authors. The efficient frontier is obtained after optimization of 30 random funds of hedge funds in 9,637 directions. Colour shadings represent (respectively) the level of the Mean (TL-skewness) on the left (right) figure.

Figure 7. First Four TL-moment Efficient Frontier in the TL-Skewness-TL-Variance plane.

extension is to be found in the development of a conditional version of our four TL-moment asset allocation model. A conditional time-varying modelisation of the four L-moment model can be achieved either by using a multivariate GARCH specification for the asset return (co)-moments (see Jondeau and Rockinger, 2009) or within a dynamic quantile regression framework (see Engle and Manganelli, 2004, Gouriéroux and Jasiak, 2008, and Taylor, 2008-a and 2008-b). A third potential extension of our work, would be in the development of an asset pricing relation that generalizes the Gini-CAPM (see Shalit and Yitzhaki, 1989, Okunev, 1990, and Benson *et al.*, 2003) in the four TL-moments direction. This can be done either by imposing some restrictions on the joint asset return distribution (see Shalit and Yitshaki, 2005-a and Fabozzi *et al.*, 2006), or by restricting the agent risk preferences to separable utility functions (see Cass and Stiglitz, 1970, Gregory-Allen and Shalit, 1999, and Shalit and Yitshaki, 1984 and 2005-b). Finally, it would be of great interest to inves-

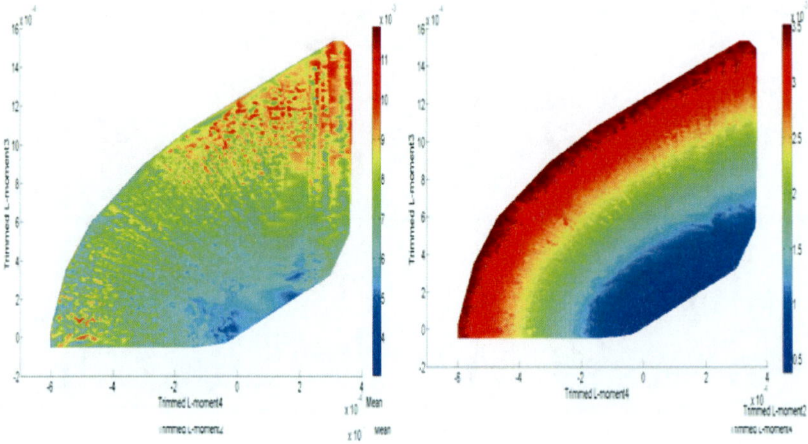


**Source**: Bloomberg, monthly net asset values (31/1998-03/2008) in USD of 94 hedge funds coming from 11 strategies;computations by the authors. The efficient frontier is obtained after optimization of 30 random funds of hedge funds in 9,637 directions. Colour shadings represent (respectively) the level of the mean (TL-variance) on the left (right) figure.

Figure 8. Four TL-moment Efficient Frontier in the TL-Skewness-TL-Kurtosis plane.

tigate the relative performance of our four TL-moment approach with respect to alternative robust non-parametric multi-moment models (see, Martellini and Ziemann, 2010, and Hurlin *et al.*, 2009) and parametric extensions (see, Adcock, 2008, Bucley *et al.*, 2008, Mencia and Sentana, 2009, and Bacmann and Benedetti, 2009). All these extensions are left to future works.

## Acknowledgements

We are grateful to Thierry Chauveau and Thierry Michel for help and encouragement in preparing this work. We also wish to thanks Bertrand Maillet and Paul Merlin who largely contributed to our research in the field of L-moments. The content of this article engages only its authors and does not necessarily reflect the opinions of their employers.

# Appendix 1

Let the local solution $(\delta^*, \mathbf{w}_p^*)$ of the following non-linear optimization program:

$$\mathbf{w}_p^* = \underset{(\mathbf{w}_p,\delta)\in(\mathfrak{F}_p \times IR_+)}{ArgMax} \{\delta\}$$

$$s.t. \begin{cases} \lambda_1^{(1)}(R_p) \geq \lambda_1^{(1)}(R_q) + \delta g_1 \\ \lambda_2^{(1)}(R_p) \leq \lambda_2^{(1)}(R_q) + \delta g_2 \\ \lambda_3^{(1)}(R_p) \geq \lambda_3^{(1)}(R_q) + \delta g_3 \\ \lambda_4^{(1)}(R_p) \leq \lambda_4^{(1)}(R_q) + \delta g_4 \end{cases} \quad (26)$$

where $\mathbf{w}_{p^*}$ is the $(N \times 1)$ weakly efficient portfolio weight vector that (weakly) maximizes the relative improvements over the evaluated portfolio TL-moment coordinates $\lambda_q^{(1)}$ in the direction vector $\mathbf{g} = (g_1;\, g_2\,;\, g_3\,;\, g_4\,)'$. Then $(\delta^*, \mathbf{w}_p^*)$ is also a global solution of $(26)$.

**Proof.** Let us denote:

$$D = \Big\{(\delta, \mathbf{w}_p) \in (IR_+ \times IR^N) : \lambda_1^{(1)}(R_p) \geq \lambda_1^{(1)}(R_q) + \delta g_1;$$
$$\lambda_2^{(1)}(R_p) \leq \lambda_2^{(1)}(R_q) + \delta g_2;\ \lambda_3^{(1)}(R_p) \geq \lambda_3^{(1)}(R_q) + \delta g_3;$$
$$\lambda_4^{(1)}(R_p) \leq \lambda_4^{(1)}(R_q) + \delta g_4;\ \text{with } \mathbf{w}_p'\mathbf{1} = 1 \text{ and } \mathbf{w}_p \geq \mathbf{0}\Big\} \quad \text{(A.1.1.)}$$

We have:

$$S_{\mathbf{g}}(\mathbf{w}_p) = Max\,\{\delta : (\delta, \mathbf{w}_p) \in D\} \quad \text{(A.1.2.)}$$

Assume that the couple $(\delta_1, \mathbf{w}_{p1})$ constitutes a local maximum, but is not a gobal one. In that case, there exists a couple $(\delta_2, \mathbf{w}_{p2}) \in D$ such that:

$$\delta_2 > \delta_1 \quad \text{(A.1.3.)}$$

But since $\mathfrak{D}_p$ satisfies the free disposal property, this implies that for all $\delta \in [\delta_1, \delta_2]$, there exists $\mathbf{w}_p \in \mathfrak{F}_p$ such that $(\delta, \mathbf{w}_p) \in D$. Therefore, there does not exist a neighbourhood $V[(\delta_1, \mathbf{w}_{p1}), \varepsilon]$ where $\varepsilon > 0$, such that $\delta_1 \geq \delta$ for all $(\delta, \mathbf{w}_p) \in V[(\delta_1, \mathbf{w}_{p1}), \varepsilon]$. Consequently, if $(\delta^*, w_p^*)$ is a local maximum, then it is also a gobal maximum.

# References

Abramowitz M. and I. Stegun, (1972), *The Handbook of Mathematical Functions*, 9th Printing, Dover Publications, New-York, 1046 pages.

Adcock C., (2008), "Asset Pricing and Portfolio Selection based on the Multivariate Skew-Student Distribution", *Proceedings of FFM08 Conference*, Aix-en-Provence, May 2008, 30pages.

Artzner P., F. Delbaen, J. Eber and D. Heath, (1999), "Coherent Measures of Risk", *Mathematical Finance* **9**, 203-228.

Athayde G. and R. Flôres, (2002), "Portfolio Frontier with Higher Moments: The Undiscovered Country", *Computing in Economics and Finance* **209**, 1-42.

Athayde G. and R. Flôres, (2003), "Incorporating Skewness and Kurtosis in Portfolio Optimization: A Multi-dimensional Efficient Set", in Stephen Satchell and Allan Scowcroft, ed.: *Advances in Portfolio Construction and Implementation (Butteworth-Heinemann)*.

Athayde G. and R. Flôres, (2004), "Finding a Maximum Skewness Portfolio a General Solution to Three-moments Portfolio Choice", *Journal of Economic Dynamics and Control* **28**, 1335-1352.

Athayde G. and R. Flôres, (2006), "On Certain Geometric Aspects of Portfolio Optimisation with Higher Moments", in *Multi-moment Asset Pricing Models*, Jurczenko-Maillet Eds, John Wiley & Sons,2006, 21 pages.

Bacmann J. and S. Benedetti, (2009), "Optimal Bayesian Portfolios of Hedge Funds", *International Journal of Risk Assessment and Management* **11**, 39-58.

Bayazit M. and B. Önöz, (2002), "LL-moments for Estimating Low Flow Quantiles", *Hydrological Sciences* **47**, 707-720.

Beedles W. and M. Simkowitz, (1978), "Diversification in a Three-moment World", *Journal of Financial and Quantitative Analysis* **13**, 927-941.

Benson K., R. Faff and P. Pope, (2003), "The Relevance of Investor Risk Classes in Ranking: Fund Performance: An Application of the Extended Mean-Gini CAPM", *Journal of Quantitative Economics* **1** (1), 20-35.

Brandouy O., W. Briec, K. Kerstens, and I. Woestyne, (2008), "Performance Appraisal with Luenberger Productivity Indexes", *Working Paper*, University of Lille, 39 pages.

Briec W. and K. Kerstens, (2007), "Portfolio Selection in Multidimensional General and Partial Moment Space", *Working Paper*, University of Lille, 44 pages.

Briec W. and K. Kerstens, (2009), "Multi-horizon Markowitz Portfolio Performance Appraisals: A General Approach", *Omega* **37**, 50-62.

Briec W., K. Kerstens and J. Lesourd, (2004), "Single-Period Markowitz Portfolio Selection, Performance Gauging, and Duality: A Variation on the Luenberger Shortage Function", *Journal of Optimization Theory and Applications* **120**, 1-27.

Briec W., K. Kerstens and O. Jokung, (2007), "Mean-Variance-Skewness Portfolio Performance Gauging: A General Shortage Function and Dual Approach", *Management Science* **53**, 135-149.

Buckley I., D. Saunders and L. Seco, (2008), "Portfolio Optimization when Asset Returns have the Gaussian Mixture Distribution", *European Journal of Operational Research* **185**, 1434-1461.

Caballé J. and A. Pomansky, (1996), "Mixed Risk Aversion", *Journal of Economic Theory* **71**, 485-513.

Cass D. and J. Stiglitz, (1970), "The Structure of Investor Preferences and Asset Returns, and Separability in Portfolio Allocation: A Contribution to the Pure Theory of Mutual Funds", *Journal of Economic Theory* **2**, 122-160.

Chunhachinda P., K. Dandapani, K. Hamid and S. Prakash, (1997), "Portfolio Selection and Skewness: Evidence from International Stock Markets", *Journal of Banking and Finance* **21**, 143-167.

Darolles S., C. Gourriéroux and J. Jasiak, (2009), "L-Performance with an Application to Hedge Funds", *Journal of Empirical Finance* **16**, 671-685.

Davies R., H. Kat and S. Lu, (2009), "Fund of Hedge Funds Portfolio Selection: A Multiple-objective Approach", *Journal of Derivatives and Hedge Funds forthcoming*, 35 pages.

Dittmar R., (2002), "Nonlinear Pricing Kernels, Kurtosis Preference, and Evidence from the Cross-Section of Equity Returns", *Journal of Finance* **57**, 369-403.

Elamir E. and A. Seheult, (2003), "Trimmed L-moments", *Computational Statistics&Data Analysis* **43**, 299-314.

Engle R. and S. Manganelli, (2004), "CAViaR: Conditional Auto-Regressive Value-at-Risk by Regression Quantiles",*Journal of Business and Economic Statistics* **22**, 367-381

Fabozzi F., S. Ortobelli, S. Rachev and H. Shalit, (2006), "Risk Probability Functionals and Probability Metrics Applied to Portfolio Theory", *Working Paper*, University of Karlsruhe, 35 pages.

Gembicki F. and Y. Haimes, (1975), "Approach to Performance and Multiobjective Sensitivity Optimization: The Goal Attainment Method", *Journal of Transactions on Automatic Control* **20**, 769-771.

Gouriéroux C. and J. Jasiak, (2008), "Dynamic Quantile Models", *Journal of*

*Econometrics* **147**, 198-205.

Gouriéroux C. and W. Liu, (2006), "Efficient Portfolio Analysis using Distorsion Risk Measures", *Working Paper*, CREST, 33 pages.

Greenwood J., J. Landweher and N. Natales, (1979), "Probability Weighted Moments: Definition and Relation to Parameters of Several Distributions Expressable in Inverse Form", *Water Ressources Review* **15**, 1049-1054.

Gregory-Allen R. and H. Shalit, (1999), "The Estimation of Systematic Risk under Differentiated Risk Aversion: A Mean-Extended Gini Approach", *Review of Quantitative Finance and Accounting* **12**, 135-157.

Guidolin M. and A. Timmermann, (2005), "Optimal Portfolio Choices under Regime Switching, Skew and *Kurtosis* Preferences", *Review of Financial Studies*, Federal Reserve Bank of St Louis, 35 pages.

Guidolin M. and A. Timmermann, (2008), "International Asset Allocation under Regime Switching, Skew and *Kurtosis* Preferences", *Review of Financial Studies* **21**, 889-935.

Guttman, N., J. Hosking and J. Wallis, (1993), "Regional Precipitation Quantile Values for the Continental US Computed from L-Moments", *Journal of Climate* **6**, 2326-2340.

Hampel F., E. Ronchetti, P. Rousseeuw and W. Stahel, (2005), *Robust Statistics: The Approach Based On Influence Functions*, Wiley-Interscience, 502 pages.

Harvey C. and S. Siddique, (2000), "Conditional Skewness in Asset Pricing Tests", *Journal of Finance* **54**, 1263-1296.

Heyde C., (1963), "On a Property of the Lognormal Distribution", *Journal of Royal Statistical Society* **29**, 392-393.

Hosking J., (1989), "Some Theoretical Results Concerning L-Moments", *Research Report RC14492*, IBM Research Division, 13 pages.

Hosking J., (1990), "L-moments: Analysis and Estimation", *Journal of the Royal Statistical Society Series* **B 52**, 105-124.

Hosking J., (2007), "Some Theory and Practical Uses of Trimmed L-moments", *Journal of Statistical Planning and Inference* **137**, 3024-3039.

Hosking J. and J. Wallis, (1997), *Regional Frequency Analysis,* Cambridge, 224 pages.

Hurlin C., P. Kouontchou and B. Maillet, (2009), "A Robust Conditional Realized Extended 4-CAPM", *Working Paper*, University of Paris 1, 44 pages.

Jondeau E. and M. Rockinger, (2003-a), "Conditional Volatility, Skewness and Kurtosis: Existence, Persistence and Comovements",*Journal of Economic*

*Dynamic and Control* **27** (10), 1699-1737.

Jondeau E. and M. Rockinger, (2003-b), "How Higher Moments Affect the Allocation of Assets", *Finance Letters* **1** (2), 1-5.

Jondeau E. and M. Rockinger, (2006), "Optimal Portfolio Allocation Under Higher Moments",*Journal of the European Financial Management Association* **12**, 29-67.

Jondeau E. and M. Rockinger, (2009), "Time-Variability in Higher Moments IS Important in Asset Allocation", *Working Paper*, University of Lausanne, 44 pages.

Joro T. and P. Na, (2006), " Portfolio Performance Evaluation in Mean-Variance-Skewness Framework", *European Journal of Operational Research* **175**, 516-542.

Jurczenko E. and B. Maillet, (2001), "The 3-CAPM: Theoretical Foundations and an Asset Pricing Model Comparison in a Unified Framework", in *Developments in Forecast Combination and Portfolio Choice*, Dunis-Timmermann-Moody Eds, John Wiley & Sons, 239-273.

Jurczenko E. and B. Maillet, (2006-a), "Theoretical Foundations of Asset Allocation and Pricing Models with Higher-order Moments", in *Multi-moment Asset Pricing Models*, Jurczenko-Maillet Eds, John Wiley & Sons, 2006, 1-36.

Jurczenko E. and B. Maillet, (2006-b), "The Four-moment Capital Asset Pricing Model: between Asset Pricing and Asset Allocation", in *Multi-moment Asset Pricing Models*, Jurczenko-Maillet Eds, John Wiley & Sons, 2006, 113- 163.

Jurczenko E., B. Maillet and P. Merlin, (2006-c), "Hedge Fund Selection with Higher-order Moments: A Nonparametric Mean-Variance-Skewness-*Kurtosis* Efficient Frontier", in *Multi-moment Asset Pricing Models*, Jurczenko-Maillet Eds, John Wiley & Sons, 2006, 51-66.

Jurczenko E., B. Maillet and P. Merlin, (2008), "Efficient Frontier for Robust Higher-order Moment Portfolio Selection", *Working Paper*, University of Paris 1, 68 pages.

Karvanen J., (2006), "Estimation of Quantile Mixtures via L-moments and Trimmed Lmoments", *Computational Statistics and Data Analysis* **51**, 947-959.

Kerstens K., A. Mounir and I. Woestyne, (2009), "Geometric Representation of the Mean-Variance-Skewness Portfolio Frontier based upon the Shortage Function",*Working Paper*, IESEG, 32 pages.

Konheim T., (1971), "A Note on Order Statistics", *American Mathematical Monthly* **78**, 524.

Koenker R. and G. Bassett, (1978), "Regression Quantiles", *Econometrica* **46**, 33-50.

Konno H. and K. Suzuki, (1995), "A Mean-variance-skewness Portfolio Optimization Model", *Journal of the Operations Research Society of Japan* **38**, 173-187.

Lai T., (1991), "Portfolio with Skewness: A Multiple-objective Approach", *Review of Quantitative Finance and Accounting* **1**, 293-305.

Kraus A. and R. Litzenberger, (1976), "Skewness Preference and the Valuation of Risk Assets", *Journal of Finance* **31**, September 1976, 1085-1099.

Lee S. and S. Maeng, (2003), "Frequency Analysis of Extreme Rainfall Using L-Moment",*Irrigation and Drainage* **52**, 219-230.

Lux T., (2000), "On Moment Condition Failure in German Stock Returns : An Application of Recent Advances in Extreme Value Statistics", *Empirical Economics* **25**, 641-652.

Lux T., (2001), "The Limiting Extremal Behaviour of Speculative Returns : An Analysis of Intra-Daily Data from the Frankfurt Stock Exchange", *Applied Financial Economics* **11**, 299-315.

Malevergne Y. and D. Sornette, (2005), "Higher-moment Portfolio Theory: Capitalizing on Behavioral Anomalies of Stock Markets", *Journal of Portfolio Management* **31**, 49-55.

Markowitz H., (1952), "Portfolio Selection",*Journal of Finance* **7**, 77-91.

Martellini L. and V. Ziemann, (2010), "Improved Forecasts of Higher Order Moments and Co-Moments of Asset Returns and Implications for Portfolio Selection", *Review of Financial Studies* **23**, 1467-1502.

Mencía J. and E. Sentana, (2009), "Multivariate Location-scale Mixtures of Normals and Mean-variance-skewness Portfolio Allocation", *Journal of Econometrics, forthcoming*, 49 pages.

Moisello U., (2007), "On the Use of Partial Probability Weighted Moments in the Analysis of Hydrological Extremes", *Hydrological Processes* **21**, 1265-1279.

Morey M. and R. Morey, (1999), "Mutual Fund Performance Appraisals: A Multi-horizon Perspective with Endogenous Benchmarking", *Omega International Journal of Management Science* **27**, 241-258.

Okunev J., (1990), "An Alternative Measure of Mutual Fund Performance", *Journal of Business Finance and Accounting Spring*, 247-264.

Pérez N., S. Ménendez and L. Seco, (2003), "A Theoretical Comparison between Moments and L-moments", *Working Paper*, RiskLab, 23 pages.

Yitzhaki S., (2003), "Gini's Mean Difference: A Superior Measure of Variability for Non-Normal Distributions", *International Journal of Statistics* **61**, 285-316.

Ryoo H., (2007), "A Compact Mean-Variance-Skewness Model for Large-scale Portfolio Optimization and its Application to the NYSE Market", *Journal of Operational Research Society* **58**, 505-515.

Serfling R. and P. Xiao, (2006), "A Contribution to Multivariate L-Moments: L-Comoment Matrices", *Working Paper*, University of Texas, 38 pages.

Serfling R. and P. Xiao, (2007), "A Contribution to Multivariate L-Moments: L-Comoment Matrices", *Journal of Multivariate Analysis* (**98**), 1765-1781.

Shalit H. and S. Yitshaki, (1989), "Evaluating the Mean-Gini Approach to Portfolio Selection",*International Jourunl of Finance* **1** (2), 15-31.

Shalit H. and S. Yitshaki, (2005-a), "The Mean-Gini Efficient Portfolio Frontier", *Journal of Financial Research* **28**, 59-75.

Shalit H. and S. Yitshaki, (2005-b), "Capital Market Equilibrium: The Mean-Gini Approach", *Working Paper*, 27 pages.

Sillitto G., (1969), "Derivation of Approximants to the Inverse Distribution Function of a Continuous Univariate Population from the Order Statistics of a Sample", *Biometrika* **56**, 641-650.

Sun Q. and X. Yan, (2003), "Skewness Persistence with Optimal Portfolio Selection", *Journal of Banking and Finance* **27**, 111-1121.

Taylor J., (2008a), "Estimating Value-at-Risk and Expected Shortfall using Expectiles", *Journal of Financial Econometrics* **6**, 231-252.

Taylor J., (2008b), "Using Exponentially Weighted Quantile Regression to Estimate Value-at-Risk and Expected Shortfall", *Journal of Financial Econometrics* **6**, 382-406.

Ulrych T., D. Velis, A. Woodbury and M. Sacchi, (2000), "L-moments and C-moments", *Stochastic Environmental Research and Risk Assessment* **14**, 50-68.

Zhang D., (2008), "Non-convex Optimal Portfolio Sets and Constant Relative Risk Aversion", *Journal of Economics and Business* **60**, 551-555.

Wang Q., (1997), "LH-moments for Statistical Analysis of Extreme Events", *Water Resources Research* **33**, 2841-2848.

Wang S., (2000a), "Premium Calculations by Transforming the Layer Premium Density", *ASTIN Bulletin*, **26**, 71-92.

Wang S., (2000b), "A Class of Distortion Operators for Pricing Financial and Insurance Risks", *Journal of Risk and Insurance* **67**, 15-36.

Whalen T., G. Savage and G. Jeong, (2004), "An Evaluation of the Self-Determined Probability Weighted Moment Method for Estimating Extreme Wind Speeds", *Journal of Wind Engineering and Industrial Aerodynamics* **92**, 219-239.

Wierzbicki A., (1986), "On the Completeness and Constructiveness of Parametric Characterizations to Vector Optimization Problems", *OR Spektrum* **8**, 73-87.

In: The Recent Trend of Hedge Fund Strategies ISBN 978-1-61668-338-2
Editor: Yasuaki Watanabe , pp. 57-95 

*Chapter 2*

# HEDGE FUND REPLICATION

***Akihiko Takahashi*[1] *and Kyo Yamamoto*[2*]**
[1] The University of Tokyo
[2] GCI Asset Management, Inc.

**Abstract**

This chapter provides a comprehensive explanation of hedge fund replication. This chapter first reviews the characteristics of hedge fund returns. Then, the emergence of hedge fund replication products is discussed. Hedge fund replication methods are classified into three categories: Rule-based, Factor-based, and Distribution replicating approaches. These approaches attempt to capture different aspects of hedge fund returns. This chapter explains the three methods.

**J.E.L. Classification:** G11, G20, G23

**Keywords:** Hedge Funds, Alternative Investments, Hedge Fund Clones

## 1. Introduction

The established cycles of the manufacturing industry has eventually made its way to the hedge fund industry. In the manufacturing industry, many companies compete to develop new products protected by patent. This is often a very

*E-mail address: kyo.yamamoto@gci.jp

expensive process involving large amounts of money invested to develop sophisticated proprietary technology. Rival companies release similar products and the prices of these products fall gradually. Eventually, the previously sophisticated technology becomes common, allowing for the products to be produced at low cost. This in turn leads to a further drop of prices. Finally, the products are mass-produced. At this stage, the companies are unable to earn sufficient profits, and look to develop new sophisticated products. This results in an endless cycle. However, some of these mass-produced products also survive due to low costs.

Hedge funds provide investment strategy as a product. Fund managers are money management professionals, and receive rewards by providing the strategy to investors. They make efforts to sophisticate their own investment strategies. Their strategies are not protected by patent, but the prevailing industry structure enables their strategies to be kept confidential. The hedge fund industry has become severely competitive with new funds launched one after another, while many others collapse. In spite of this, the fees of investing into hedge funds are still at high levels and have not fallen down. For a typical case, investors need to pay 2% as management fee and 20% as incentive fee. This seems peculiar, when compared with the manufacturing industry. The reason for this lies in the difficulty of evaluating hedge fund performances. All fund managers believe that the high fees charged are justifiable as they are capable of earning high returns through their strategy. Investors in return invest in the fund because they believe that the fund manager will provide returns that will justify the high cost. To evaluate a hedge fund's performance, at leaset a few years of performance track record is needed. However, even if the track record is outstanding, there is no consensus on the persistence of a fund manager's skill. It is this difficulty in evaluating the performance of hedge funds that has kept fees unusually high despite the highly competitive nature of the industry.

In recent years, investment banks and investment companies have released hedge fund replication products, which provide investors access to hedge fund returns at lower costs. In addition, these products avoid some shortcomings of hedge funds that will be discussed later. Some replication products mimic a simple trading strategy of hedge funds while others attempt to infer the actual investment positions of hedge funds and take similar positions. Given the highly competitive nature of the hedge funds industry, the emergence of hedge fund clones can be considered a natural progression that has been long overdue when compared to the business cycle of the manufacturing industry.

The development of such techniques has proven to be a challenging task. Currently, the biggest banks such as Goldman Sachs, Merrill Lynch, and JP Morgan, and some large investment companies such as, Partners Group, have launched such products. (See, for example, [15].) Some of these institutions developed cloning technique collaborating with the pioneers in hedge fund research such as William Fung, David Hsieh, and Narayan Naik. (See also [15].) They and other researchers have proposed various methods, but these techniques are still work-in-progress. This chapter explores the methods of hedge fund replication in detail.

In the following section, we review the empirical characteristics of hedge fund returns, and reconfirm the properties of replication targets. Section 3 describes how and why hedge fund clones emerged and classifies replication methodologies into three distinct approaches. Sections 4 till 6 are devoted to explaining in detail the three approaches. Section 7 concludes the chapter.

## 2. Empirical Characteristics of Hedge Fund Returns

This section reviews the empirical characteristics of hedge fund returns before the aim and methodologies of hedge fund replication products are discussed. Originally, hedge fund managers seek absolute returns, i.e. they try to earn profits under any market circumstances. These managers make use of their unique insights into financial markets to find investment opportunities and extract returns. Since managers' abilities and insights are unique, employed financial instruments and investment strategies exhibit a wide variety. Some managers invest in stocks, bonds, or currencies, and others invest in complex structured products. Common investment strategies include long/short equities, event driven, global macro, relative value arbitrage, and so on. Due to the variety of investment tools and strategies, hedge funds exhibit a spectrum of risk-return profiles. Large investors, such as university endowments and pension funds, determine asset allocations to various asset classes. Recently, hedge funds have been included as one of the asset classes. Therefore, those investors also need to understand the return characteristics of hedge funds in broad terms.

Although investment instruments and strategies that hedge funds employ are wide-ranging, investment styles that capture absolute returns can be classified into two categories. The first is dynamically changing exposure to markets. Some managers predict market directions and take long or short positions accordingly. They realize profits when the markets move in line with their predictions. These managers are referred to as directional traders.

The second is exploiting market inefficiencies, i.e. mispriced securities. There are mainly two approaches that exploit market inefficiency: These are relative value and security selection. Relative value is finding two or more securities or portfolios that have the same value but are priced differently in markets. Relative value traders create positions when there is mispricing and close positions when the two market values converge. Security selection is finding undervalued or overvalued securities, taking long or short positions respectively and closing these positions when the manager judges the prices to have reached fair value.

There is much literature that has tried to define the characteristics of hedge fund returns. Their challenge has been extracting unique properties of hedge fund returns from cross-sectional and time-series data. These works can be classified into two main approaches that help to explain hedge fund returns. The first approach is through analyzing distribution and time-series properties of hedge fund returns. The second approach is through identifying factors and understanding how these factors drive hedge fund returns. This approach is also commonly referred to as style analysis.

The most outstanding find from returns distribution analysis is the non-normality characteristic of hedge fund returns. This is documented by [23], in which the authors calculated skew and kurtosis of hedge fund returns by strategy and tested for normality of returns. The result showed most strategies to exhibit negative skew and high kurtosis, and hence, their hypotheses of normality were rejected. The sign of skew is also dependent on data sample. [23] used TASS database, which covers mainly US and European hedge funds and reported negative skew of returns. [17] analyzed the return of hedge funds in Eurekahedge Asia-Pacific database and showed positive skew of returns. While there exists inconsistency in the signs of skew, it is recognized that the returns of hedge funds exhibit skew and fat-tails, leading to non-normality. Time-series analysis has been carried out by [16]. Their research showed the returns of hedge funds that hold illiquid assets to exhibit positive autocorrelation.

For further analysis, we compared the performance of Asian hedge funds against stock indices. AsiaHedge Indices (AsiaHedge composite, Asia excluding Japan, Japan Long/Short index) were used for this purpose. The panel A, B, and C of figure 1 graph asset value growth of the respective indices against relevant stock indices. The reason why stock indices are used is that most hedge funds in Asia-Pacific region employ equity-oriented strategies as noted in [17].

The graphs show that hedge funds returns closely match stock returns in up markets but decline less that stock returns in down markets. This in turn leads to higher returns than stocks in the long run. Figure 2 shows statistics of monthly excess returns of hedge fund and stock indices. Mean excess returns of hedge funds are higher than stock indices with lower standard deviations. They exhibit positive skew, fat-tails and positive correlation with the stock indices (0.73-0.84). Their serial correlations, which are measured by AR (1), is not high.

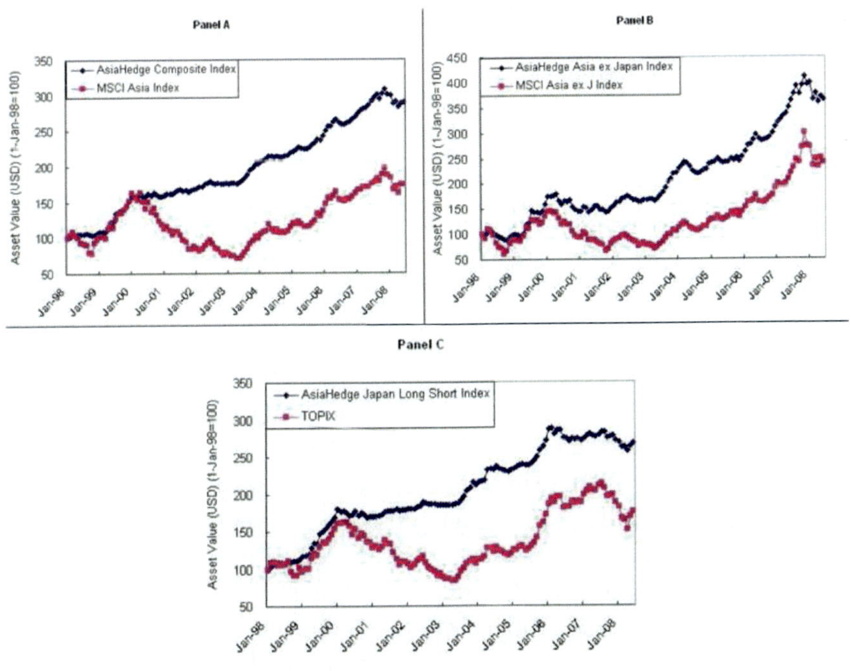


Figure 1. Asset value growth of AsiaHedge indices [Data source: Bloomberg and homepage of AsiaHedge (http://www.asiahedge.net/)].

Style analysis decomposes hedge fund returns into some common risk factors. The most fundamental and heavily-used model is the linear factor model;

$$R_i = \alpha_i + \sum_k \beta_{ik} F_k, \tag{1}$$

where $R_i$ is the return of fund $i$, $F_k$ is the return of factor $k$, $\beta_{ik}$ is the exposure of fund $i$ to factor $k$, and $\alpha_i$ is the rest of the return $R_i$. In considering the portfolio

| | AsiaHedge Composite Index | MSCI Asian Index | AsiaHedge Asia ex-J Index | MSCI Asia ex-J Index | AsiaHedge Japan L/S Index | TOPIX |
|---|---|---|---|---|---|---|
| Mean | 0.54% | 0.25% | 0.79% | 0.63% | 0.49% | 0.24% |
| Std. dev. | 1.73% | 5.19% | 4.02% | 7.10% | 2.09% | 4.84% |
| Skew | 1.11 | 0.10 | 0.94 | 0.09 | 1.12 | 0.06 |
| Kurtosis | 8.57 | 3.13 | 7.09 | 3.42 | 6.47 | 2.92 |
| Max | 9.29% | 17.30% | 18.81% | 21.10% | 9.96% | 13.12% |
| Min | -4.11% | -12.55% | -8.82% | -16.15% | -3.88% | -12.37% |
| AR (1) | 0.19 | 0.13 | 0.21 | 0.16 | 0.18 | 0.15 |
| Correlation with the stock index | 0.76 | | 0.84 | | 0.73 | |

Figure 2. Monthly statistics of excess returns of hedge fund and stock indices (Jan/98-May/08) [Data source: Bloomberg and homepage of AsiaHedge (http://www.asiahedge.net/)].

of hedge funds, the risk is captured by the factors and other components as follows.

$$\sum_{i=1}^{n} w_i R_i = \sum_{i=1}^{n} \alpha_i + \sum_{k} (w_1 \beta_{1k} + \cdots + w_n \beta_{nk}) F_k,$$

where $w_i$ is the weight on fund $i$.

Before proceeding to explore the empirical results of style analysis for hedge funds, we review the results of such analysis done on mutual funds by [30]. In that research, the returns of mutual funds were decomposed by linear regressions into twelve asset class factors: Bills, Intermediate-term government bonds, Long-term government bonds, Corporate bonds, Mortgage-related securities, Large-capitalization value stocks, Large-capitalization growth stocks, Medium-capitalization stocks, Small-capitalization stocks, Non-US bonds, European stocks, and Japanese stocks. The research showed that a large part of mutual fund returns are explained by the twelve asset class factors. $R^2$ levels were at 60%-97%.

[7] implemented style analysis for hedge funds for the first time. First, they performed Sharpe's style regression on mutual fund and hedge fund returns. While more than half the mutual funds had $R^2$s above 75%, nearly half (48%) of the hedge funds had $R^2$s below 25%. The reasons why Sharpe's style regression does not work for hedge funds are due to their dynamic trading strategies (changing exposures to asset class factors) and spread trading strategies

(long/short strategies). In order to find style factors unique to hedge funds, the literature extracted mutually orthogonal principal components, and constructed style factors whose returns were highly correlated to the principal components. It showed that the style factors related non-linearly to the underlying market factors.

Some other research papers reported non-linear relations of specific investment strategies to the market. For example, [9] studied trend-following funds. A trend-follower tries to capture market trends. A trend is a time-series of asset prices that move persistently in one direction over a given time interval, where price changes exhibit positive serial correlation. A trend-follower attempts to identify developing price patterns with this property and trade in the direction of the trend when this occurs. Figure 3 describes the non-linear relationship between trend-following funds and the equity market. Morgan Stanley (MS) World Equity Index is used as a proxy for the world equity market and its returns are sorted into five states. State 1 consists of the worst months, and State 5 the best months. This figure graphs the average monthly returns of an equally weighted portfolio of the six largest trend-following funds, along with that of the world equity markets, for each state. Trend-follower funds earn high returns in the worst state and the best state, and low returns in normal states.

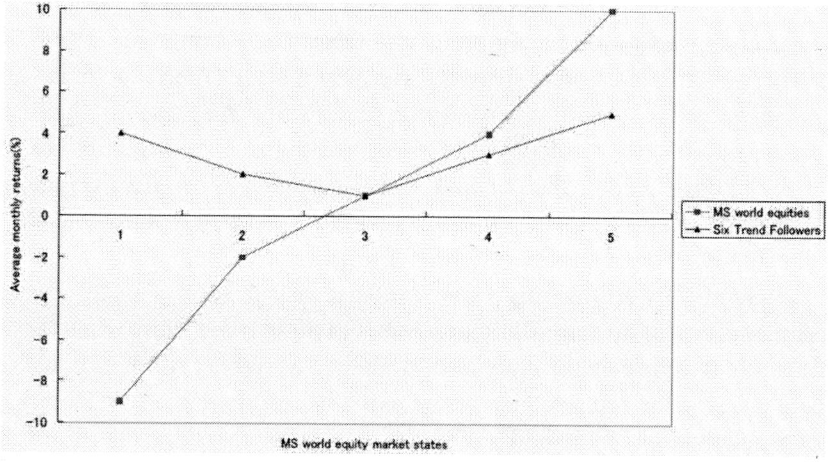


Figure 3. Average monthly returns of six large trend-following funds in five different MS world equity market states [The authors created based on [9].]

Another strategy with non-linear characteristics is active risk arbitrage (merger arbitrage) as reported by [24]. After the announcement of a merger or acquisition, the target company's stock typically trades at a discount to the price offered by the acquiring company. The difference between the target's stock price and the offer price is known as the arbitrage spread. Risk arbitrage refers to an investment strategy that attempts to profit from this spread. If the merger is successful, the arbitrageur captures the arbitrage spread. However, if the merger fails, the arbitrageur incurs a loss, usually much greater than the profits obtained if the deal succeeds. As mentioned in the article, risk arbitrage funds earn profits in both flat and appreciating markets, but suffer large losses in depreciating markets.

As just described, the strategies that employ dynamic trading or bet on corporate events induce the non-linear relationships with the markets. Poor or non-linear relationships with the markets make it difficult to find style factors for hedge funds. Hedge fund researchers navigate this challenging environment to discover style factors by mainly following two methodologies.

The first method is extracting factors from data of hedge fund returns using a statistical method. [7] found style factors by principal component analysis, and [3] by cluster analysis. Using these statistical methods, we can find style factors that explain large parts of hedge fund returns. These style factors can be considered orthogonal or remote with each other.

The second method is constructing style factors based on asset classes like [30]. These factors are referred to as asset based style (ABS) factors. ABS factors can be observed in markets. To be able to find ABS factors that drive hedge fund returns, and to identify the exposures to these factors, allow for the risk of each hedge fund or the portfolio of hedge funds to be effectively monitored. This is useful information for the portfolio construction and rebalancing of hedge funds. More aggressively, this allows for the prediction of fund returns by having forward looking views on these risk factors. This also allows for risk management by controlling exposures to these risk factors when they or securities highly correlated to them are tradable. Moreover, in theory, we can replicate parts of the returns that can be explained by tradable risk factors, or extract excellent alpha by hedging the exposures to these risk factors. For these purposes, ABS factors have been researched more than statistical approaches.

For style analysis of hedge funds, we need the factors that capture arbitrage and dynamic trading strategies. The representative examples of factors that catch spread trading are small-minus-big (SMB), high-minus-low (HML), and credit spread factors. SMB is the difference of returns between small and big cap stocks. Therefore, it represents a strategy that longs small stocks and shorts large stocks. This is a typical long/short strategy that captures the small stock premium. HML is the difference of returns between high book-to-market ratio stocks minus low book-to-market ratio stocks. High and low book-to-market ratio stocks are referred to as value and growth stocks, respectively. HML is a return of the typical strategy that longs value stocks and shorts growth stocks to realize the value premium. Credit spread represents a return of the strategy that buys corporate bond and sells government bonds. It can be inferred that above three factors explain some parts of hedge fund returns. However, there still remains the question of what additional factors can effectively explain arbitrage and dynamic trading strategies non-linear characteristics with the markets.

The terms of non-linearity and dynamic trading strategies remind us of derivative products. Figure 4 shows the profit/loss of contracts of European options at the maturity date. These P/Ls exhibit non-linear relationships to the underlying asset. Moreover, these P/Ls can be replicated using dynamic replication strategies. Figures 3 and 4 show the returns of trend-following funds to resemble the P/Ls of a straddle contract. In addition, a strategy that shorts put options on the stock market earns profits constantly in flat or appreciating markets, and incurs losses in depreciating markets. This P/L characteristic resembles the returns of risk arbitrage funds. From the above examples, we can assume that these derivative products can be used as factors for dynamic trading strategies even if the funds do not trade the products in practice. [1] analyzed risk exposures of equity-oriented hedge funds categorized by investment strategies: Event arbitrage, Restructuring, Event driven, Relative value arbitrage, Convertible arbitrage, Equity hedge, Equity non-hedge, and Short selling. They used SMB, HML, momentum, credit spread, the return of rolling ATM and OTM European call and put options on S&P 500 composite index in addition to asset class indices as ABS factors. The research showed that some parts of returns for all of the strategies were explained by some spread factors. In addition, option factors were significant for six out of the eight strategies. Some returns of event arbitrage, restructuring, event driven, and relative value arbitrage were explained by a shorting strategy of OTM put options on S&P 500 composite index. Convertible arbitrage and short selling were significantly explained by a shorting strategy of ATM put options and OTM call options, respectively. The $R^2$s of the regressions ranged between 40-92%, which was higher than the results of [7] using Sharpe's asset class factor model. [9] introduced an interesting ABS factor, a lookback straddle, that captures the returns of trend following funds in

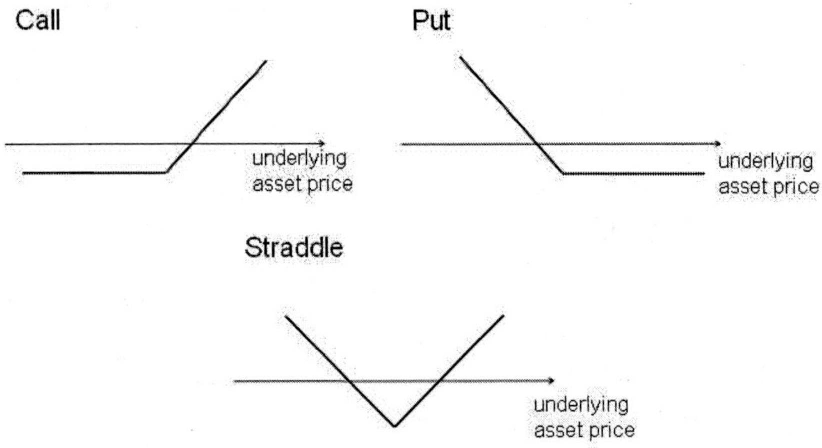


Figure 4. The Profit/Loss of contracts of European options at the maturity date.

addition to a straddle of European options. Lookback straddle is a product that gives the difference between the maximum and minimum prices of an underlying asset within the contract period at maturity date. Figure 5 shows the delta of lookback straddle that replicates the payoff. The parameter setting is same with [9]. Panel A describes the delta in the scenario that the underlying asset price rose to 130, fell down to 115, and rose to 145. Panel B graphs the scenario that the underlying asset price rose to 130, and fell back to 100. In both scenarios, the deltas of lookback straddle tend to increase and decrease in line with asset prices. And since it seems logical to assume that trend followers also change their positions as mentioned above, the rolling strategy of lookback straddle can be a powerful ABS factor in explaining the returns of trend following funds.

As just described, ABS factors, such as options, explain some parts of the return of dynamic trading and arbitrage strategies. Hedge fund exposures to traditional factors such as stocks and bonds are called traditional beta. Those to ABS factors such as long/short and option factors are called alternative beta. The remainder is referred alternative alpha. In many cases, the risk and performance of hedge funds are analyzed through decomposing the returns into the three above mentioned parts. [1], [11] and [13] show that large parts of hedge fund returns are explained by traditional and alternative beta on an aggregate basis.

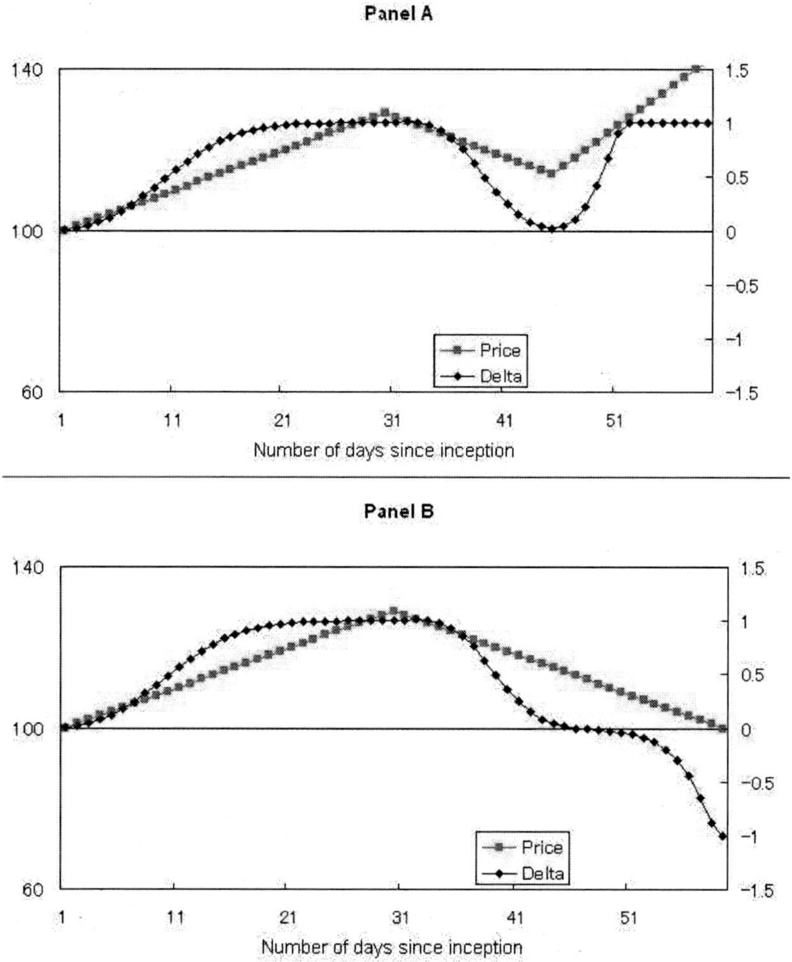


Figure 5. Delta of lookback straddle [The authors created based on [9].]

## 3. Emergence of Hedge Fund Replication Products and the Approaches

Hedge fund investing has been common for large investors, such as university endowments and institutional investors. Although there is no consensus on the exact reason for investing into hedge funds, we have identified two main possibilities: High absolute return and Low correlation to other asset classes. As described in the previous section, hedge fund returns can be decomposed into risk factors and alternative alpha. Therefore, we can consider hedge funds to be efficient portfolios comprised of risk factors and alternative alpha. With this reasoning, we can determine that the actual worth of hedge funds is their accessibility to alternative risk premium, their ability to control exposures to risk factors, and their accessibility to alternative alpha. We define alternative risk premium as risk premium that "buy and hold" asset class strategies cannot access. Combining these three, a skilled fund manager can deliver high absolute returns and low correlation to other asset classes. However, there are some demerits of hedge fund investing. The most common ones are high costs, low transparency, and low liquidity. These are structural problems of hedge funds. Moreover, low transparency adds to manager selection risk. In the worst case, investors end up selecting a fraudulent fund manager. These structural problems make the process for fund selection, due diligence, and risk monitoring very tough. There is also the issue of capacity constraint. Some hedge fund managers set limits on the fund size as they have difficulty managing large amounts of assets. In fact, [14] and [25] clarified that capital inflows attenuated the alpha generating ability of some hedge funds and funds of hedge funds. As a result, these funds do not accept new investments upon reaching their limits. Questions are being raised whether hedge funds deliver returns above and beyond these shortcomings. Moreover, slumps and scandals within the hedge fund industry accelerate flight to quality.

In recent years, asset management firms and investment banks have provided hedge fund replication products. They aim to deliver hedge fund returns without the demerits of hedge funds. They invest in transparent and liquid assets, such as index futures, ETFs, currencies, and offer the products at low costs. They disclose the replication strategy and composition of the portfolio. The use of highly liquid assets also reduces capacity constraints and allows for quick liquidation. Since it is hardly possible to exactly replicate hedge fund returns month-to-month, there are some approaches, which aim to replicate the different characteristics of hedge fund returns instead. As mentioned previously, the worth of hedge funds can be separated into three categories: Accessibility to alternative risk premium, Control over exposures to risk factors, and Alternative alpha.

The first of these approaches is a rule-based approach that aims to replicate hedge fund accessibility to alternative risk premium. Hedge funds can take exposures to risk factors, which a "buy and hold" strategy of traditional asset classes cannot access, by employing long/short, dynamic trading, or relative value strategies. Rule-based hedge fund clones mimic typical trading strategies that hedge funds employ. For example, Merrill Lynch equity volatility arbitrage index mimics the volatility arbitrage strategy based on some simple rules. (See [2].)

The second approach is factor-based replication that seeks to replicate hedge fund accessibility to alternative risk premium and control exposures to risk factors. In other words, they try to deliver both traditional and alternative beta of hedge funds returns. This approach needs three steps. The first step is to find ABS factors that can explain hedge fund returns. They are for example, market indices, spread factors, and option trading and hedging strategies. Moreover, rule-based clones themselves can be considered as ABS factors. The second step is to estimate the factor exposure of the replication target. This procedure is based on statistical techniques, such as regression and filtering. The final step is creating the estimated factor exposures using tradable instruments.

The third approach is distribution replication that aims to replicate the distribution of hedge fund returns. This approach differs from factor-based clones that try to fit their returns to the target hedge fund returns on a month-to-month basis. These distribution replicating clones generate returns sampled from the same distribution as target hedge fund returns. Moreover, the clones replicate correlation structure between hedge funds and investors' portfolio. This is ideal for investors who look to benefit from the low correlation properties of hedge funds.

The above mentioned methodologies are still work-in-progress. The following sections discuss these replication approaches in greater detail.

## 4. Rule-Based Approach

As stated in the previous section, the rule based approach mimics typical hedge fund investment strategies, which access alternative risk premium. The recent growth in ETFs allows for us to take exposures to hedge fund style factors that were previously inaccessible. Through these ETFs, we can try to mimic the equity long/short strategies of hedge funds. For example, we can create a SMB factor by longing a small cap stock index and shorting a large cap stock index, and a HML factor by longing a value stock index and shorting a growth stock index. ETFs that track these indices are mainly listed in US and Europe.

These are typical equity-oriented strategies that extract small and value stock premiums.

Dynamic trading strategies can be replicated by using listed index options. If an index option is not listed, we can replicate its payoff through a delta-hedging strategy of the underlying asset. For example, simple trend following strategies can be replicated through the delta of a lookback straddle, which is described in Figure 5. Currently, such rule-based clone methodologies used in practice are proprietary. For example, Merrill Lynch provides its equity volatility arbitrage index. The index exploits the market anomaly present in the volatility of S&P 500 index. The high demand for S&P index options has historically led to higher prices, which in turn leads to high implied volatilities. As a result, the implied volatility of S&P index options has tended to be higher than its realized volatility. Merrill Lynch equity volatility arbitrage index extracts returns by systematically shorting variance swaps. According to [15], besides Merrill Lynch, rule based clones are also provided by Deutsche Bank, Rydex Investments, IndexIQ, and so on. There has been little academic research done on rule-based clones. The reason for this is that these clones aim to mimic trading strategies thought to be employed by hedge funds and hence cannot be discussed under a theoretical framework. There is however an academic article that researched the risk/returns of arbitrage strategies. [4] studied five fixed income arbitrage strategies: Swap spread, Yield curve, Mortgage, Fixed income volatility, Capital structure arbitrage. The paper determines trading strategies based on models and rules, implements them on a historical simulation basis, and examines the risk/return characteristics. We can think of these strategies as rule-based clones. The following paragraph is a brief summary of the strategies.

A swap spread arbitrageur enters into a position when the spread between the swap rate and the coupon rate of a Treasury bond is larger than the expected average short term spread. He then closes the position when the spread converges to the expected average value. A yield curve arbitrageur tries to exploit mis-valuations along the yield curve. He assumes a term structure model and fits the model to match exactly certain points along the swap curve for each month. Then, the other swap rates are plotted to identify their distance from the fitted curve. If a swap rate is far from the model value, he takes a position to capture this mispricing until the market swap rate converges to its theoretical value. MBS arbitrage strategy consists of buying MBS passthroughs while hedging their interest rate exposure. In [4], the authors concluded that discount securities, that have weaker negative convexity than premium securities, are more profitable. Fixed income volatility arbitrage strategy is similar to the method employed by Merrill Lynch's equity volatility arbitrage index. For this strategy, the arbitrageur exploits the difference between implied and realized volatility of interest rates, while Merrill Lynch's index does the same for equities. Also, as in the case for equities, the implied volatility for interest rates tends to be higher than the realized volatility. The arbitrageur enters into a sequence of one-month variance swaps that pays him the difference between the initial implied variance of an interest rate caplet and the realized variance for the corresponding Eurodollar futures contract for each month. He earns profits when the realized volatility is less than the implied volatility of interest rate caps. Capital structure arbitrageur exploits mispricing between a company's debt and its listed equity. He computes the theoretical credit default swap (CDS) spread and the size of an equity position needed to hedge changes in the value of the CDS using a model. Following this, the arbitrageur compares the theoretical CDS spread with the level quoted in the market. If the market spread is higher (lower) than the theoretical spread, he shorts (longs) the CDS contract, while simultaneously maintaining the equity hedge. The strategy becomes profitable when the market spread and the theoretical spread converges. Details of these strategies are further explained in the paper.

The main risk and return characteristics of the five above mentioned strategies implemented in the paper are as follows. All five of the strategies on average generate positive excess returns under the 10% volatility levels. Sharpe ratios range from about 0.3 to 0.9, which is comparable with the ratio of 0.72 reported by [31] for a broad set of fixed income arbitrage funds. Most excess returns are positively skewed as even though these strategies produce large negative returns from time to time, they tend to generate even larger offsetting positive returns. After risk adjusting for both equity and bond market factors, the article found significant alpha levels for the yield curve, mortgage, and capital structure arbitrage strategies. These strategies require more "intellectual capital" to implement, whereas swap spread and volatility arbitrage strategies that require less "intellectual capital" resulted in insignificant alpha levels.

As described earlier, one can create rule-based clones by mimicking basic investment strategies thought to be employed by hedge funds. Since trading strategies are implemented based on some rules, there are no style drift and manager's investment misjudging. However, these products have several problems. Firstly, profit-earning opportunities disappear as more people recognize and exploit these opportunities. For example, equity and fixed income volatility arbitrage capture the tendency that implied volatility is higher than realized volatility. As the number of arbitrageurs who short options or variance swaps in order to exploit the market anomaly increases, these investment opportunities will disappear. [4] found that strategies that require more "intellectual capital" to implement resulted in significant alpha, whereas others do not. This problem derives the following problem.

The second problem is that the product provider may not disclose the trading rule sufficiently. High transparency is one of the original strengths of hedge fund replication products. However, the product development process requires the use of portfolio optimization methods or the use of models to find mispricings and calculating hedge ratios. If such methods were made fully transparent and became common, market inefficiencies will disappear. In addition, if many rule-based clones come to market, the providers will seek ways to differentiate themselves by developing proprietary models and optimization programs. Eventually, this process might lead to black box methods that will not allow investors to identify risks adequately. It is difficult to earn profits using common strategies, while strategies using proprietary models often provide low transparency. Investors should select products with a full realization of this trade-off.

# 5. Factor-Based Approach

As described in section 3, the factor-based hedge fund clone providers try to replicate hedge fund accessibility to alternative risk premium and control exposures to risk factors. In other words, they attempt to deliver $\sum_k \beta_{ik} F_k$ in equation (1). This is a three step process described below.

Firstly, these providers find risk factors that drive hedge fund returns. Asset class factors such as stock and bond indices, and non-linear factors such as index options and lookback straddles can explain hedge fund returns. Rule-based clones can also be powerful risk factors. It is desirable to find the factors through tradable instruments at this stage. Secondly, they estimate the current exposures of hedge funds to the factors. For this, they need to employ statistical techniques. For example, [22] tried to capture dynamically changing exposures by rolling regression using 24 monthly data. We can assume that proprietary methods have been developed for this purpose. Finally, they create and manage the factor exposures using tradable instruments. If these providers were able to fund factors through tradable instruments during the first step, then this final step is a straightforward process. These steps are used to replicate month-to-month hedge fund returns.

Several firms have launched factor-based clones, which try to replicate aggregate hedge fund returns. Figure 6 graphs the performance of these clones. Although the replication targets are not disclosed exactly, we compare them with HFRI fund weighted composite and HFRI FoF indices for example. Most of these clones successfully approximate the returns of HFRI indices, while Clone 2 and Clone 5 do not. Clone 2 outperforms hedge fund indices. In contrast, Clone 5 underperforms the indices due to large drawdowns, although its correlation with HFRI fund weighted composite index is 0.90.

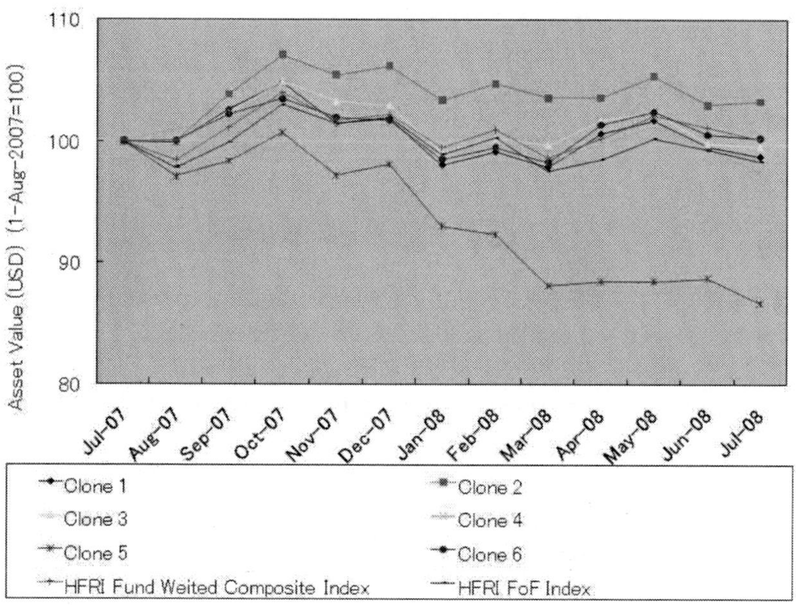


Figure 6. Performance of factor-based clones (Data source: Bloomberg).

As just described, the factor-based clones can fail to track hedge fund returns. Furthermore, the potential of these replication methods cannot be evaluated sufficiently due to their short track records. To find a reason for this failure, we considered the mis-estimation of the current exposures to factors. For example, if we estimate the current exposure by regression using the most recent 24 monthly returns, the estimated exposures are reflective of the average exposures in the previous two years. Hence in this case, we are not able to capture intermediate exposure changes during this period in a timely manner. However, even though data for a shorter time period can estimate more recent exposure changes, such data is prone to large estimation errors. It is therefore a challenging task to estimate the current exposure levels with high accuracy.

In this section, we report our attempt to replicate AsiaHedge Asia excluding Japan and Japan Long/Short Indices. Firstly, we searched for investable risk factors for AsiaHedge Asia excluding Japan Index. Since most of hedge funds in Asia are equity-oriented, we can infer that Asian stock indices explain a substantial part of the hedge fund index return. Figure 7 plots the excess return of the hedge fund index against MSCI Asia Pacific excluding Japan index. There exists a strong linear relation between both indices. This result is consistent with [17]. The MSCI Asia Pacific excluding Japan index is tradable through ETFs. Figure 8 describes the tracking pattern of Lyxor ETF MSCI AC Asia Pacific to the index. Historically, the ETF exhibits minimal tracking error and this allows us to conclude that the Lyxor ETF has almost the same movement as that of the benchmark MSCI index. This in turn allows us to use the historical returns of the MSCI index for performance analysis as the index has a longer track record than the Lyxor ETF. To further improve the explanatory factor, we ran a linear regression adding an additional bond index factor that is represented by iBoxx ABF Pan Asia unhedged total return index. However, as this did not improve the explanatory power, we decided to use MSCI Asia Pacific excluding Japan index as the single factor to replicate AsiaHedge Asia excluding Japan Index.

Panel A of figure 9 graphs the excess return of the AsiaHedge Japan Long/Short Index against the TOPIX, which is tradable by futures or ETFs. The result showed the explanatory power to be insufficient and to improve it, we added the SMB factor, which is represented by the return of the Russell/Nomura small cap index minus the Nikkei 225 Index. Both the Russell/Normura and Nikkei indices are also tradable by ETFs. We were not able to add HML factors as value/growth style indices in Japan are not tradable. Figure 10 describes the tracking pattern of ETFs to these indices. As shown, tracking errors for these cases are very small. The excess return of the hedge fund index is regressed to TOPIX and SMB factors using the data from January 2002 to May 2008 period. The resulting regression coefficients are 0.34 and 0.25 respectively. Panel B of Figure 9 plots the excess return of the hedge fund index against the portfolio that is constructed by 34% to TOPIX and 25% to SMB factors. The explanatory power as measured by $R^2$ is 0.81. We judge this to be sufficient and therefore make use the two factors for the replication of the AsiaHedge Japan Long/Short Index.

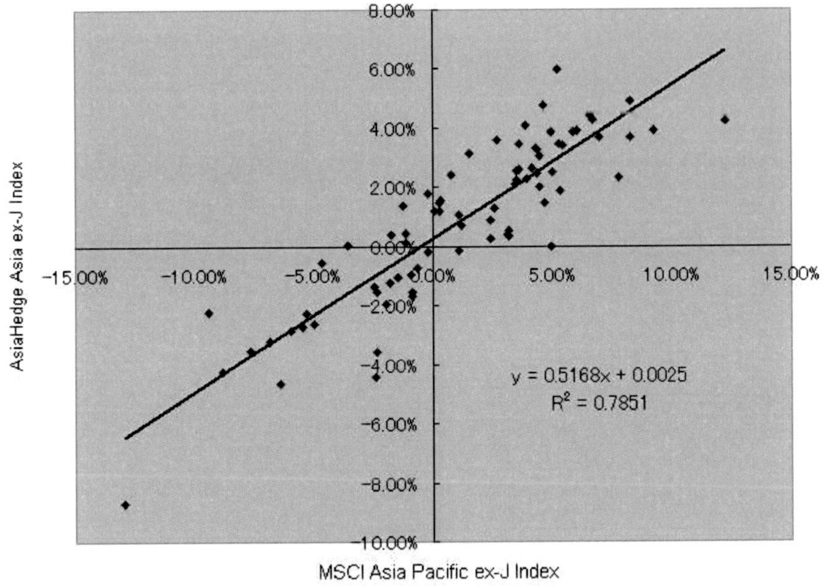


Figure 7. Monthly excess return of AsiaHedge Asia ex Japan Index against MCSI Asia ex-J Index (Jan/2002-May/2008).

When we attempt to replicate the hedge fund index in practice, we cannot use future data. Therefore, we estimate the hedge fund returns exposure on the identified risk factors by using past data. The easiest estimation method is known as rolling window regression, where we make use of 24 monthly returns data for example. For the purposes of this replication, we set the intercept in the regression at zero. As mentioned previously, the use of 24 monthly returns data is only reflective of the average exposure during past two years and does not capture recent exposure changes. To remedy this problem, we also estimated the exposure changes by using Kalman filter, which is able to capture dynamic exposure changes. The model and estimation procedures used in this replication are as follows.

We model the exposure change by state space model. Let $R_t$ denote the hedge fund returns, $F_t$ be the $K$ dimensional vector that represents factor returns, $\beta_t$ be unobservable $K$ dimensional factor exposure vector. Let us assume that the exposures change as follows.

$$\beta_t = \beta_{t-1} + \epsilon_t, \tag{2}$$

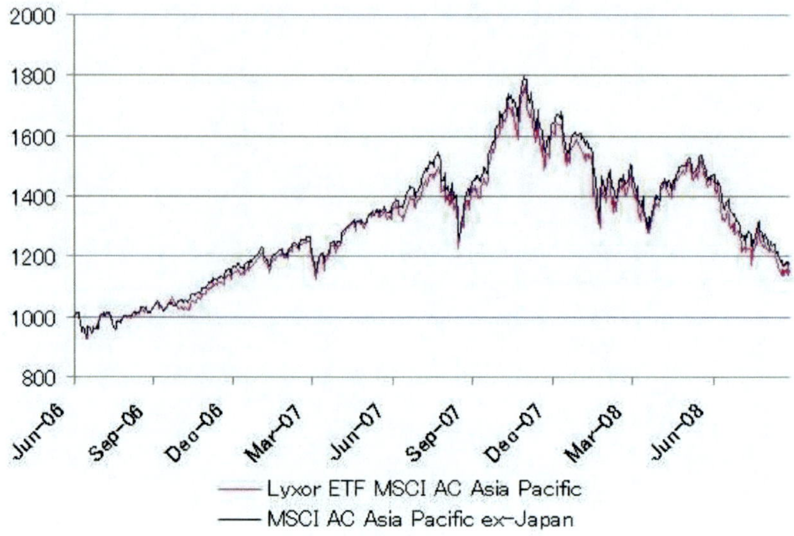


Figure 8. Tracking of Lyxor ETF to MSCI AC Asia Pacific Index (Data source: Bloomberg).

$$R_t = \beta_t' F_t + \eta_t, \tag{3}$$

where $\epsilon_t$ is representative of white noise that follows $K$ dimensional Gaussian distribution with mean $\mathbf{0}$, and covariance matrix $\Sigma$, and $\eta_t$ is a random variable that follows one dimensional normal distribution with mean 0 and variance $\sigma_\eta^2$. Our aim is to estimate unobservable factor exposures by using observable return data of $R_t$ and $F_t$. For a replicating purpose, we assumed that expected hedge fund alpha is zero.

We use Kalman filter for the estimation. Let $Y_t = \{R_1, \cdots, R_t, F_1, \cdots, F_t\}$ be observed values. We represent conditional expectation and covariance matrix as

$$\beta_{t|s} = E[\beta_t | Y_s],$$

$$V_{t|s} = E[(\beta_t - \beta_{t|s})(\beta_t - \beta_{t|s})' | Y_s].$$

$\beta_{t|s}$ is called prediction if $s < t$, and filtering if $s = t$. We can obtain these values sequentially by repeating prediction for one period ahead and filtering one after another. First, the prediction for the following period is obtained by

$$\beta_{t|t-1} = \beta_{t-1|t-1},$$

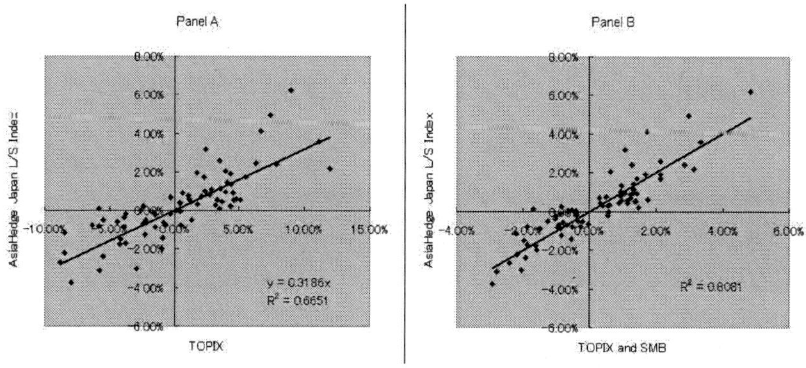


Figure 9. Monthly excess return of AsiaHedge Japan Long/Short Index against TOPIX and the portfolio of 34% TOPIX and 25% SMB (Jan/2002-May/2008).

$$V_{t|t-1} = V_{t-1|t-1} + \Sigma.$$

In the prediction algorithm, $\beta_{t|t-1}$ is same with filter $\beta_{t-1|t-1}$, while $V_{t|t-1}$ consists of two terms. The first is filter $V_{t-1|t-1}$ and the second is the effect of white noise $\eta_t$. Then, filtering is calculated as

$$\beta_{t|t} = K_t R_t + (I - K_t F_t')\beta_{t|t-1},$$

$$V_{t|t} = V_{t|t-1} - K_t F_t' V_{t|t-1},$$

where $K_t = (F_t' V_{t|t-1} F_t + \sigma_\eta^2)^{-1} V_{t|t-1} F_t$, which is referred to as Kalman gain. Therefore, filtering $\beta_{t|t}$ is a weighted average of new observation $R_t$ and prediction $\beta_{t|t-1}$, where the weight on the new observation is Kalman gain. The second term for filtering $V_{t|t}$ represents the improvement of state estimation accuracy due to new observation. We estimate the parameters $\Sigma$ and $\sigma_\eta^2$ by maximum likelihood, and then exposures to risk factors from January 2002 to May 2008. Figure 11 graphs the exposure changes of AsiaHedge Asia ex-Japan Index to MSCI Asia Pacific excluding Japan index estimated using rolling window regression and Kalman filter. Figure 12 does the same comparison between AsiaHedge Japan Long/Short Index and the two factors (TOPIX and SMB). These graphs show that on average, the Kalman filter captures exposure changes earlier than the rolling window regression.

Finally, we proceed to back test the performance of our replication models through making investments into the identified ETFs at levels estimated by the statistical methods. Figure 13 and 14 exhibit statistics of the replication

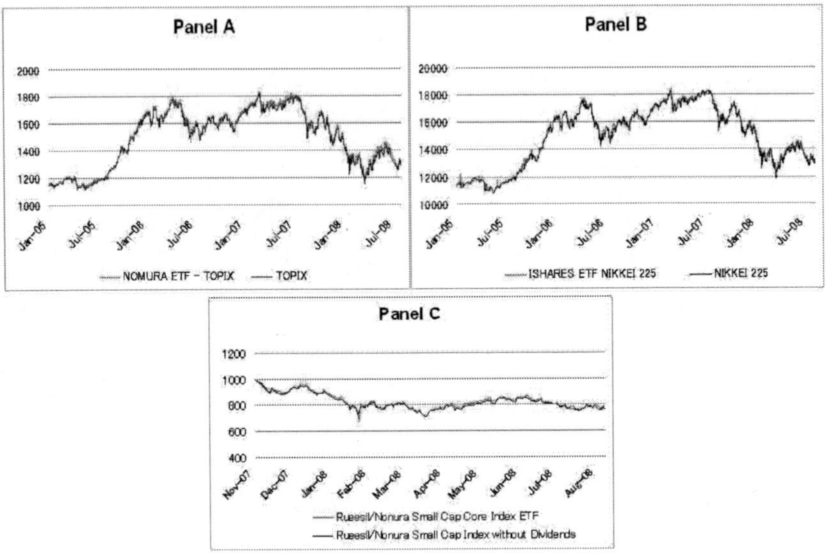


Figure 10. Tracking of ETFs to Japanese benchmark indices (Data source: Bloomberg).

results for AsiaHede Asia ex-Japan and Japan Long/Short indices respectively. In-sample figures refer to static exposures estimated through regression analysis using data from January 2002 to May 2008 period. Data of future periods is not available in practice, but we have included the estimated value using such data for comparative purposes. Rolling-window and Kalman filter capture dynamic exposures using past data. These are available methods in practice. One of the most important statistics is the correlation with the replication target, which is shown at the bottom of the table. The replicated returns by Kalman filter have higher correlation than rolling-window regression for both cases. Other statistics also show Kalman filter to be the better replicator. Especially, using Kalman filter succeeded in replicating skew and kurtosis better than rolling window. We conclude that the current exposure of both AsiaHedge hedge fund indexes can be captured more accurately by Kalman filter than by rolling-window regression. Moreover, statistics of Kalman filter is better than that of in-sample regression. In-sample regression uses future data, which does not allow for it to capture changing exposures within the period, leading to worse results. Rolling-window regression underperforms in-sample regression, which effec-

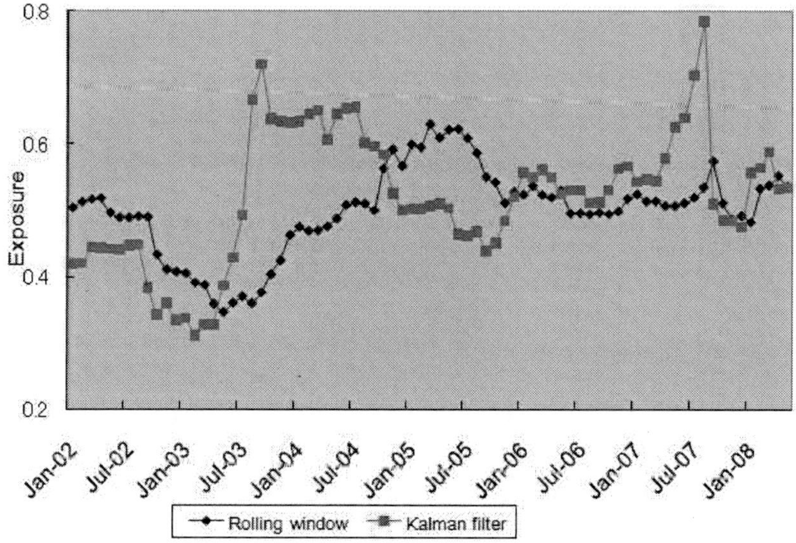


Figure 11. Exposure change of AsiaHedge Asia ex-Japan Index to MSCI Asia Pacific excluding Japan index estimated by rolling window regression and Kalman filter.

tively means that the loss incurred by the delay of capturing exposure change is larger than by inability to capture dynamic changes of exposure.

If one could find appropriate risk factors and capture the change of exposures to them quickly, he can replicate the target hedge fund returns on a month-to-month basis. Although exposure estimation by Kalman filter was the best in this example, it can be insufficient for some cases. The state space model that Kalman filter uses is for the case of normal white noise. Therefore, this model cannot capture drastic exposure changes. [21] estimated the exposure changes of mutual funds for non-Gaussian white noise cases using the Monte Carlo filter. Similar research should be done for hedge funds using Monte Carlo and other non-linear filtering methods to catch drastic exposure changes appropriately. Moreover, as long as we use monthly hedge funds return data, we cannot take into account dynamic exposure changes that occur within a month. Hedge fund managers monitor risk on a weekly, daily, or a more frequent basis, and adjust their investment positions according to these risk levels especially when prominent financial events occur. Some investable hedge fund indices report

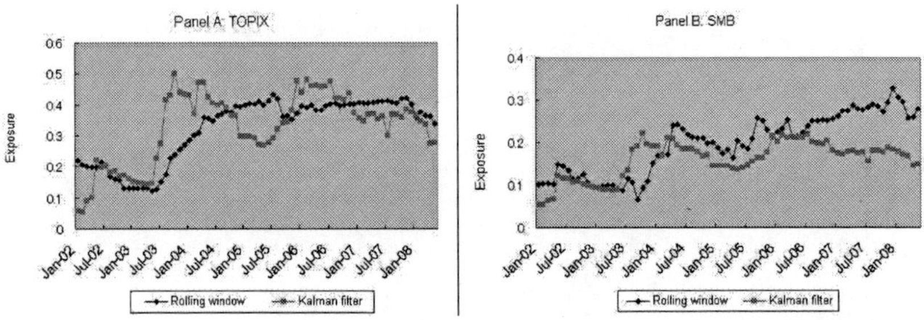


Figure 12. Exposure change of AsiaHedge Japan Long/Short Index to SMB estimated by rolling window regression and Kalman filter.

| | AsiaHedge Asia ex Japan Index | In-sample | Rolling window | Kalman filter |
|---|---|---|---|---|
| Annual return | 14.16% | 11.07% | 10.50% | 11.71% |
| Annual std. dev. | 9.53% | 8.66% | 8.28% | 8.57% |
| Sharpe ratio | 1.16 | 0.92 | 0.90 | 1.01 |
| Skew | -0.77 | -0.55 | -0.39 | -0.58 |
| Kurtosis | 3.70 | 3.33 | 3.48 | 3.80 |
| Max drawdown | 12.33% | 11.58% | 10.61% | 12.12% |
| Correlation | | 0.89 | 0.86 | 0.93 |

Figure 13. Statistics for replicated returns and the AsiaHedge Asia ex-J Index.

daily returns, but it is on an estimation basis. In many cases, these daily estimated returns are revised at a future date. The development of methods that incorporate dynamic exposure change within a month is also challenging task.

# 6. Distribution Replicating Approach

This section discusses the distribution replicating methodology that aims to replicate the joint distribution of an investor's portfolio and hedge fund returns. Unlike the factor-based approach, the distribution replication approach does not aim to replicate the target hedge fund returns on a month-to-month basis. Instead, this method aims to generate returns that have the same distribution pattern as the hedge fund returns. When it is difficult to find to risk factors that

| | AsiaHedge Japan Long/Short Index | In-sample | Rolling window | Kalman filter |
|---|---|---|---|---|
| Annual return | 6.41% | 5.42% | 4.71% | 5.39% |
| Volatility | 6.00% | 5.44% | 5.15% | 5.51% |
| Sharpe ratio | 0.55 | 0.43 | 0.32 | 0.42 |
| Skew | 0.61 | 0.20 | 0.05 | 0.36 |
| Kurtosis | 4.68 | 2.90 | 3.14 | 4.37 |
| Max drawdown | 10.78% | 9.26% | 10.92% | 9.70% |
| Correlation | | 0.90 | 0.88 | 0.95 |

Figure 14. Statistics for replicated returns and the AsiaHedge Japan Long/Short Index.

explain the target hedge fund returns, factor-based approach cannot work. This approach would be a powerful replication method for that case. Since investors expect hedge funds to have low correlation with their existing portfolio, it is also desirable to replicate the dependence between the investor's portfolio and hedge fund returns. One way of achieving this is to replicate the joint distribution of investor's portfolio and hedge fund returns.

The above mentioned methodology is proposed by [20]. In short, the basic concept is to price the distribution of hedge fund's payoff and replicate it through the dynamic trading of tradable securities. The theoretical framework is based on [5]'s payoff distribution pricing model. A given payoff distribution can be replicated by many different payoff functions. It showed that the cheapest way to get a payoff distribution is to allocate terminal wealth as a decreasing function of the state price density. [20] extended the payoff distribution pricing model to a bivariate setting, and considered the joint distribution with investor's portfolio. Details of the theoretical background are described in the papers. [27] proposed an alternative way to perform [20]'s replication methodology.

The following explains their attempt at using the distribution replicating approach. First, we describe the settings. Let us assume asset $S^1$ is the investor portfolio, asset $S^2$ is a reserve asset and asset $S^3$ is a hedge fund. Our goal is to replicate the joint distribution of monthly returns of $S^1$ and $S^3$ through the dynamic trading of $S^1$ and $S^2$. We set 0 as the start of the month and $T$ as the end of the month. The monthly logarithmic returns of the three assets are represented by $R_i$ for $i = 1, 2, 3$. We denote the distribution function for $R_i$ by

$F_i$ and the copula function with respect to the joint distribution of $(R_1, R_3)$ by $C$. To dynamically trade $S^1$ and $S^2$, we need to identify the asset price process of $S^1$ and $S^2$. They are denoted by $\{S_t^1\}_{t=0}^T$ and $\{S_t^2\}_{t=0}^T$. We set $S_0^1 = S_0^2 = 1$.

To implement the replicating strategy, we need to proceed with the following steps. We first obtain the joint distribution of investor's portfolio and hedge fund returns ($R_1$ and $R_3$). This is the target distribution to replicate. Next, we choose a reserve asset $S^2$ and infer the stochastic processes $\{S_t^1\}_{t=0}^T$ and $\{S_t^2\}_{t=0}^T$. Following that, we also obtain the joint distribution of $R_1$ and $R_2$. We then determine the payoff function, which transform the joint distribution of $(R_1, R_2)$ to that of $(R_1, R_3)$. Finally, we price the payoff distribution and replicate the payoff through the dynamic trading of $S^1$ and $S^2$. In the following, we explain the each step more in detail.

There are several ways to determine the joint distribution of $R_1$ and $R_3$. The easiest is to model them using the bivariate probability distribution. However, hedge funds exhibit different return characteristics to traditional asset classes, such as skews and fat-tails, and are nonlinearly related in some cases as shown in section 2. Therefore, [20] proposed modeling investor's portfolio and hedge fund returns separately, and connecting them by copula. Some copulas can capture asymmetric dependence structure flexibly. For example, Clayton copula has more dependence in the lower tail than in the upper tail. This allows for the copula to capture the strong dependence in bear markets and weak dependence in bull markets. Risk arbitrage funds tend to exhibit a similar dependence structure.

For hedge fund returns, it is desirable to use the distribution class that can capture its skewness and fat-tails. For example, the previous research by [20] and [27] used Gaussian distribution, Student-t, Gaussian mixture and Johnson distribution. We denote the distribution function of standard normal distribution by $N(\cdot)$, and the density of Gaussian distribution with mean $\mu$ and variance $\sigma^2$ by $\phi(x; \mu, \sigma^2)$. Gaussian distribution is determined by only mean and variance, and therefore does not capture skewness and fat-tails. Student-t captures can capture some kurtosis but cannot model skewness. Gaussian mixture with $m$ regimes and parameters $\{\pi_k\}_{k=1}^m$, $\{\mu_k\}_{k=1}^m$, $\{\sigma_k^2\}_{k=1}^m$ has the density

$$f(x) = \sum_{k=1}^{m} \pi_k \phi(x; \mu_k, \sigma_k^2),$$

where $\phi(x; \mu, \sigma^2) = \frac{1}{\sqrt{2\pi}\sigma} \exp\{-\frac{(x-\mu)^2}{2\sigma^2}\}$ is the density of Gaussian distribution with mean $\mu$ and variance $\sigma^2$. The intuitive interpretation of this distribution is as follows. It is assumed that there are $m$ regimes (states), which happen with probability $\{\pi_k\}_{k=1}^{m}$. If regime $k$ occurred, the conditional distribution is Gaussian whose density is $\phi(x;\mu_k,\sigma_k^2)$. Allowing multi-regimes, this distribution class can capture skewness and kurtosis. The distribution functions of Johnson distributions are given by

$$F(x) = N\left(\gamma + \delta h\left(\frac{x-\xi}{\lambda}\right)\right),$$

where $\gamma$ and $\delta$ are shape parameters, $\xi$ and $\lambda$ are location and scale parameter respectively, and $h(\cdot)$ is one of the following functions:

$$h(z) = \begin{cases} \log z & \text{(log-normal)} \\ \log\left(z + \sqrt{z^2+1}\right) & \text{(unbounded)} \\ \log\left(\frac{z}{1-z}\right) & \text{(bounded)} \end{cases}$$

Johnson distributions are often used for analysis of non-normal behavior of hedge fund returns as seen in [19], [28], and [29].

For investor's portfolio, we have to use a well-fitted probability distribution of monthly returns, and model its stochastic process thereafter. To carry this out, we should model the monthly returns to be consistent with the stochastic process. [27] pointed out that [20] had modeled the monthly return and stochastic process inconsistently. To correct the inconsistency, [27] modeled the daily and monthly returns using a Gaussian mixture. The most consistent way is to model the stochastic process of the investor's portfolio and then derive the probability distribution of the month end logarithmic returns from the stochastic process.

Copula integrates the marginal distribution of investor's portfolio and hedge fund returns, and defines the joint distribution. The copula function $C$ of the random vector $(R_1, R_3)$ is the joint distribution function of the random vector $(U, V)$, where $U = F_1(R_1)$ and $V = F_3(R_3)$. Then, the joint distribution function of $(R_1, R_3)$ satisfies

$$F_{1,3}(r_1, r_3) = C(F_1(r_1), F_3(r_3)).$$

The previous works used Gaussian, Student-t, Gumbel, Clayton, Frank, and symmetrised Joe-Clayton copulas. The characteristics of these copula is explained in [20]. Further details are argued in [18] and [26].

There are some ways to estimate the parameters and select model. [20] and [27] used different parameter estimation and model selection procedures. [20] estimated the parameter for copula and marginal distribution of $R_1$ and $R_3$ all together by maximum likelihood. They then selected the final model by AIC. On the other hand, [27] estimated the parameters separately. First, they estimated the parameter for the marginal distributions and selected the model using a goodness-of-fit test. They then ranked the time-series data of the returns to determine the copula. Through this method, they hoped to work around the copula selection without the effect of mis-specification and estimation error of the marginal distributions. Further detail regarding these procedures is described in the papers.

After we determine the copula, we need to infer the stochastic process of investor's portfolio $S^1$ and reserve assets $S^2$. Remember that the time-series structure of these assets is required because we aim to replicate the payoff of hedge funds through the dynamic trading of these assets. The strategy is derived through using methods of pricing and hedging of derivatives such as tree models, Monte Carlo simulation and others. The easiest way is to model the asset price process by geometric Brownian motion and estimating the parameters. In using the tree model, we approximate the stochastic process using a bivariate binomial or trinomial tree. For both these cases, it is only necessary to estimate some of the statistics of instantaneous (or daily) return such as mean, standard deviation, and correlation. On the other hand, if one uses Monte Carlo simulation, one has to make assumptions and infer the stochastic process so as to fit the sample data.

After estimating the parameters and selecting models of the asset returns and price processes, we have to next determine a payoff function. Since we are trying to obtain the joint distribution of investor's portfolio and hedge fund returns through the dynamic trading of the investor's portfolio and reserve assets, we require a function $\tilde{g}$ such that

$$P\left(R_1 \leq x,\ \tilde{g}\left(R_1, R_2\right) \leq y\right) = P(R_1 \leq x, R_3 \leq y) \ \text{ for any } x, y,$$

or equivalently,

$$P\left(\tilde{g}\left(R_1, R_2\right) \leq y \middle| R_1 = x\right) = P(R_3 \leq y | R_1 = x) \ \text{ for any } x, y.$$

Then, $\tilde{g}(\cdot,\cdot)$ is given by

$$\tilde{g}(x, y) = Q\left\{x, P(R_2 \leq y | R_1 = x)\right\},$$

where $Q(x, \alpha)$ is the order $\alpha$ quantile of the conditional law of $R_3$ given $R_1 = x$. In terms of asset prices, the payoff function is represented as

$$g(S_T^1, S_T^2) = \exp\{\tilde{g}(\log S_T^1, \log S_T^2)\}. \tag{4}$$

Given the payoff function, the problem comes down to pricing and hedging of contingent claim. Therefore, we can utilize methods developed for option pricing. The present value of the objective payoff can be obtained by the discounted expectation of the payoff under risk-neutral measure. If one modeled the market to be complete, the payoff can be perfectly replicated through a delta hedging strategy. [20] recommended to implement these processes using Monte Carlo simulation or a trinomial tree, while [27] proposed the use of a quadratic hedging strategy with a combined method of tree model and Monte Carlo simulation. If the present value of the payoff is equal to one, the replication strategy delivers a return that has the same distribution with that of the target hedge fund. If it exceeds one, we need additional cost to replicate the payoff. Otherwise, we are able to get hedge fund returns at lower cost.

Through the steps described above, one can theoretically replicate the distribution of hedge fund returns. However, there can exist replication errors due to the following reasons. First, the estimation error can exist in the inference of both the hedge fund return distributions and the stochastic process of investor's portfolio and reserve assets. Furthermore, even when the returns are generated from known population distribution data and parameters are estimated using simulated data, these estimated parameters can include some errors especially in the case of small samples. The inference process is performed using some assumptions such as stationarity. If there is a structural break in the sample data period used for parameter estimations, the inference process would fail. Second, approximation errors can occur when the tree model is used to calculate both the value of the payoff and size of position, and numerical errors can occur if Monte Carlo simulation is used instead. The accuracy of replication can be evaluated through comparing some statistics of the target hedge fund returns and the replicated returns.

[20] studied the effects estimation errors, derived from inference using small sample data. They assumed the true population distribution of asset returns to be stationary. The investor's portfolio and reserve assets log returns were assumed to follow a bivariate Gaussian distribution with a parameter set. As for hedge fund returns and the copula between those of hedge fund and investor's portfolio, they considered two cases. The first is that the hedge fund log returns follow

a Gaussian distribution and the copula is a symmetrised Joe-Clayton copula with some parameter sets. This copula's dependence in the upper tail is stronger than in the lower tail. The second is that hedge fund log returns follows a Johnson unbounded distribution with parameters that set skewness levels at 2.0 and excess kurtosis levels at 10. The copula in this case is a Gaussian copula, which has a dependence structure similar to that of a bivariate Gaussian distribution. In their study, return samples were drawn from the population using different sample sizes of N (= 24, 48, 72, 96, 120, 240), to examine the effect of small samples. Using the data samples, they inferred return distributions, and derived payoff functions by (4). They took 2000 observations from the investor's portfolio and reserve assets, substituted them into the payoff function, and obtained the payoff outcomes.

They then calculated the mean, standard deviation, skewness, kurtosis, and correlation with the investor's portfolio. These procedures were repeated 100 times for each N, and the different sets of statistics were compared and evaluated. They showed that, for the case of Gaussian distribution and symmetrised Joe-Clayton copula, the larger the sample, the more accurate the payoff function is. Even with a relatively small sample the procedure still works quite well. For the case of Johnson unbounded distribution and Gaussian copula, they could not conclude that a larger sample improves the payoff function accuracy as like the previous example. Moreover, the replication accuracy of skewness and kurtosis was low, because small samples do not contain enough information on tail events. These results imply that if we succeed in calculating the present value of the payoff and position size, we can replicate the joint distribution of investor's portfolio and hedge fund return with good accuracy excluding tail events.

Following their simulation analysis, [20] attempted to replicate an actual fund of hedge funds and a further two hedge funds on an out-of-sample basis. To achieve this, they estimated parameters and selected models using only preceding sample data of the month they tried to replicate. Therefore, their results are reflective of actual replication that can be done. They assumed that the investor's portfolio consisted 50% of a S&P 500 tracking portfolio and 50% of a long-dated US Treasury bonds, and used the nearest Eurodollar futures as the reserve asset. As for replicating the fund of hedge funds, they succeeded in cloning the joint distribution of investor's portfolio and the fund returns in most cases except for three large losses from 1987 to 2004. As for replicating the two hedge funds, [20] generated similar statistical properties as the fund returns, although the returns appeared in a different order. Further detailed results are described in the paper.

[27] tested their replication accuracy using an in-sample test. For example, they performed parameter estimation and model selection using sample data from 2002 to 2006, and attempted to replicate hedge fund returns during that period. Note that we cannot get the result when we implement their replication strategy in practice. Their methodology was applied to HFRI and EDHEC hedge fund indices by strategy. The volatility and the dependence coefficients (Kendall's tau) were replicated with great precision, and the skewness and kurtosis were with slightly less accuracy. The choice of reserve asset impacted the initial cost of investing in the replicating portfolio, leading to the difference of mean returns.

Separately, we attempted to clone Eurekahedge global CTA/managed futures and macro indices on an out-of-sample basis. [17] showed that it was difficult to find risk factors that explained returns of hedge funds for these strategies. Hence, we used a distribution replicating approach instead of attempting to replicate the returns of these indices on month-to-month basis using a factor-based approach. The inception month of these indices is January 2000. We used the data from the first two years since inception to estimate the return distributions while the monthly log-returns from January 2002 to May 2008 were replicated. We assumed the investor's portfolio $S^1$ to be composed of 50% Japanese stocks and 50% Japanese government bonds (JGB). Since we are required to dynamically trade these assets, TOPIX futures and long-term JGB futures were used as proxies. Both these securities are listed on the Tokyo Stock Exchange. The reserve asset $S^2$ is made up of 25% S&P 500 futures, 25% NYMEX WTI crude oil futures, 25% COMEX gold futures, and 25% JPY against USD spot currency. All data is obtained from Bloomberg. Log-returns on futures are calculated by rolling the front contract. The front contract is rolled on the last trading day of the maturity month. Our base currency is USD. And since TOPIX and JGB futures are denominated in JPY, we applied a currency hedge. Accordingly, the log returns of these assets are adjusted by the difference between the interest rates of USD and JPY. Libor rates were used for the interest rates. We ran a linear regression of the monthly log-returns of the two indices against the above mentioned six assets using data from January 2002 to May 2008. The adjusted $R^2$s for the global CTA/Managed futures and macro indices were 0.22 and 0.48 respectively. The statistics for monthly log-returns of investor's portfolio and reserve asset January/2002-May 2008 are shown in Figure 15, where

Kendall's tau is a dependence coefficient defined by

$$\tau = P[(X_1 - X_2)(Y_1 - Y_2) > 0] - P[(X_1 - X_2)(Y_1 - Y_2) < 0],$$

where $(X_1, Y_1)$ and $(X_2, Y_2)$ are independent and identically distributed random vectors.

| | Investor's portfolio | Reserve asset |
|---|---|---|
| Mean | 0.75% | 1.19% |
| Std. Dev. | 2.04% | 2.68% |
| $\frac{\text{Mean}}{\text{Std. Dev.}}$ | 0.37 | 0.44 |
| Skew | -0.15 | 0.05 |
| Kurtosis | 2.68 | 2.33 |
| Correlation with investor's portfolio | 1.00 | 0.35 |
| Kendall's tau with investor's portfolio | 1.00 | 0.19 |
| Min | -3.87% | -4.17% |
| Max | 5.37% | 7.39% |
| Number of positive return months (Total: 77) | 53 | 50 |

Figure 15. Statistics for the log-returns of investor's portfolio and reserve asset (January/2002-May/2008).

We implemented the following replication procedure for each month using past data. First, parameter estimation and model selection for the marginal distribution of monthly log-returns of hedge fund were performed using the same method mentioned in [27]. The best fitting model is chosen from a Gaussian mixture with $m$ regimes ($m = 1, 2, 3, 4, 5$) and Johnson unbounded distribution. Next, the copula model between monthly log-returns of hedge fund and investor's portfolio is estimated and selected in the same manner as in [27], which is through the ranking of time-series data. The copula is selected from Gaussian, Student, Clayton, Frank and Gumbel. Following that, we modeled the stochastic process of the investor's portfolio and reserve asset through a bivariate log-normal process;

$$\frac{dS_t^1}{S_t^1} = \mu_1 dt + \sigma_{11} dW_t^1,$$
$$\frac{dS_t^2}{S_t^2} = \mu_2 dt + \sigma_{21} dW_t^1 + \sigma_{21} dW_t^2$$

with $S_0^1 = S_0^2 = 1$. The parameters were estimated using daily data. Then, the monthly log-return of investor's portfolio is obtained by $N(\mu_1 - \sigma_{11}^2/2, \sigma_{11}^2)$ as a byproduct. Finally, we replicated the payoff function (4) by using a delta-hedging strategy on a daily basis. We calculated the present value and delta of the payoff using Monte Carlo simulation. Figure 16 describes the obtained investment weights on the investor's portfolio and reserve asset. Panel A and B are the weights for global CTA/Managed futures and global macro respectively.

The results of our replication process are as follows. Figure 17 exhibits the monthly log-returns and the growth of the asset value of the target hedge fund indices and the clones. Panel A is the result for Eurekahedge global CTA/Managed futures, and Panel B is that for Eurekahedge global macro. Panel 1 describes the time-series of monthly log-returns. The correlation between the log-returns of target hedge fund index and its clone are included in the panel. The correlations for CTA/Managed futures and global macro are 0.38 and 0.52 respectively, which show that the clones do not replicate the returns of target on a month-to-month basis. Panel 2 exhibits the growth of asset values of the target hedge fund indices and the clones. The CTA/Managed futures clone achieved the same amount of profits with the target in the long run. Though, the shapes of their equity curves are similar, the timing of their returns differs. On the other hand, the global macro clone earns less return than the target. In this case, though their equity curves are also similar, there are differences in return levels. Figure 18 exhibits the statistics for the returns of the target hedge fund and the replicas. For the case of CTA/Managed futures, mean and standard deviation are replicated with great accuracy. Minimum and maximum returns and the number of positive returns are also close. The skewness, kurtosis and the dependence coefficients (correlation and Kendall's tau) were slightly less accurate. For the case of global macro, the result is similar to that of CTA/Managed futures except for the mean and skewness. The mean return is slightly less than the target, and the sign of skewness is opposite from the target. However, many of the other statistics are replicated with better accuracy than in the case of CTA/Managed

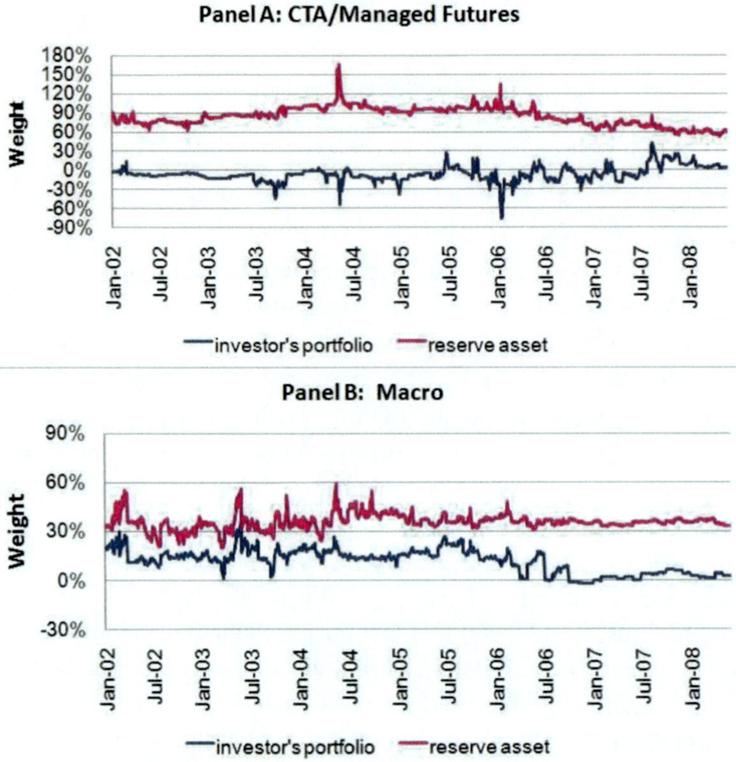


Figure 16. The investment weights on the investor's portfolio and reserve asset.

futures. These include standard deviation, kurtosis, dependence coefficients, and minimum value.

In summary, the above mentioned methodology enables us to obtain the joint distribution of the investor's portfolio and the target hedge fund's returns. The merit of this approach is that we can gain access to the statistical properties of hedge fund returns even if we are not able to find risk factors that explain hedge fund returns. This method, since it clones the dependence structure between the investor's portfolio and hedge fund returns, is able to satisfy investor's expectation that hedge fund returns have low correlation with their existing portfolio. Moreover, this methodology allows positions to be adjusted dynamically. However, there are still areas for improvement within this methodology. For example, the reserve asset is constructed through an equal weighted portfolio

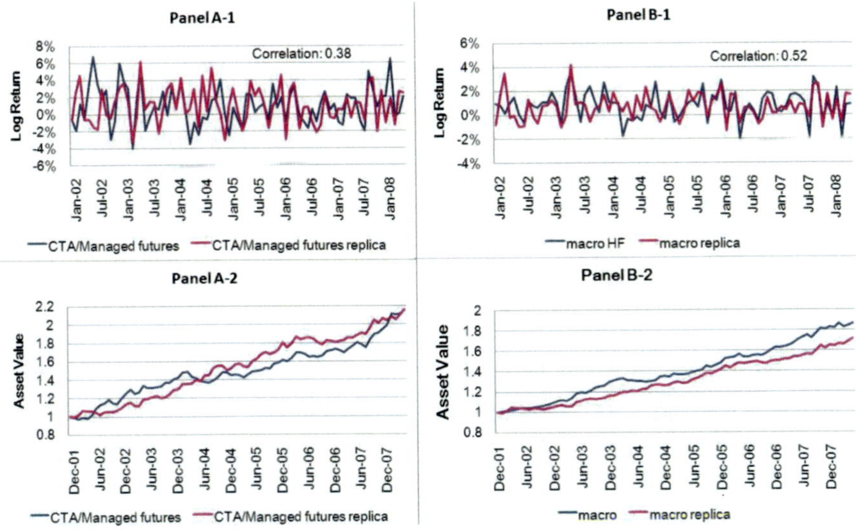


Figure 17. Monthly log-returns and growth of asset values of the target hedge fund indices and the replicas.

| | CTA/ Managed futures | CTA/Managed futures replica | Macro | Macro replica |
|---|---|---|---|---|
| Mean | 0.99% | 1.00% | 0.81% | 0.70% |
| Std. Dev. | 2.27% | 2.18% | 1.16% | 1.11% |
| $\frac{\text{Mean}}{\text{Std. Dev.}}$ | 0.44 | 0.46 | 0.70 | 0.63 |
| Skew | 0.29 | 0.14 | -0.20 | 0.46 |
| Kurtosis | 2.99 | 2.36 | 3.08 | 3.32 |
| Correlation with investor's portfolio | 0.04 | 0.28 | 0.41 | 0.52 |
| Kendall's tau with investor's portfolio | 0.07 | 0.16 | 0.24 | 0.32 |
| Min | -4.05% | -3.28% | -1.99% | -1.35% |
| Max | 6.77% | 6.22% | 3.49% | 4.19% |
| Number of positive return months (Total: 77) | 49 | 50 | 59 | 57 |

Figure 18. Statistics for log-returns of the target hedge fund and the replicas (January/2002-May/2008).

of assets that it is assumed that the target hedge funds invest in. The selection of these assets is an important determination in the construction of the reserve asset. To determine the appropriate assets is a challenging task. Going forward, developments in modeling and estimating the asset returns or price processes, and dynamic replication techniques will further improve the performance of replication.

## 7. Conclusion

In this paper, we discussed hedge fund replication. As long as the return characteristics of hedge funds are appealing, hedge fund clone products would prove beneficial and useful. Since hedge fund returns cannot be replicated perfectly, a number of different methods have surfaced. These methods are classified into three approaches: Rule-based, Factor-based, and Distribution replication based approaches. These approaches aim to replicate different aspects of hedge fund returns. In the above sections, we explained each method in detail. The methodologies are work-in-progress. Future research may lead to improvisation of these techniques that in turn will generate replicated returns with properties much closer to target hedge fund returns than current clones. We also eagerly await the development of hybrid methods that are able to combine the advantages of each of the various mentioned methods. Furthermore, new developments in this arena should not only be limited to existing hedge fund replications. It is going to be important to develop new investment strategies, which meet a wide range of investors' needs, through the use of transparent and liquid assets.

### Acknowledgements

We thank Mr. Hideki Yamauchi, Mr. Takahiko Suenaga, Mr. Tetsuya Aoki, and Mr. Takeshi Hakamada in GCI Group for their constant support. We are greatfull to Mr. Nandakumar Lokanathan and Mr. Allen Zheng in GCI Group for extensive help in improving English in this version.

## References

[1] Agarwal, V. and Naik, N.Y. (2004). Risks and Portfolio Decisions Involving Hedge Funds. *The Review of Financial Studies*, Vol. 17(1), pp. 63-98.

[2] Bowler, B. (2007), The Emergence of Synthetic Hedge Funds. http://www.pacificprospect.com/jsp_2007/downloads/a/2.pdf

[3] Brown, S.J. and Goetzmann, W.N. (2003). Hedge Funds With Style. *The Journal of Portfolio Management*, Vol. 29(2), pp. 101-112.

[4] Duarte, J., Longstaff, F. and Yu, F. (2007). Risk and Return in Fixed Income Arbitrage: Nickels in front of a Steamroller? *The Review of Financial Studies*, Vol. 20(3), pp. 769-811.

[5] Dybvig, P. (1988a). Distributional Analysis of Portfolio Choice. *Journal of Business*, Vol. 61, pp. 369-393.

[6] Dybvig, P. (1988b). Inefficient Dynamic Portfolio Strategies or How to Throw Away a Million Dollars in the Stock Market. *Review of Financial Studies*, Vol. 1, pp. 67-88.

[7] Fung, W. and Hsieh, D.A. (1997). Empirical Characteristics of Dynamic Trading Strategies: The Case of Hedge Funds. *The Review of Financial Studies*, Vol. 10(2), pp. 275-302.

[8] Fung, W. and Hsieh, D.A. (2000). Performance Characteristics of Hedge Funds and Commodity funds: Natural vs. Spurious Biases. *The Journal of Financial and Quantitative Analysis*, Vol. 35(3), pp. 291-307.

[9] Fung, W. and Hsieh, D.A. (2001). The Risk in Hedge Fund Strategies: Theory and Evidence from Trend Followers. *The Review of Financial Studies*, Vol. 14(2), pp. 313-341.

[10] Fung, W. and Hsieh, D.A. (2002). The Risk in Fixed-Income Hedge Fund Styles. *The Journal of Fixed Income*, Vol. 12, pp. 6-27.

[11] Fung, W. and Hsieh, D.A. (2003). Benchmark for Alternative Investments: A Risk Factor-Based Approach. Working Paper.

[12] Fung, W. and Hsieh, D.A. (2004). Extracting Portable Alphas from Equity Long-Short Hedge Funds. *Journal of Investment Management*, Vol. 2, pp. 57-75.

[13] Fung, W. and Hsieh, D.A. (2007). Will Hedge Funds Regress towards Index-like Products? *Journal of Investment Management*, Vol. 5(2), pp. 46-55.

[14] Fung, W. Hsieh, D.A., Naik, N.Y. and Ramadorai, T. (2008). Hedge Funds: Performance, Risk and Capital Formation. *Journal of Finance*, Vol. 63(4), pp. 1777-1803.

[15] Géhin, W. (2007). Hedge Fund Clones: Key Issues in Distinguishing between Them. http://www.edhec-risk.com/latest_news/RISKArticle.2007-10-11.3936?newsletter=yes

[16] Getmansky, M., Lo, A. and Makarov, I. (2004). An Econometric Analysis of Serial Correlation and Illiquidity in Hedge-Fund Returns. *The Journal of Financial Economics*, Vol. 74, pp. 529-609.

[17] Hakamada, T., Takahashi, A. and Yamamoto, K. (2007), Selection and Performance Analysis of Asia-Pacific Hedge Funds. Journal of Alternative Investments, Vol. 10(3), pp. 7-29.

[18] Joe, H. (1997). *Multivariate Models and Dependence Concepts.* Chapman and Hall.

[19] Kaplan, P.D. and Knowles, J.A. (2004). Kappa: A Generalized Downside Risk-Adjusted Performance Measure. Working Paper.

[20] Kat, H.M. and Palaro, H.P. (2005), Who Needs Hedge Funds? A Copula-Based Approach to Hedge Fund Return Replication. Working Paper.

[21] Kobayashi, T., Sato, S., and Takahashi, A. (2005). Style Analysis Based on a General State Space Model and Monte Carlo Filter. Working Paper.

[22] Lo, A. and Hasanhodzic, J. (2006). Can Hedge-Fund Returns Be Replicated?: The Linear Case. Working Paper.

[23] Malkiel, B.G. and Saha, A. (2005). Hedge Funds: Risk and Return. *The Financial Analysts Journal*, Vol. 61(6), pp. 80-88.

[24] Mitchell, M. and Pulvino, T. (2001). Characteristics of Risk in Risk Arbitrage. *Journal of Finance*, Vol. 56, pp. 2067-2109.

[25] Naik, N.Y., Ramadorai, T., and Stromqvist, M. (2007). Capacity constraints and hedge fund strategy returns. *European Financial Management*, 13(2), pp. 239-25.

[26] Nelsen, R.B. (1999). *An introduction to copulas: Vol. 139 of Lecture Notes in Statistics*. Springer-Verlag, New York.

[27] Papageorgiou, N., Remillard, B. and Hocquard, A. (2008). Replicating the properties of hedge fund returns. *Journal of Alternative Investments*, forthcoming.

[28] Passow, A. (2005). Omega Portfolio Construction with Johnson distributions. *Risk*, Vol. 18(4), pp. 85-90.

[29] Pérez, P. G. (2004). An approach to the non-normal behavior of hedge fund indices using Johnson distributions. Working Paper.

[30] Sharpe, W. (1992). Asset Allocation: Management Style and Performance Measurement. *The Journal of Portfolio Management*, (Winter,1992), pp. 7-19.

[31] Tremont/TASS (2004), Fourth Quarter Asset Flows Report. Tremont Capital Management, New York, NY.

In: The Recent Trend of Hedge Fund Strategies ISBN: 978-1-61668-338-2
Editor: Yasuaki Watanabe, pp. 97-131 

*Chapter 3*

# HEDGE FUND STYLE ANALYSIS WITH THE GAP STATISTIC

***Robert J. Bianchi*[*1], Michael E. Drew[1], Madhu Veeraraghavan[2] and Peter Whelan[3]***

[1]Department of Accounting, Finance and Economics, Griffith University
Brisbane, Queensland, Australia
[2]Department of Accounting and Finance, Monash University
Melbourne, Victoria, Australia
[3]School of Economics and Finance, Queensland University of Technology,
Brisbane, Queensland, Australia

* E-mail address: r.bianchi@griffith.edu.au; (Corresponding author) Tel: +61-7-3735 7078; Fax: +61-7-3735 3719; Postal address: Griffith Business School, Department of Accounting, Finance and Economics, Nathan campus, Griffith University, 170 Kessels Road, Nathan, Brisbane, Queensland, 4111, Australia. We thank Stephen Brown, Adam Clements, Edwin Elton, Martin Gruber, Paul Lajbcygier, Rodney Sullivan, Terry Walter, two anonymous referees, and seminar participants at the 2005 Global Finance Conference, the 2005 European Financial Management Association Conference, the 2005 Australian Conference of Economists and New York University for helpful comments. The authors thank Credit Suisse First Boston, Lehman Brothers, Citigroup and Tremont TASS Europe Ltd for providing data. We thank the QUT High Performance Computing staff for programming, hardware and software assistance. We gratefully acknowledge the Applied Modeling in Economics & Finance Research Centre, Pension and Investment Management Project, School of Economics and Finance, Faculty of Business, QUT for financial assistance. Finally, we thank the numerous hedge fund managers who have provided insightful information in our understanding of hedge fund investment styles. Any remaining errors are our own.

## Abstract

We propose a new approach to investment style analysis by classifying the hedge fund universe with the Tibshirani, Walther and Hastie (2001) Gap Statistic. This study finds the statistical presence of only three broad hedge fund investment styles for the period 1994 to 2001. The investment styles can be best described as: quasi-long-equity; non-directional; and, global-directional. We validate the findings of the Gap Statistic by passively replicating the systematic returns of these three investment styles with traditional asset classes.

**Key words**: Hedge Funds, Investment Style Analysis

**JEL Classification:** *C19, G10, G11, G15*

# 1. Introduction

One of the fastest areas of growth in funds management is the global hedge fund industry where the U.S. Securities and Exchange Commission (2003) estimate its size at approximately $600 to $650 billion in funds under management in the United States alone.[1] These specialist fund managers provide a wide range of investment styles and strategies to investors, or do they? The analysis of hedge fund investment style is an emerging issue given its importance to a plan sponsor's asset allocation process. The objective of this study is to ask the fundamental question of, how many different hedge fund investment styles are truly available to investors? This study analyzes returns with a new classification technique known as the Gap Statistic and finds the presence of only three broad investment styles in the hedge fund industry. We examine the economic rationale behind these investment styles and reveal the investment philosophies that dominate the hedge fund universe. The three hedge fund investment styles can be best described as (i) quasi-long-equities, (ii) non-directional and (iii) global-directional. Furthermore, we demonstrate that a large proportion of the systematic returns of these investment styles can be passively replicated with traditional asset classes.

In practice, the classification of hedge fund investment styles are determined by market participants who construct their own peer-group based classification

[1] The United States Securities Exchange Commission (S.E.C.) (2003) expects the hedge fund industry to grow to over $1 trillion in the next five to ten years. As at 31 December 2002, the S.E.C.(2003) valued the U.S. stock market at $11.8 trillion, making the size of the hedge fund industry in the U.S. at approximately 5% of the value of the U.S. stockmarket.

methods. This means that there are neither generally accepted groupings of hedge funds nor methods available to accurately group these fund managers. For instance, Tremont TASS Europe Ltd (hereafter TASS) classify hedge funds into 11 broad categories, the Hennessee Group classify the industry into 23 different investment styles, while Hedge Fund Research, Inc. (HFR) has 30 classifications. Despite market participants developing their own hedge fund style categories, the debate over investment styles widens further when the academic literature is considered. While there are specific investment style studies in the hedge fund literature, there is almost no investment style analysis of the hedge fund universe.[2] The recent work of Brown and Goetzmann (2003) remains the only industry-wide study. They provide evidence of eight hedge fund investment styles. These divergent views on hedge fund investment styles remains an unresolved issue which this study seeks to address.

Style analysis has a long tradition in industry and has been researched in the early performance studies including Carlson (1970), Elton and Gruber (1970, 1971) and McDonald (1974). However, the importance of style analysis was not fully appreciated until the seminal work of Sharpe (1992). The Sharpe (1992) framework employs a constrained OLS regression which relates funds with their factor loadings in order to determine style attributes. The Sharpe (1992) model remains the dominant investment style framework which assumes full knowledge of the risk factors and unconditional linearity in the relationship between portfolio returns and the common style factor loadings.

Although Sharpe (1992) remains the benchmark investment style framework, it is must be operationalised under restrictive conditions which are not accommodative towards hedge fund style analysis. The Sharpe (1992) model assumes full knowledge of the risk factors, returns must exhibit normality and its linear-based framework may not adequately model portfolio dynamics. The Sharpe (1992) model has motivated researchers to develop competing frameworks. Lo (2001) and Fung and Hsieh (2002b) inform us that returns which depart from normality, fund dynamics and returns which are not easily related to independent risk factors are inherent in hedge fund returns. An alternative investment style model which competes with Sharpe (1992) is the principal component analysis (PCA) framework from Fung and Hsieh (1997a, 2000). The unique feature of the PCA framework is the estimation of investment styles without the knowledge of factor loadings. Although PCA is a viable alternative to

[2] Various style-specific studies include Fung and Hsieh (1997a, 2001, 2002a) who examine trend following CTAs, Mitchell and Pulvino (2001) evaluate a hedge fund investment strategy referred to as merger or risk arbitrage, Fung and Hsieh (2002c) and Kao (2002) investigate the fixed income hedge fund style.

Sharpe (1992), studies by Brown (1989) and MacKinlay (1995) demonstrate the inference problems encountered by researchers when identifying the accurate number of principal components.

In another approach, Brown and Goetzmannn (1997, 2003) and Brown, Goetzmann, Hiraki, Otsuki and Shiraishi (2001) employ a *k*-means hard cluster analysis with a generalised least squares procedure in order to adjust for a fund's time-varying variance or heteroskedasticity. The Brown and Goetzmannn (1997, 2003) model (hereafter 'BG') has three characteristics which makes it more conducive for hedge funds than the Sharpe (1992) approach. First, it is able to relax the assumption of normally distributed returns. Second, the estimation of factor loadings (or style attributes) is not required, and, finally, factor loadings can be time-varying.[3] The BG model employs the conventional likelihood ratio (LR) test statistic to estimate the number of investment styles.

A key element in all investment style frameworks is the method by which funds are classified into their respective style attributes. The classification methodology therefore becomes the primary determinant of an investment style analysis. In this study we show that the BG model can be extended with a new classification test statistic which provides new insights in the appropriate grouping of hedge funds. Recently, a new test statistic known as the Tibshirani, Walther and Hastie (2001) Gap Statistic (hereafter 'Gap Statistic') has been developed which is specifically designed to estimate the optimal number of groups in a dataset. Tibshirani *et. al.,* (2001) demonstrate the robustness of the Gap Statistic against other classification statistics and therefore makes it an ideal candidate to address the issues in investment style analysis. This study adds a new dimension to the literature by considering this newly developed classification test statistic.[4]

---

[3] The contribution of the Brown and Goetzmann (1997) model is important as it expresses the classic modern asset pricing model in the form of a modified k-means hard cluster analysis procedure. Modern asset pricing models take the mathematical form that returns are equal to a conditional (group) expected return plus an idiosyncratic error. The work of Brown and Goetzmann (1997) employs a standard k-means cluster analysis on monthly return data, which inherently has the characteristics and styles of each fund embedded in the monthly returns. The k-means cluster analysis classifies data using cross-sectional attributes of the data, and when the procedure is restricted to cluster solely on returns as the attribute, the Brown and Goetzmann (1997) model interprets this k-means cluster analysis as grouping return data based on conditional group mean returns, which is consistent with standard modern asset pricing theory. By considering this new mathematical framework, Brown and Goetzmann (1997) have developed an investment style analysis tool which is useful when the risk factors are not fully identified.

[4] Of the three investment style models, the BG model seems most likely to accommodate the Gap Statistic. The BG model employs the conventional Quandt (1960) likelihood ratio (LR) test statistic to estimate the optimal number of investment styles, however, there are limitations with this test statistic. Specifically, the LR test assumes that returns are normally distributed and

This study finds the statistical presence of three broad investment styles in the hedge fund universe over the long-term. We re-classify the individual funds into their respective hedge fund styles and we find that the systematic returns of the three investment style portfolios can be passively replicated with traditional asset classes. The first hedge fund style consists of funds who are effectively long global equities and those who earn the small firm and momentum risk premia. The second investment style consists of funds whose returns are determined by *relative-value* investment decisions. That is, these funds are generally not exposed to directional-risk, but rather, derive their return and risk characteristics from the relative relationship of two assets or more. The third hedge fund investment style consists of fund managers who develop dynamic long/short directional positions across the four global investment classes of bonds, equities, commodities and currencies. Furthermore, we estimate that 42 to 83 percent of the variation of the systematic returns of these three hedge fund investment styles can be passively replicated with traditional asset classes.

This study makes a number of contributions to the literature. First, we perform an investment style analysis on the hedge fund universe where little research has been undertaken. Second, this study extends the BG model by substituting the LR test statistic with the more effective Gap Statistic. This study is the first to consider the Gap Statistic on a sample of hedge funds. Third, the introduction of the Gap Statistic in the investment style literature provides researchers with a new tool specifically designed to determine the optimal number of groups in a dataset. Fourth, the issue of survivorship is well documented in the performance literature, however, it has been neglected in the area of investment style analysis. This study reports the impact of non-survivors on an investment style analysis for the first time. Fifth, the modelling of trend following CTA returns has been problematic in the literature due to the dynamic nature of their long/short directional positions. Studies such as Fung and Hsieh (2001) have proposed lookback option strategies to model the dynamics of these fund managers. This study contributes to the literature by proposing a naïve moving average investment strategy which explains the dynamic investment behaviour of these fund managers. We demonstrate its explanatory power and ease of use across equities, bonds, currencies and commodities without having to resort to an

there is ambiguity in the appropriate degrees of freedom in such a test. The inherent limitations of the LR test motivates this study by extending the BG model with the Gap Statistic in order to more accurately estimate the number of hedge fund investment styles. The only known study to employ the Gap Statistic in a finance setting is Lajbcygier and Ong (2003) who considered the BG model with the Gap Statistic on Japanese mutual funds. This paper is the first to employ this framework to estimate the optimal number of hedge fund investment styles.

option-based framework. Finally, an important aspect of this study demonstrates that a large proportion of the systematic returns of these three hedge fund investment styles can be passively replicated with traditional asset classes.

The format of the study is as follows. Section 2 describes the data and methodology, Section 3 provides the results of the Gap Statistic, Section 4 validates the Gap Statistic investment styles, Section 5 outlines the passive replication of these styles, while Section 6 provides a summary of the conclusions.

# 2. Data and Methodology

This study employs the TASS dataset of individual hedge fund survivors and non-survivors for the period January 1994 to August 2001, consisting of ninety-two monthly observations. This paper follows Fung and Hsieh (2000) and Liang (2000, 2001) by analysing hedge fund returns from January 1994 onwards in order to incorporate hedge fund survivorship bias.[5] A total of 3,012 hedge funds were available for analysis consisting of 1,836 survivors and 1,176 non-survivors. Within the cohort of survivors, 371 hedge funds possessed a complete performance history spanning the full ninety-two month sample.

The TASS dataset is similar to other fund databases whereby fund performance histories commence and cease at various points in time. This feature of the dataset reflects the normal life cycle of funds in the mutual and hedge fund industries. The issue of hedge fund survivors and non-survivors entering and exiting the dataset is not a trivial matter as it may cause serious problems and biases when employing various methods of analysis.[6] Addressing these data and computational issues are important considerations. Some researchers elect to make assumptions and construct hypothetical return data where there are no available performance figures. The decision to create synthetic data for these funds would require the modeling of the source and the shape of the distribution of hedge funds returns to various risk factors and asset classes (such as stockmarket and bond proxies). The work of Lo (2001) and Fung and Hsieh (2002b) suggest that the use of standard econometrics to model hedge fund returns may be regarded as dubious and controversial, at best. If at all, the introduction of synthetic returns into the dataset would itself impose 'survivability' into the data,

---

[5] See Liang (2000) and Fung and Hsieh (2000) for comprehensive reviews on why hedge funds cease to report.

[6] An example of this is conventional matrix algebra which relies on a complete dataset to be available in order for the computation to be performed.

which therefore would create a new form of bias. This study actively confronts these data issues by making no assumptions or modifications to the original data.

The BG Generalised Style Classification model is employed in this study as we are interested in quantifying the number of hedge fund investment styles without imposing restrictive assumptions.[7] Recall that the BG model is a $k$-means hard cluster analysis which clusters on monthly returns and has been modified as a generalised least squares (GLS) procedure in order to account for time-varying and fund-specific residual return variance. The GLS procedure accounts for heteroskedasticity by scaling the data observations by the inverse of the estimated standard deviation. The GLS methodology also reduces the impact that outliers may have on the classification algorithm thereby improving the results of the cluster analysis. The original BG model employs the LR test as the important test statistic which estimates the number of hedge fund styles. In this study, we estimate the number of groups with the BG model, however, we substitute the LR test with the Gap Statistic.[8]

The Gap Statistic's method in estimating the optimal number of groups in a dataset has intuitive appeal. While the euclidean distance in a conventional cluster analysis measures the distances of each observation to its cluster mean, the Gap Statistic differs as it measures the distance between each individual observation within each cluster. This calculation is referred to as the pooled within-cluster sum of squares known as $W$ for $k$ groups, resulting in $\log(W_k)$. The Gap Statistic then mathematically compares $\log(W_k)$ against its expectation under a null reference distribution of the data. The expectation under a null reference distribution is calculated by generating $B$ reference samples from the original data and estimating the pooled within-cluster sum of squares of each sample $W^*_{kb}$, and calculating its expected value $(1/B)\sum\log(W^*_{kb})$. The Gap Statistic therefore becomes $Gap(k) = (1/B)\sum\log(W^*_{kb}) - \log(W_k)$. After an adjustment for sampling and simulation error, $s_k$, the Gap Statistic estimates the optimal number of groups in a dataset as $\hat{k}$ = smallest $k$ such that $Gap(k) \geq Gap(k+1) - s_{k+1}$. The Gap Statistic thus estimates the statistical benefit of increasing the number of

---

7 Refer to Brown and Goetzmann (1997) for a full specification of the Generalised Style Classification (GSC) model.

8 Although Ben-Hur, Elisseeff and Guyon (2002) acknowledge the robustness of the Gap Statistic, they identify its sum squared distance criterion as its weakness as this numerical technique makes it biased towards compact clusters or groups rather than sparse data relationships.

groups while $Gap(k) < Gap(k+1) - s_{k+1}$. The appendix provides a technical specification of the Gap Statistic.

# 3. Results

The results are structured to consider the following issues. First, what is the impact of survivorship bias when estimating the number of hedge fund styles? Second, how many hedge fund investment styles are there in the long-term and are there any short-term dynamics? To address these considerations, the estimates of the Gap Statistic are calculated on two subsets of the original data. The first subset of data consists of the full sample of survivors and non-survivors so that the impact of survivorship bias can be quantified. The second subset of data consists of the 371 hedge fund survivors who have a complete performance history over the full sample period. The second subset of data is employed in order to calculate the Gap Statistic over the long-term.

## A. Full Sample

Table 1 reports summary statistics on the full sample of survivors and non-survivors.[9] The results provide well-known but nevertheless striking features of hedge fund returns. Table 1 shows that the distributions of hedge fund returns are wide and varied with some funds exhibiting negative skewness and severe excess kurtosis. The Jarque-Bera tests reject the assumption of normality across the majority of the TASS investment style categories. The non-normality of returns is a key feature of hedge funds which is consistent with previous research from Lo (2001) and Lochoff (2002).

We proceed to estimate the Gap Statistic on the full sample of survivors and non-survivors. Calculations on this dataset is limited because the Gap Statistic requires a complete data matrix. That is, the Gap Statistic requires a full performance history of each fund in its calculation.

[9] Refer to the works of Edwards and Park (1996), Liang (2000), Fung and Hsieh (2000) and Edwards and Caglayan (2001) for detailed analyses of the variety of hedge fund biases being, survivorship, instant history and multiperiod sampling bias.

**Table 1. Descriptive Statistics (Survivors and Non-survivors)**

| Categories | Mean | Max. | Min. | Std. Dev. | Skew. | Kurtosis | J- Bera |
|---|---|---|---|---|---|---|---|
| All Funds (inc FOFs) | 0.96 | 6.63 | -5.11 | 1.87 | 0.26 | 4.01 | 4.898 |
| All Funds (ex FOFs) | 1.04 | 6.84 | -5.31 | 1.92 | 0.21 | 4.06 | 4.959 |
| Convertible Arbitrage | 0.99 | 3.80 | -3.90 | 1.27 | -0.93 | 4.76 | 25.145** |
| Dedicated Short Bias | 0.40 | 22.48 | -12.10 | 5.60 | 0.69 | 4.51 | 16.014** |
| Emerging Markets | 0.67 | 12.09 | -21.61 | 5.03 | -0.77 | 6.02 | 44.140** |
| Equity Market Neutral | 1.09 | 3.38 | -1.03 | 0.84 | 0.01 | 2.99 | 0.002 |
| Event Driven | 1.06 | 4.27 | -6.90 | 1.41 | -1.81 | 12.39 | 388.332** |
| Fixed Income Arb. | 0.79 | 2.67 | -6.29 | 1.10 | -3.34 | 21.02 | 1415.385** |
| Fund of Funds ( FOFs) | 0.64 | 5.63 | -4.16 | 1.73 | 0.34 | 3.59 | 3.132 |
| Global Macro | 0.75 | 7.11 | -3.79 | 2.09 | 1.02 | 4.35 | 22.838** |
| Long/Short Eq. Hedge | 1.51 | 11.55 | -8.52 | 3.11 | 0.25 | 4.56 | 10.297** |
| Managed Futures | 0.64 | 7.79 | -4.05 | 2.43 | 0.34 | 2.86 | 1.884 |
| Other | 0.74 | 6.66 | -6.57 | 2.29 | -0.15 | 3.47 | 1.186 |

This table presents the descriptive statistics of hedge fund returns from monthly observations from 1994-2001 and classified in their TASS Tremont investment style classifications. The sample consists of 3,012 funds consisting of 1,836 survivors and 1,176 non-survivors. The final column is the Jarque-Bera test statistic for normality. * and ** denote statistical significance at the 5% and 1% levels, respectively.

**Table 2. Gap Statistic (Survivors and Non-survivors)**

| | | Estimated Number of Groups (Investment Styles) | | | | | | |
|---|---|---|---|---|---|---|---|---|
| Period | Funds | 1 | 2 | 3 | 4 | 5 | 6 | 7 |
| 1994-1996 | 665 | 0% | 0% | 17.3% | 82.7% | 0% | 0% | 0% |
| 1995-1997 | 827 | 0% | 99.5% | 0.5% | 0% | 0% | 0% | 0% |
| 1996-1998 | 963 | 98.1% | 1.9% | 0% | 0% | 0% | 0% | 0% |
| 1997-1999 | 1,092 | 0% | 7.1% | 0% | 92.9% | 0% | 0% | 0% |
| 1998-2000 | 1,204 | 0% | 0% | 90.2% | 7.8% | 0% | 0% | 0% |
| 1999-2001 | 1,296 | 0% | 22.4% | 0% | 77.6% | 0% | 0% | 0% |

This table reports the Gap Statistic estimates on the dataset containing survivors and non-survivors across various three year time periods. The calculations of the Gap Statistic are based on 10 reference sets and 1,000 trials. The dominant Gap Statistic estimate for each time period is highlighted. The second column reports the number of surviving and non-surviving funds available for each Gap Statistic estimate.

To circumvent the issue of funds entering and exiting the database at various time intervals, the length of the tests were restricted to three year time horizons so that both surviving and non-surviving funds that possessed a full three year performance history were included in the calculation.[10] The estimate of the Gap Statistic on the full sample is presented in Table 2. The results show that the Gap Statistic persistently estimates between one and four hedge fund investment styles over the various time periods. Although the results vary for each time period, the Gap Statistic consistently estimates four hedge fund styles or less, which are persistently lower than the previous findings in Brown and Goetzmann (2003).

While the inclusion of non-survivors in the Gap Statistic minimises the impact of survivorship bias, it also limits the calculation to short time intervals. The Gap Statistic requires a full performance history for each fund and this is problematic considering that funds begin and terminate at various time intervals. In order to calculate the Gap Statistic over the long-term, we consider the 371 survivors that possess a full performance history for the 1994-2001 period.

## B. Survivors Only

To estimate the Gap Statistic over the long-term, we must employ funds with a complete performance history, however, this introduces data biases. To calculate the long-term Gap Statistic, there is a tradeoff by introducing survivorship bias into the analysis. However, this long-term Gap Statistic estimate provides investors with pertinent information content regarding the types of 'surviving' investment styles available in the hedge fund universe. The summary statistics of the sample of funds with a complete performance history are presented in Table 3.

As expected, the descriptive statistics of these funds are consistent and similar with the previous results of the full sample. Once again, the skewness, kurtosis and Jarque-Bera statistics of the survivors suggest that a majority of hedge fund returns are not normally distributed. The similarities of Tables 1 and 3 suggest that survivorship bias does not influence the non-normality characteristics of hedge fund returns.

The estimates of the Gap Statistic on the funds with a complete performance history are presented in Table 4. The results show that over short-term time horizons, the Gap Statistic calculates the presence of up to five investment styles. The marginal difference in Table 2 and 4 demonstrates the small upward bias in the estimation of the Gap Statistic when one excludes non-survivors from the analysis.

---

[10] As the Gap Statistic calculation cannot accept funds with missing observations, this test excludes hedge fund survivors and non-survivors who may have had a partial performance history over the various test periods. While this study attempts to incorporate survivorship effects by including hedge fund non-survivors, a residual level of bias still exists in the calculation.

**Table 3. Descriptive Statistics (Funds With Complete History)**

| Categories | Mean | Max. | Min. | Std. Dev. | Skew. | Kurtosis | J-Bera |
|---|---|---|---|---|---|---|---|
| All Funds (inc FOFs) | 0.95 | 6.12 | -5.36 | 1.88 | 0.09 | 3.68 | 1.917 |
| All Funds (ex FOFs) | 1.02 | 6.53 | -5.71 | 1.96 | 0.06 | 3.76 | 2.268 |
| Convertible Arbitrage | 0.80 | 3.13 | -3.89 | 1.38 | -0.80 | 3.65 | 11.369** |
| Dedicated Short Bias | 0.25 | 23.56 | -15.02 | 5.41 | 0.67 | 6.03 | 41.934** |
| Emerging Markets | 0.26 | 16.02 | -27.71 | 6.28 | -0.66 | 6.38 | 50.298** |
| Equity Market Neutral | 1.11 | 4.57 | -2.08 | 1.45 | 0.07 | 2.56 | 0.824 |
| Event Driven | 1.06 | 4.28 | -7.27 | 1.43 | -2.07 | 13.94 | 524.721** |
| Fixed Income Arb. | 0.64 | 7.99 | -3.06 | 1.24 | 2.06 | 16.19 | 731.607** |
| Fund of Funds ( FOFs) | 0.73 | 5.46 | -4.29 | 1.73 | 0.21 | 3.44 | 1.441 |
| Global Macro | 0.87 | 9.87 | -2.82 | 2.19 | 1.28 | 5.15 | 42.818** |
| Long/Short Eq. Hedge | 1.37 | 11.70 | -8.77 | 3.16 | 0.22 | 4.42 | 8.464* |
| Managed Futures | 0.80 | 7.66 | -5.86 | 3.17 | 0.04 | 2.42 | 1.334 |
| Other | 0.98 | 4.32 | -4.77 | 1.46 | -1.06 | 5.74 | 45.885** |

This table presents the descriptive statistics of hedge fund funds from monthly observations from 1994-2001 and classified in their TASS Tremont investment style classifications. The sample consists of 371 funds that possess a complete performance history for the full sample period. The final column is the Jarque-Bera test statistic for normality. * and ** denote statistical significance at the 5% and 1% levels, respectively.

**Table 4. Gap Statistic (Funds with Complete History)**

| | | Estimated Number of Groups (Investment Styles) | | | | | | |
|---|---|---|---|---|---|---|---|---|
| Period | Funds | 1 | 2 | 3 | 4 | 5 | 6 | 7 |
| 1994-1996 | 371 | 0% | 0% | 98.0% | 2.0% | 0% | 0% | 0% |
| 1995-1997 | 371 | 0% | 0% | 92.8% | 7.2% | 0% | 0% | 0% |
| 1996-1998 | 371 | 0% | 17.6% | 8.8% | 29.7% | 44.0% | 0% | 0% |
| 1997-1999 | 371 | 0% | 91.5% | 0% | 8.5% | 0% | 0% | 0% |
| 1998-2000 | 371 | 0% | 0% | 16.2% | 83.8% | 0% | 0% | 0% |
| 1999-2001 | 371 | 0% | 0% | 99.6% | 0.4% | 0% | 0% | 0% |
| 1994-2001 | 371 | 0% | 0% | 84.0% | 0.0% | 0% | 10.9% | 5.1% |

This table reports the Gap Statistic estimates on the dataset containing all funds with a complete performance history. The calculations of the Gap Statistic are based on 10 reference sets and 1,000 trials. The Gap Statistic was estimated on various three year time periods and also for the full 1994-2001 sample period. The dominant Gap Statistic estimate for each time period is highlighted. The second column reports the number of funds available for each Gap Statistic estimate.

The long-term Gap Statistic for the full 1994-2001 period is reported in the last row of Table 4. The result shows that 84% of the 1,000 Gap Statistic simulations calculated the statistical presence of three hedge fund investment styles over the long-term. This statistical finding of only three hedge fund styles over the long-term is significant as it differs to Brown and Goetzmann's (2003) finding of eight styles and is in stark contrast to current industry practice. It is noteworthy that the Gap Statistic for the full 1994-2001 period finds the presence of six and seven hedge fund investment styles at times, however, these simulations are not statistically significant. These insignificant estimates of six and seven styles partially explain the results from Brown and Goetzmann (2003) who employ the LR test statistic which tends to over-estimate the number of groups, thus causing an upward bias in the number of investment styles.

**Table 5. Cross-Tabulation of Styles and Correlations**

| | **Total** | **Style 1** | **Style 2** | **Style 3** |
|---|---|---|---|---|
| *Panel A: Cross-Tabulation with TASS Styles* | | | | |
| Convertible Arbitrage | 13 | 2 | 11 | 0 |
| Dedicated Short Bias | 6 | 0 | 5 | 1 |
| Emerging Markets | 20 | 17 | 3 | 0 |
| Equity Market Neutral | 7 | 1 | 6 | 0 |
| Event Driven | 60 | 11 | 49 | 0 |
| Fixed Income Arb. | 6 | 0 | 6 | 0 |
| Fund of Funds (FOFs) | 91 | 41 | 36 | 14 |
| Global Macro | 15 | 3 | 7 | 5 |
| Long/Short Eq. Hedge | 102 | 76 | 25 | 1 |
| Managed Futures | 50 | 9 | 8 | 33 |
| Other | 1 | 0 | 1 | 0 |
| Total Number of Funds | 371 | 160 | 157 | 54 |
| *Panel B: Correlation to the S&P 500 All Return Index* | | | | |
| All Months: Mean Correl. | | 0.461 | 0.156 | -0.055 |
| All Months: 95% Percentile | | 0.655 | 0.498 | 0.148 |
| All Months: 5% Percentile | | 0.254 | -0.331 | -0.194 |
| Up Months: Mean Correl. | | 0.233 | 0.045 | -0.020 |
| Up Months: 95% Percentile | | 0.440 | 0.317 | 0.137 |
| Up Months: 5% Percentile | | -0.033 | -0.234 | -0.188 |
| Down Months: Mean Correl. | | 0.389 | 0.148 | -0.128 |
| Down Months: 95% Percentile | | 0.632 | 0.501 | 0.208 |
| Down Months: 5% Percentile | | 0.074 | -0.369 | -0.374 |

**Table 5. Continued**

| | Total | Style 1 | Style 2 | Style 3 |
|---|---|---|---|---|
| *Panel C: Correlation to Lehman Bros. U.S. Gov. Long Term Bond Index* | | | | |
| All Months: Mean Correl. | | 0.023 | 0.031 | 0.201 |
| All Months: 95% Percentile | | 0.199 | 0.210 | 0.348 |
| All Months: 5% Percentile | | -0.125 | -0.146 | -0.003 |
| Up Months: Mean Correl. | | -0.044 | 0.031 | 0.195 |
| Up Months: 95% Percentile | | 0.135 | 0.210 | 0.436 |
| Up Months: 5% Percentile | | -0.224 | -0.146 | -0.106 |
| Down Months: Mean Correl. | | 0.196 | 0.119 | 0.157 |
| Down Months: 95% Percentile | | 0.400 | 0.377 | 0.333 |
| Down Months: 5% Percentile | | -0.051 | -0.147 | -0.072 |

Panel A presents the number of funds classified in the three Gap Statistic investment styles versus their original TASS investment style classifications. Panel B reports the distribution of the correlation coefficient between funds and the S&P 500 All Return Index while Panel C reports the distribution in the correlation coefficient between funds and the Lehman Brothers U.S. Government Long Term Bond Index. The reported correlation coefficient is the mean, 5th and 95th percentile correlation coefficient of the individual funds against these traditional asset classes for all, up and down months.

## C. Fund Behaviour Based on Gap Statistic Style Classifications

Table 5 provides a preliminary examination of fund behaviour based on their long-term Gap Statistic classifications. Panel A of Table 5 cross-tabulates the funds in their original TASS groupings with their associated Gap Statistic style categories. Panel A shows that style 1 is dominated with Equity Long/Short funds which suggests that some equity factor may determine the returns of this investment style. A striking feature of Panel A is that a large proportion of the sample (ie. 160 of the 371 funds) are classified in this investment style. The style 2 category contains a large proportion of relative-value or non-directional style funds.[11] Finally, style 3 is dominated by the funds in the managed futures TASS classification.

[11] Gatev, Goetzmann and Rouwenhorst (1999), Mitchell and Pulvino (2001), Lo (2001), Kao (2002) and Fung and Hsieh (2002c) inform us that these investment styles possess non-directional characteristics as they tend to hold a combination of long/short positions of similarly related assets. See Shleifer and Vishy (1997) for the theoretical rationale of the inherent risks involved in arbitrage. For an empirical example, refer to Mitchell and Pulvino (2001) who examine the return and risks in merger arbitrage.

Panel B of Table 5 reports the correlation behaviour of the individual funds in the three styles against the stockmarket proxy of the Standard and Poors 500 All Return Index. The funds in style 1 demonstrate a strong and positive correlation to US equities which reflects the dominance of Equity Long/Short funds in this style classification. The funds in style 2 report little or no correlation to US equities which is expected considering that many relative-value or non-directional funds were classified in this group. The funds in style 3 report little or no correlation to US equities, however, the negative correlation coefficients for all, up and down months reveals an interesting dynamic reflecting the dynamic long and short directional investment behaviour of managed futures funds.[12] Panel C of Table 5 is similar to Panel B and reports the correlation of funds to a bond proxy. The funds in the sample are generally not correlated with US government bond returns.

Overall, Table 5 shows that funds in style 1 are dominated by Equity Long/Short funds which possess a positive association with equities. The funds in style 2 are relative-value style funds which tend to exhibit little or no association with stocks and bonds. Finally, the funds in style 3 also exhibit little or no correlation with stocks and bonds, however, they possess a small but negative association with US stock returns which will be explored further in the proceeding sections.

## 4. Validation of Gap Statistic Hedge Fund Styles

The economic rationale of the three Gap Statistic categories must be examined to ensure that these investment styles are meaningful to investors. To consider these categories in a conventional finance framework, three style index portfolio returns are constructed. We eliminate the idiosyncratic risk of individual hedge funds by forming the systematic returns of these three investment styles. The equal weighted returns of each classification group is calculated to form the three investment style portfolio returns. These three investment style index portfolios form the basis of much of the analysis for the remainder of the study. The three style portfolio indices are presented in Figure 1 and their summary statistics are reported in Table 6.

---

[12] This interesting relationship with the S&P500 is consistent with similar characteristics in trend followers found in Edwards and Liew (1999) and Fung and Hsieh (1997a, 2002a). Elton, Gruber and Rentzler (1987) and Fung and Hsieh (1997b) inform us that these fund managers employ trend-following or momentum based strategies which are directional in nature and tend to exhibit reasonable volatility in returns.

**Table 6. Summary Statistics of Style Index Portfolio Returns**

| Style | Mean | Max. | Min. | S.D. | Skew. | Kurt. | Jarque Bera | Sharpe | First Auto. | 95% VaR | 95% CVaR |
|---|---|---|---|---|---|---|---|---|---|---|---|
| 1 | 1.03 | 11.70 | -14.47 | 3.70 | -0.483 | 5.598 | 29.45** | 0.585 | 0.144 | -4.40 | -7.25 |
| 2 | 0.90 | 2.41 | -2.32 | 0.71 | -0.984 | 6.191 | 53.88** | 2.372 | 0.395** | -0.25 | -0.82 |
| 3 | 0.85 | 12.82 | -7.45 | 4.02 | 0.534 | 3.291 | 4.70 | 0.378 | -0.026 | -4.97 | -6.27 |

This table presents the summary statistics of the style index portfolio returns. The first column indicates the style index portfolio. The second to the sixth columns are the four moments of the distribution of monthly returns. Jarque-Bera denotes the hypothesis test statistic for normality. The column heading Sharpe is the annualised Sharpe Ratio of the monthly returns. The column heading First Auto. reports the first-order autocorrelation. The 95% VaR denotes the historical 95% Value-at-Risk of the monthly returns. The 95% CVaR reports the historical 95% Conditional Value-at-Risk of the monthly returns. ** denotes statistical significance at the 1% level.

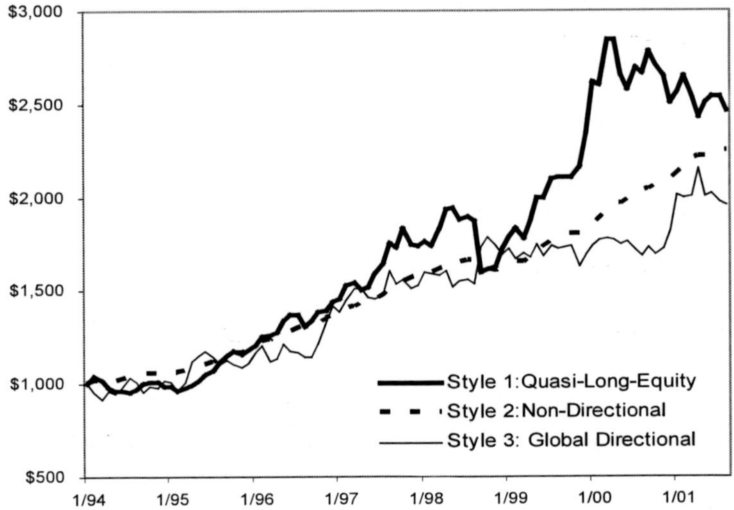


Figure 1. Performance of the Gap Statistic Style Indexes, 1994-2001. (Initial Wealth 1/1994 = $1,000).

Table 6 shows that the portfolio returns of styles 1 and 3 have considerable variance in comparison to their mean. Styles 1 and 2 possess negative third moments in their return distributions which differs to style 3. The Jarque-Bera test for normality is rejected for style 1 and 2 due to the negative third moments and significant excess kurtosis. Style 2 generates 90 percent of the returns of style 1 with only a fraction of the volatility. This translates to an attractive sharpe ratio for the style 2 index portfolio in comparison to styles 1 and 3. Table 6 also reports the historical 95% VaR and 95% CVaR of style 2 at only a fraction of those of the style 1 and 3 portfolios.[1] The impressive statistics for style 2 must be tempered with the inherent risks in hedge fund returns which are located in the third and fourth moments of the return distributions.[2] Another striking feature of the style 2 index portfolio is the strong first-order autocorrelation of returns relative to the other style portfolios. Conversely, the style 3 portfolio exhibits a positive third moment and a relatively normal distribution of returns. Overall, the summary statistics in Table 6 provides evidence to suggest that the systematic returns of these three style portfolios are indeed different.

---

[1] The skewed distributions of the three style index portfolio returns makes the CVaR more conducive than VaR as a risk metric.

[2] Refer to Geman and Kharoubi (2003) for a discussion of hedge fund risks and the third and fourth moments of the return distribution.

## A. Evaluation of Funds and Associated Styles

As a form of validation, we examine the individual funds in each style to ensure that they have been classified in a way which is consistent with modern portfolio theory. We calculate the correlation coefficient of each fund with their respective style index portfolio return. We would expect a high correlation coefficient between the funds and their respective style index returns. Funds with a low correlation with its style portfolio returns would indicate that they may have been misclassified by the Gap Statistic. Table 7 reports the distribution of correlation coefficients between the funds and their respective style index portfolio returns.

Table 7 shows that the correlations in styles 1 and 3 are very high. Table 7 also reports a less pronounced correlation of funds in style 2 which is a surprising finding. The funds in style 2 exhibit a lower correlation to their respective style index across all reported percentiles in comparison to funds in styles 1 and 3.

**Table 7. Distribution of Correlations between Funds and Style Portfolio**

| Style | Min. | $5^{th}$ | $10^{th}$ | $25^{th}$ | $50^{th}$ | $75^{th}$ | $90^{th}$ | $95^{th}$ | Max. |
|---|---|---|---|---|---|---|---|---|---|
| 1 | 0.28 | 0.40 | 0.46 | 0.55 | 0.67 | 0.78 | 0.84 | 0.85 | 0.92 |
| 2 | -0.26 | -0.08^ | 0.06 | 0.22 | 0.38 | 0.52 | 0.65 | 0.69 | 0.79 |
| 3 | 0.27 | 0.30 | 0.36 | 0.55 | 0.71 | 0.80 | 0.88 | 0.89 | 0.91 |

This table reports the percentile distribution of correlation coefficients between the fund returns with their associated style index returns across various percentile intervals. ^ denotes that eleven funds in style 2 at or below the sixth percentile exhibit correlations of less than zero to their respective style index returns.

Second, there are 11 (ie. 7 percent) out of the 157 funds in style 2 that possess a negative correlation with their style 2 index portfolio, although they are located at the sixth percentile and lower in the distribution.[3] The effect of a broad-based estimate of three hedge fund styles must result in a small number of funds with a negative correlation (ie. 2.96% of the entire sample). One would expect to find a small number of funds that may not fit these three broad investment styles. Overall, Table 7 illustrates the merit of the Gap Statistic's precision in accurately classifying these funds into three investment styles.

[3] These 11 funds have the following TASS Tremont investment styles: 4 fund of funds, 3 long-short equity hedge, 2 event-driven, 1 convertible arbitrage and 1 dedicated short bias. The Gap Statistic has determined that it is not statistically viable to increase the number of investment styles to accommodate these 11 funds which represent 2.96% of the 371 fund sample.

## B. Correlation between Style Index Portfolio Returns

To further examine the validation of the three investment style portfolios, Table 8 presents the correlations and equality tests of the three style index portfolio returns. A perfect classification scheme would form three style portfolio returns that are uncorrelated. Table 8 reports weak correlation between the style index portfolios with the exception of style 1 and 2. Despite the high correlation between style 1 and 2, the equality test in Panel C indicates that style 1 and 2 exhibit statistically significant variances. Overall, the statistically significant correlation between styles 1 and 2 is a surprising result which contradicts the findings in Tables 6 and 7. Although correlation measures the association between returns, it does not consider causation which is examined in the following section.

**Table 8. Style Portfolio Correlations and Equality Tests**

| *Panel A: Pearson Correlations* | | | | |
|---|---|---|---|---|
| $\rho$ (Pearson) | | Style 1 | Style 2 | Style 3 |
| | Style 1 | 1 | | |
| | Style 2 | 0.604** | 1 | |
| | Style 3 | -0.056 | 0.193 | 1 |
| *Panel B: Spearman Rank Correlations* | | | | |
| $\rho$ (Spearman) | | Style 1 | Style 2 | Style 3 |
| | Style 1 | 1 | | |
| | Style 2 | 0.524** | 1 | |
| | Style 3 | 0.078 | 0.345** | 1 |
| *Panel C: Equality Tests* | | | | |
| | Styles | Mean | Median | Variance |
| | 1-2 | 0.858 | 0.685 | 0.000** |
| | 1-3 | 0.730 | 0.419 | 0.555 |
| | 2-3 | 0.766 | 0.389 | 0.000** |

Panel A presents the Pearson correlation coefficients of the returns of the three Gap Statistic style portfolios. Panel B provides the Spearman rank-correlation coefficients. The test performed on Panel A and B is the two-tail hypothesis test of the correlation is not zero. Bonferroni corrected critical values were employed in order to mitigate the effect of a Type I error when testing across three investment styles. Panel C reports the p-values of the equality test in means, median and variance of the style index portfolio returns. The p-values reported for the mean difference is the parametric two-tailed test for equality of means. The p-values reported for the median difference is the nonparametric Wilcoxon Signed Rank two-tailed test for equality of medians. The p-values reported for the variance difference is the two-tailed F-test for equality of variances. * and ** denote statistical significance at the 95% and 99% confidence levels.

## Table 9. Regression: Funds on Three-Factor Style Index Model

| Dependent Variables | | Independent Variables | | | | | | | | |
|---|---|---|---|---|---|---|---|---|---|---|
| Funds | No. | Mean Intercept | Mean Style 1 Coeff. | Mean Style 2 Coeff. | Mean Style 3 Coeff. | Sig./Insig. Intercept | Sig/Insig. Style 1 Coeff. | Sig/Insig. Style 2 Coeff. | Sig/Insig. Style 3 Coeff. | Mean Adj. $R^2$ |
| *Panel A: Gap Statistic Styles* | | | | | | | | | | |
| Style 1 | 160 | -0.14% | 1.02 | -0.01 | -0.00 | 13/147 | 159/1 | 74/86 | 35/125 | 0.78 |
| Style 2 | 157 | -0.03% | 0.00 | 1.00 | 0.00 | 15/142 | 81/76 | 153/4 | 57/100 | 0.90 |
| Style 3 | 54 | -0.17% | 0.01 | 0.00 | 0.99 | 3/51 | 9/45 | 15/39 | 54/0 | 0.76 |
| All Funds | 371 | -0.10% | 0.44 | 0.42 | 0.14 | 31/340 | 249/122 | 242/129 | 146/225 | 0.83 |
| *Panel B: TASS Styles* | | | | | | | | | | |
| Conv.Arb | 13 | -1.67% | 0.20 | 0.81 | -0.04 | 5/8 | 6/7 | 12/1 | 4/9 | 0.93 |
| Ded. Sh.Bias | 6 | 1.94% | -1.33 | 2.16 | 0.23 | 0/6 | 6/0 | 6/0 | 1/5 | 0.74 |
| Em. Mkts. | 20 | 2.40% | 1.39 | -0.09 | -0.21 | 1/19 | 18/2 | 9/11 | 6/14 | 0.69 |
| Eq. Mkt. Ntrl. | 7 | 0.70% | 0.07 | 0.96 | -0.02 | 0/7 | 4/3 | 6/1 | 0/7 | 0.84 |
| Ev. Driven | 60 | 0.28% | 0.22 | 0.87 | -0.09 | 3/57 | 31/29 | 55/5 | 28/32 | 0.92 |
| F.I.Arb | 6 | -0.82% | -0.11 | 1.13 | -0.04 | 2/4 | 4/2 | 6/0 | 2/4 | 0.89 |
| FOFs | 91 | -0.40% | 0.34 | 0.47 | 0.18 | 11/80 | 66/25 | 67/24 | 46/45 | 0.91 |

## Table 9. Continued

| Dependent Variables | | Independent Variables | | | | | | | | |
|---|---|---|---|---|---|---|---|---|---|---|
| Funds | No. | Mean Intercept | Mean Style 1 Coeff. | Mean Style 2 Coeff. | Mean Style 3 Coeff. | Sig./Insig. Intercept | Sig/Insig. Style 1 Coeff. | Sig/Insig. Style 2 Coeff. | Sig/Insig. Style 3 Coeff. | Mean Adj. $R^2$ |
| G.Macro | 15 | -0.52% | 0.16 | 0.48 | 0.35 | 0/15 | 5/10 | 9/6 | 9/6 | 0.81 |
| LSEQ | 102 | -0.32% | 0.79 | 0.17 | 0.02 | 8/94 | 88/14 | 51/51 | 13/89 | 0.76 |
| MFutures | 50 | -0.31% | 0.27 | 0.00 | 0.73 | 1/49 | 20/30 | 20/30 | 37/13 | 0.74 |
| Other | 1 | 1.12% | -0.18 | 1.25 | -0.05 | 0/1 | 1/0 | 1/0 | 0/1 | 0.96 |

This table presents the summary of various OLS multi-factor regressions. The dependent variable in these regressions are the excess returns of each fund as classified in their respective investment styles. The three independent variables are the time series of monthly excess returns associated with (1) style 1 index portfolio, (2) style 2 index portfolio, and (3) the style 3 index portfolio. The mean value of the intercept and the coefficients of all regressions are reported. The second column denotes the number of funds in each category. The columns with the headings Sig./Insig. denote the number of funds with a statistically significant or insignificant (at the 5% level) regression coefficient for each variable. The mean adjusted coefficient of determination of all regressions is reported in the final column of this table.

## C. Explanatory Power of Style Index Portfolio Returns

We examine the explanatory power of the systematic returns of the style index portfolios and the way they jointly describe the returns of the hedge fund universe. One would expect that the systematic returns of these three investment styles would capture a large proportion of the variation in hedge fund returns. We regress the returns of individual funds against the systematic returns of the style index portfolios to form the following three-factor model.

$$R_i - R_F = \alpha_i + \beta_{i1}(R_1 - R_F) + \beta_{i2}(R_2 - R_F) + \beta_{i3}(R_3 - R_F) + e_i$$

In this model, $R_i$ is the return on the individual hedge fund, $R_F$ is the risk-free rate of return derived from the 1 month T-Bill rate from Ibbotson and Associates, $R_1$ is the style 1 portfolio return, $R_2$ is the style 2 portfolio return, $R_3$ is the style 3 portfolio return, $\beta_i$ is the sensitivity of fund $i$ to the relevant style index, and $e_i$ is the residual risk. To address the multicollinearity concerns from the high correlation between style 1 and 2, the style 2 index returns in his model are made orthogonal to the style 1 index returns.[1] The orthogonalization captures the marginal effect of style 2 over and above the factor loading of the style 1 portfolio return.

Panel A of Table 9 demonstrates that the three-factor style model has high explanatory power for funds when classified under the Gap Statistic. Panel B of Table 9 demonstrates that the three Gap Statistic investment style portfolio returns have high explanatory power when funds are grouped in their original TASS classifications, however, the statistically significant beta coefficients are more dispersed and are not concentrated as in Panel A. Overall, these findings suggest that the systematic returns of the three Gap Statistic investment styles captures the variation of fund returns in the hedge fund universe. These findings provide the motivation to consider the opportunity of passively replicating these systematic returns which is examined in a subsequent section of this study.

[1] Refer to Elton, Gruber, Das and Hlavka (1993) and Chapman and Pearson (2000) for excellent treatments of orthogonalization in finance settings.

## D. Evaluation of Style Consistency

Although the three-factor style model exhibits strong explanatory power, we need to consider the consistency of these three investment styles. Table 10 reports the mean $R^2_{adj}$ values of the fund regressions and their associated style index portfolio return segregated across various time horizons. The results show that the style portfolio returns can effectively explain the cross-sectional variance of the respective individual funds over short-term periods and for the full 1994-2001 period also.

As a second test of style consistency, we follow Gallo and Lockwood (1999) and employ the Chow (1960) test to detect investment style drift between funds and their associated investment styles. The Chow (1960) test examines the stability of regression coefficients over two distinct time periods. Funds with statistically significant p-values under a Chow (1960) test possess regression coefficients that are statistically different, which suggests the evidence of changing investment style with respect to its associated style portfolio returns. The Chow (1960) test is estimated under a single-factor model. We perform the Chow (1960) tests on the funds in their Gap Statistic classification scheme in Panel A of Table 11 versus their original TASS style classifications in Panel B.

**Table 10. Cross-Sectional Variance**

| | | Mean Adj. R Squared | |
|---|---|---|---|
| **Time Period** | **Style 1** | **Style 2** | **Style 3** |
| 1994-1996 | 0.498 | 0.639 | 0.582 |
| 1995-1997 | 0.510 | 0.797 | 0.622 |
| 1996-1998 | 0.519 | 0.794 | 0.694 |
| 1997-1999 | 0.489 | 0.810 | 0.742 |
| 1998-2000 | 0.618 | 0.765 | 0.794 |
| 1999-2001 | 0.619 | 0.668 | 0.798 |
| 1994-2001 | 0.565 | 0.741 | 0.707 |

This table reports the mean adjusted coefficient of determination of the individual regressions of funds against their respective style index. The time periods are the same as those employed to calculate the Gap Statistic. The last row of this Table reports the cross sectional variance for the full 1994-2001 sample period.

Panel A of Table 11 reports that 10.78 per cent of funds were found to exhibit style inconsistency when classified in the three Gap Statistic classifications. As a comparison, Panel B reports 10.24 per cent of funds to exhibit style inconsistency when regressed against their TASS peer-group equal weighted portfolio returns.

The results in Table 11 provide compelling evidence that little or no loss of style consistency exists when re-classifying the hedge fund universe from eleven TASS styles to three Gap Statistic styles.[2]

**Table 11. Chow Test**

| Funds | No. | Independent Variable | Chow Test: No. Insignif. | Chow Test: No. Signif. | % |
|---|---|---|---|---|---|
| *Panel A:* | | | | | |
| Style 1 | 160 | Style 1 Portfolio | 141 | 19 | |
| Style 2 | 157 | Style 2 Portfolio | 142 | 15 | |
| Style 3 | 54 | Style 3 Portfolio | 48 | 6 | |
| | | | 331 | 40 | 10.78% |
| *Panel B:* | | | | | |
| Convertible Arb. | 13 | EW. Conv. Arb. | 12 | 1 | |
| Dedicated Short Bias | 6 | EW. Ded. Sh. Bias | 5 | 1 | |
| Emerging Markets | 20 | EW. Em. Mkts | 20 | 0 | |
| Equity Market Neutral | 7 | EW. Eq. Mkt. Ntrl. | 6 | 1 | |
| Event Driven | 60 | EW. Ev. Driven | 55 | 5 | |
| Fixed Income Arb. | 6 | EW. F.I. Arb. | 5 | 1 | |
| Fund of Funds | 91 | EW. FOFs | 74 | 17 | |
| Global Macro | 15 | EW. G. Macro | 14 | 1 | |
| Long/Short Eq. Hedge | 102 | EW. LS. Eq. Hdg. | 93 | 9 | |
| Managed Futures | 50 | EW. M.Fut. | 48 | 2 | |
| Other | 1 | EW. Other | 1 | 0 | |
| | | | 333 | 38 | 10.24% |

This table reports the Chow (1960) breakpoint test as a form of style consistency test. The test was performed by dividing the sample into two periods of 46 months. EW denotes the equal weighted portfolio of funds within each TASS style classification. The penultimate and final columns report the number of funds with statistically insignificant vs. significant p-values at the 5% level, respectively.

[2] We also interpret this as evidence to indicate that hedge funds, as a group, generally do not attempt to engage in strategic investment style drift.

# 5. Passive Replication of Style Portfolio Returns

The final analysis of this study is the passive replication of these three investment styles with traditional asset classes. If these three investment style portfolios can be replicated then this must surely provide a meaningful validation of their very existence. To passively replicate these three styles, we exploit the previous findings in Agarwal and Naik (2004), Capocci and Hubner (2004) and Fung and Hsieh (2004) and the information content in Tables 5 and 6. The systematic returns of style 1 tends to be positively correlated with equities, style 2 exhibits low volatility and tends to be exposed to relative risks, and style 3 may possess directional exposures across global investments. We employ a parsimonious approach to the following sections which report the significant risk factors that capture the variation of returns of these three style portfolio returns.

## A. Style 1: Quasi-Long-Equity

The correlations and style classifications in Table 5 suggest that these funds are strongly associated with equities. We construct a three-factor style model based on equity risk factors in the following form.

$$R_t - R_{Ft} = \alpha + \beta_1 (MACWEI_t - R_{Ft}) + \beta_2 SMB_t + \beta_3 UMD_t + e_t$$

where $R_t$ is the style 1 portfolio return, $R_{Ft}$ is the risk-free 1 month T-Bill return earned at month $t$, MACWEI is the return on the MSCI All Country World Equity Index, SMB is the Fama and French (1993) value-weighted zero investment mimicking portfolios for size, and UMD is the Fama-French based Carhart (1997) value weighted, zero investment, factor mimicking portfolio for one-year return momentum.[3]

[3] The Fama-French (1993) HML mimicking portfolio for book-to-market equity ('high minus low') was found to be statistically insignificant.

## Table 12. Passive Replication of Style Portfolios

| | Intercept | MACWEI | SMB | UMD | FFSVMLG | LHYMWA | VIX | DJAIG | CWBI | SP | DX | Adj R-Sq |
|---|---|---|---|---|---|---|---|---|---|---|---|---|
| Panel A: Style 1 three-factor model | | | | | | | | | | | | |
| Style 1 | 0.29% | 0.73** | 0.39** | 0.11** | | | | | | | | 0.84 |
| | (0.00) | (0.04) | (0.04) | (0.03) | | | | | | | | |
| Panel B: Style 2 five-factor model | | | | | | | | | | | | |
| Style 2 | 0.41%** | 0.09** | | | 0.06** | 0.10** | 0.01** | 0.08** | | | | 0.61 |
| | (0.00) | (0.01) | | | (0.01) | (0.03) | (0.00) | (0.01) | | | | |
| Panel C: Style 3 four-factor model | | | | | | | | | | | | |
| Style 3 | 0.22% | | | | | | | 0.31** | 1.68** | 0.21** | 0.30** | 0.40 |
| | (0.00) | | | | | | | (0.90) | (0.38) | (0.06) | (0.08) | |

**Table 12. Continued**

| | Intercept | MACWEI | SMB | UMD | FFSVMLG | LHYMWA | VIX | DJAIG | CWBI | SP | DX | Adj R-Sq |
|---|---|---|---|---|---|---|---|---|---|---|---|---|
| Panel D: Combined model | | | | | | | | | | | | |
| Style 1 | 0.17% | 0.67** | 0.26** | 0.11** | 0.05 | 0.47** | 0.00 | 0.14** | -0.01 | 0.06 | -0.05 | 0.91 |
| | (0.00) | (0.04) | (0.04) | (0.02) | (0.04) | (0.06) | (0.01) | (0.04) | (0.18) | (0.03) | (0.03) | |
| Style 2 | 0.38** | 0.10** | -0.01 | 0.02 | 0.06** | 0.11** | 0.01* | 0.08** | 0.07 | -0.00 | 0.00 | 0.61 |
| | (0.00) | (0.02) | (0.01) | (0.01) | (0.01) | (0.03) | (0.00) | (0.01) | (0.06) | (0.01) | (0.01) | |
| Style 3 | 0.23% | -0.14 | 0.08 | 0.01 | -0.09 | 0.15 | -0.00 | 0.30** | 1.79** | 0.23** | 0.30** | 0.37 |
| | (0.00) | (0.14) | (0.11) | (0.04) | (0.08) | (0.15) | (0.03) | (0.09) | (0.38) | (0.07) | (0.10) | |

This table presents the risk factors which are found to capture the variation of returns of the three Gap Statistic style portfolio returns. Panel A is the parsimonious three-factor model of the style 1 portfolio. Panel B describes the parsimonious five-factor model for the style 2 portfolio. Panel C is the parsimonious four-factor model for the style 3 portfolio. Panel D reports the regression output of the combined risk factors for each style portfolio. The independent risk factors are the excess return on the MSCI All Country World Equity index (MACWEI), Fama-French small-minis big portfolio (SMB) and Fama-French based Carhart (1997) 12 month return momentum risk factor (UMD), Fama-French small high book-to-market minus large cap low book-to-market portfolio (FFSVMLG), excess returns of the Lehman Global High Yield index minus the excess returns of the Lehman Global Aggregate Index (LHYMWA), log change in the VIX volatility index (VIX), the excess returns of the Dow Jones AIG Commodity Total Return index (DJAIG), the excess return from the daily 50 period moving average investment strategy in the Citigroup World Bond index (CWBI), S&P 500 All Return index (SP) and the US Dollar index (DX). Newey-West (1987) heteroscedasticity and autocorrelation adjusted standard errors are in parentheses. The final column reports the adjusted r-square for each regression. * and ** denote statistical significance at the 5% and 1% levels, respectively.

The regression results in Panel A of Table 12 demonstrate that the style 1 portfolio returns can be replicated with the excess returns from the MSCI World Equity Index (MACWEI) and the Fama French (1993, 1996) small firm (SMB) and momentum (UMD) zero-cost portfolios. In particular, the excess returns from the MACWEI exhibits a very high factor loading. In tests not reported here, the MACWEI risk factor as a single-factor model explains 65 per cent of the variation in returns of style 1. The $R^2_{adj}$ of 0.84 reported in Panel A demonstrates the high explanatory power of this equity based style model and suggests that nearly half of the hedge funds in this sample can be explained by these common equity risk factors. This strong and positive relationship with stocks is consistent with similar findings from Asness, Krail and Liew (2001), Fung and Hsieh (2002a, 2004) and Agarwal and Naik (2004). A closer inspection of the mean and median management fees of funds classified in this style are 1.16 and 1.00 per cent, while the mean and median incentive fees are 12.81 and 15.00 per cent, respectively.[1] Plan sponsors allocating capital to this hedge fund style must consider whether the fees charged by these funds can be justified, given that a similar exposure can be passively replicated with well known equity risk factors. Due to the strong explanatory power of the equity risk factors, the style 1 portfolio can be referred to as 'Quasi-Long-Equity'.

## B. Style 2: Non-Directional

To examine the non-directional nature of Style 2, we develop risk factors which are based on relative-risks. We construct the following five-factor model.

$$R_t - R_{Ft} = \alpha + \beta_1(MACWEI_t - R_{Ft}) + \beta_2(FFSVMLG_t - R_{Ft}) + \beta_3(LHYMWA_t - R_{Ft})$$
$$+ \beta_4 \ln chgVIX_t + \beta_5(DJAIGTR_t - R_{Ft}) + e_t$$

Panel B of Table 12 reports the regression results which reveal significant factor loadings (at the 1 per cent level) towards a relative long position in the Fama-French small-cap/high book-to-market ratio portfolio and a short portfolio position in the large cap/low book-to-market ratio portfolio.

[1] Only 31 funds or 8.4% of the 371 hedge fund survivors disclosed a high water mark incentive fee structure.

These factor loadings reflect the underlying relative-risk exposure in equities which is consistent with similar findings in Capocci and Hubner (2004). Another relative-risk factor is the positive coefficient in the Lehman Global High Yield Index and the negative coefficient reported in the Lehman Global Treasury index (at the 1 per cent level). The style index captures the credit risk premium in global bonds. This finding is also consistent with similar results found in Capocci and Hubner (2004) and Fung and Hsieh (2002c).

Panel B of Table 12 also finds that the Dow Jones AIG Commodities index, the log change in the VIX volatility index and global equity risk factors are also significant. Although the systematic returns of this style index portfolio exhibits low volatility, there seems to be a small degree of directional-risk exposure inherent in this investment style. Overall, these risk factors estimate a $R^2_{adj}$ of 0.61 which provides reasonable explanatory power. The statistically significant intercept term in this regression suggests that hedge funds in this style are able to earn high levels of alpha or there is an omitted explanatory variable which has not yet been identified. The latter of these two views seems most likely. This remains an area for future research.

To address the strong correlations in Table 8, the style 2 portfolio returns were regressed against the risk factors identified for style 1 with a reported $R^2_{adj}$ of 0.18. This test demonstrates that the systematic returns of style 2 are less reliant on common equity risk factors in comparison to style 1. Given the explanatory power of the relative-based risk factors, the style 2 portfolio is referred to as 'Non-Directional'.

## C. Style 3: Directional

This investment style has been problematic for researchers in the past due to the dynamic long/short investment behaviour of trend following managed futures funds. Fung and Hsieh (2001, 2004) have recently overcome these issues by replicating these fund managers with option-based lookback straddle strategies. We take another approach to this problem by capturing the dynamic nature of these fund managers in a more simplified framework. We mimic the long/short dynamics of managed futures funds by introducing a simple moving average investment strategy across the major investment classes. We construct a four-factor style model which represents the risk factors of the four broad investment classes in the following form.

$$R_t - R_{Ft} = \alpha + \beta_1(CWBI50p_t - R_{Ft}) + \beta_2(SP50p_t - R_{Ft}) + \beta_3(DX50p_t - R_{Ft})$$
$$+ \beta_4(DJAIG_t - R_{Ft}) + e_t$$

where $R_t$ is the style 3 portfolio return, CWBI is the mimicking portfolios of the Citigroup world bond index, SP is the S&P 500 All Return Index, DX is the US Dollar Index and DJAIG is the Dow Jones AIG Commodity Index. To mimic the long/short dynamics, the 50 period moving average of the index values were constructed from *daily* data on the CBWI, SP and DX risk factors. Long positions were simulated when the index was above its moving average and short positions when the index value was below their moving average. The *daily* returns were then consolidated into *monthly* returns and then employed as the independent risk factors in the above OLS estimation.

The regression results in Panel C of Table 12 demonstrate that these four risk factors explain 40 per cent of the variation of returns of style 3.[2] Other results not reported shows that statistically similar results are achievable with moving averages ranging from 20 to 100 periods, thus demonstrating the robustness of this approach. This simple framework contributes to the literature by capturing the cross-variation of returns of managed futures funds without having to resort to option-based strategies.

## 6. Conclusion

The growing interest in hedge funds makes investment style analysis an important area of research for practitioners, academics and regulators. This study provides a new dimension to the hedge fund investment style debate. This research introduces a new approach to hedge fund style analysis by employing the recently developed Gap Statistic. The statistical evidence suggests that the hedge fund universe is broadly dominated by three investment styles. To evaluate the Gap Statistic classification, various tests were performed on the systematic returns of these investment styles to ensure

[2] In a static traded (ie. low turnover) portfolio, the alpha and beta regression coefficients describe the behaviour of the underlying assets in the investment portfolio. In a dynamic investment portfolio, the alpha and beta coefficients describe the dynamics of the fund manager and not the underlying securities or assets in the portfolio.

that they were economically meaningful to investors. As a further method of validation, evidence exists that the systematic returns of these three investment styles can be passively replicated with traditional asset classes. We show that the first investment style can be readily replicated with long global equities exposure and the small firm and momentum risk premia. The second hedge fund investment style can be passively replicated with relative-risk exposures across various asset classes. Finally, the third investment style can be mimicked with a simple moving average investment strategy across global investment classes.

Our findings have several implications for the hedge fund industry. First, the statistical presence of three investment styles provides a deeper understanding of the common risk factors that determine hedge fund returns. Second, the results demonstrate that underneath the idiosyncratic layer of hedge fund returns, common risk factors can be identified by re-classifying funds with the Brown and Goetzmann (1997, 2003) model and the Gap Statistic. The ability to passively replicate the hedge fund investment styles brings into question the justification of high management fees. The consideration for future research lies in the mimicking of these three investment styles with traditional asset classes in a performance evaluation framework. We posit that plan sponsors must carefully consider whether the hedge fund returns in their investment portfolios can be passively replicated at low cost.

# Technical Appendix

The Gap Statistic can be simply described as a test statistic derived from a bootstrapped grouping procedure. The Gap Statistic effectively measures the most probable within sum-of-square distances from a set of Monte Carlo samples which are derived from the original dataset. After the adjustment for the simulation and estimation error, the optimal number of clusters or groups is calculated.[3] The estimation of the Gap Statistic is operationalised by employing the following procedure;

[3] Refer to Tibshirani et al (2001) for a full specification of the Gap Statistic.

*Step 1*:Group the observed data and vary the number of categories from $k = 1, 2,..., K$, thus generating the within-dispersion measures $W_k$, where $k = 1, 2, \ldots, K$.[4]

*Step 2*:Generate $B$ reference data sets, using either the uniform distribution or the singular variance decomposition (SVD) method, and then cluster each one giving within-dispersion measures $W^*_{kb}$, where $b = 1, 2, \ldots, B$, and $k = 1, 2, \ldots, K$. The Gap Statistic can be estimated as $Gap_n(k) = E^*_n\{\log(W_k)\} - \log(W_k)$ where $E^*_n$ is the expectation under a sample of size $n$ drawn from the reference distribution.

*Step 3:*Estimate $\bar{l}$ as the average pooled within-cluster sum of squares from $B$ samples, $sd_k$ as the standard deviation, and $s_k$ as a form of standard error estimation.[5]

*Step 4*:The estimate $\hat{k}$ (i.e. the optimal estimated number of groups) will be the value maximising $\text{Gap}_n(k)$ after the adjustment for the sampling distribution in $E^*_n\{\log(W_k)\}$. This means that the optimal estimated number of groups can be expressed as $\hat{k}$ = smallest $k$ such that $Gap(k) \geq Gap(k+1) - s_{k+1}$.

---

[4] Each observation in a dataset is denoted as i, let the distance between observation i and observation $i'$ equate to $d_{ii'}$. The squared Euclidean distance in the Gap Statistic can therefore be mathematically described as $d_{ii'} = \sum_j (x_{ij} - x_{i'j})^2$. For a dataset grouped into k clusters, $C_r = C_1, C_2, \ldots C_k$, where $C_r$ denotes the indices of observations in cluster r, and $n_r$ refers to the number of observations in $C_r$, then the sum of the pairwise distances for all datapoints in cluster r is denoted as $D_r = \sum_{i,i' \in C_r} d_{ii'}$. Thus, the pooled within-cluster sum of squares around the cluster mean for cluster k is mathematically described as $W_k = \sum_{r=1}^{k} \frac{1}{2n_r} D_r$.

[5] Let $\bar{l} = (1/B)\sum_{b=1}^{B} \log(W^*_{kb})$ be the average pooled within-cluster sum of squares, $sd_k = [(1/B)\sum_b \{\log(W^*_{kb}) - \bar{l}\}^2]^{1/2}$ is the standard deviation, and $s_k = sd_k\sqrt{(1+1/B)}$ is the standard error estimation.

The Gap Statistic provides two choices of reference distribution, namely, the uniform distribution and the singular value decomposition (SVD) method to derive a set of principal components of the data.[6] Although the uniform method has minor limitations, this study estimates the reference distribution by employing the more thorough SVD method. This study generates ten reference datasets for each Gap Statistic trial and 1,000 trials for each test to ensure its accuracy.[7]

## References

Agarwal, V., and Naik, N.Y. (2004). Risks and Portfolio Decisions Involving Hedge Funds. *Review of Financial Studies,* **17**, 63-98.

Asness, C., Krail, R. and Liew, J. (2001). Do Hedge Funds Hedge?. *Journal of Portfolio Management,* **28**, 6-19.

Ben-Hur, A., Elisseeff, A. and Guyon, I. (2002). A Stability Based Method For Discovering Structure in Clustered Data. *Paper presented at the Pacific Symposium on Biocomputing,* Hawaii, U.S.A., January 03-07.

Brown. S. (1989). The Number of Factors in Security Returns. *Journal of Finance,* **44**, 1247-1262.

Brown. S. (1997). Mutual Fund Styles. *Journal of Financial Economics,* **43**, 373-399.

Brown. S. and Goetzmann, W. (2003). Hedge Funds with Style. *Journal of Portfolio Management*, **29**, 101-112.

Brown, S., Goetzmann, W., Hiraki, T., Otsuki, T. and Shiraishi, N. (2001). The Japanese Open-End Fund Puzzle. *Journal of Business*, **74**, 59-77.

Buetow, G., Johnson, R. and Runkle, D. (2000). The Inconsistency of Return-Based Style Analysis. *Journal of Portfolio Management*, **26**, 61-77.

Capocci, D., and Hubner, G. (2004). Analysis of hedge fund performance. *Journal of Empirical Finance*, **11**, 55-89.

[6] The uniform distribution approach draws samples uniformly over the range of funds for each time period and has the advantage that it is straight-forward and simple to employ, however, the uniform distribution may contain datapoints which are not representative of the original dataset. The second method of reference distribution for the Gap Statistic is the SVD method, which involves the generation of principal components of the data. The SVD method has the advantage of taking into account the shape of the data distribution and makes the procedure rotationally invariant. The advantage derived from a rotationally invariant procedure is that the sample datasets drawn from the SVD reference distribution method are more likely to replicate the distribution of the original dataset.

[7] The trials were limited to 1,000 trials for each test due to the large computational time involved in estimating each single trial.

Carhart, M. (1997). On Persistence in Mutual Fund Performance. *Journal of Finance*, **52**, 57-82.

Carlson, R. (1970). Aggregate Performance on Mutual Funds, 1948-1967. *Journal of Financial and Quantitative Analysis*, **5**, 1-32.

Chapman, D. and Pearson, N. (2000). Is the Short Rate Drift Actually Nonlinear?. *Journal of Finance*, **55**, 355-388.

Chow, G. (1960). Tests of Equality between Sets of Coefficients in Two Linear Regressions. *Econometrica*, **28**, 591-605.

Christopherson, J. (1995). Equity Style Classifications. *Journal of Portfolio Management*, **21**, 32-43.

Connor, G. and Korajczyk, R. (1991). The Attributes, Behaviour, and Performance of U.S. Mutual Funds. *Review of Quantitative Finance and Accounting*, **1**, 5-26.

diBartolomeo, D. and Witkowski, E. (1997). Mutual Fund Misclassification: Evidence Based on Style Analysis. *Financial Analysts Journal*, **53**, 32-43.

Edwards, F. and Liew, J. (1999). Hedge Funds versus Managed Futures as Asset Classes. *Journal of Derivatives*, **6**, 45-64.

Edwards, F. and Park, J. (1996). Do Managed Futures Make Good Investments?. *Journal of Futures Markets*, **16**, 475-517.

Elton, E. and Gruber, M. (1970). Homogeneous Groups and the Testing of Economic Hypotheses. *Journal of Financial and Quantitative Analysis*, **4**, 581-602.

Elton, E. and Gruber, M. (1971). Improved Forecasting Through the Design of Homogeneous Groups. *Journal of Business*, **44**, 432-450.

Elton, E., Gruber, M., Das, S. and Hlavka, M. (1993). Efficiency with Costly Information: A Reinterpretation of Evidence from Managed Portfolios. *Review of Financial Studies*, **6**, 1-22.

Elton, E., Gruber, M. and Rentzler, J. (1987). Professionally Managed, Publicly Traded Commodity Funds. *Journal of Business*, **60**, 175-199.

Fama, E. and French, K. (1992). The Cross-Section of Expected Stock Returns. *Journal of Finance*, **47**, 427-465.

Fama, E. and French, K. (1993). Common Risk Factors in the Returns on Bonds and Stocks." *Journal of Financial Economics*, **33**, 3-56.

Fung, W. and Hsieh, D. (1997a). Survivorship Bias and Investment Style in the Returns of CTAs. *Journal of Portfolio Management*, **24**, 30-41.

Fung, W. and Hsieh, D. (1997b). Empirical Characteristics of Dynamic Trading Strategies: The Case of Hedge Funds. *The Review of Financial Studies*, **10**, 275-302.

Fung, W. and Hsieh, D. (2000). Performance Characteristics of Hedge Funds and Commodity Funds: Natural vs. Spurious Biases. *Journal of Financial and Quantitative Analysis*, **35**, 291-307.

Fung, W. and Hsieh, D. (2001). The Risk in Hedge Fund Strategies: Theory and Evidence from Trend Followers. *The Review of Financial Studies*, **14**, 313-341.

Fung, W. and Hsieh, D. (2002a). Asset Based Style Factors for Hedge Funds. *Financial Analysts Journal*, **58**, 16-27.

Fung, W. and Hsieh, D. (2002b). Hedge Fund Benchmarks: Information Content and Biases. *Financial Analysts Journal*, **58**, 22-34.

Fung, W. and Hsieh, D. (2002c). Risk in Fixed Income Hedge Fund Styles. *Journal of Fixed Income*, **12**, 6-27.

Fung, W. and Hsieh, D. (2004). Hedge Fund Benchmarks: A Risk-Based Approach. *Financial Analysts Journal*, **60**, 65-80.

Gallo, J. and Lockwood, L. (1999). Fund Management Changes and Equity Style Shifts, *Financial Analysts Journal*, **55**, 44-52.

Gatev, E., Goetzmann, W. and Rouwenhorst, G. (2006). Pairs Trading: Performance of a Relative Arbitrage Rule. *Review of Financial Studies*, **19**, 797-827.

Geman, H. and Kharoubi, C. (2003). Hedge Funds Revisited: Distributional Characteristics, Dependence Structure and Diversification, *Journal of Risk* **5**(4).

Kao, D. (2002). Battle for Alphas: Hedge Funds versus Long-Only Portfolios. *Financial Analysts Journal*, **58**, 16-34.

Lajbcygier, P. and Ong, M. (2003). Estimating the Number of Mutual Fund Styles Using the Generalised Style Classification Approach and the Gap Statistic. *Paper presented at the Conference on Computational Intelligence for Financial Engineering, Hong Kong, March 21-23.*

Liang, B. (2000). Hedge Funds: The Living and the Dead. *Journal of Financial and Quantitative Analysis*, **35**, 309-326.

Liang, B. (2001). Hedge Fund Performance: 1990-1999. *Financial Analysts Journal*, **57**, 11-18.

Lo, A. (2001). Risk Management for Hedge Funds: Introduction and Overview. *Financial Analysts Journal*, **57**, 16-33.

Lochoff, R. (2002). Hedge Funds and Hope. *Journal of Portfolio Management*, **28**, 92-99.

MacKinlay, A. (1995). Multifactor Models Do Not Explain Deviations from the CAPM. *Journal of Financial Economics*, **38**, 3-28.

McDonald, J. (1974). Objectives and Performance of Mutual Funds, 1960-1969. *Journal of Financial and Quantitative Analysis*, **9**, 311-333.

Mitchell, M. and Pulvino, T. (2001). Characteristics of Risk and Return in Risk Arbitrage. *Journal of Finance*, **56**, 2135-2175.

Newey, W. and West, K. (1987). A Simple, Positive Semi-definite, Heteroskedasticity and Autocorrelation Consistent Covariance Matrix, *Econometrica*, **55**, 703-708.

Quandt, R. (1960). Tests of the Hypothesis that a Linear Regression System Obeys Two Separate Regimes." *Journal of the American Statistical Association*, **55**, 324-330.

Sharpe, W. (1992). Asset Allocation: Management Style and Performance Measurement. *Journal of Portfolio Management*, **18**, 7-19.

Shleifer, A. and Vishny, R. (1997), The Limits of Arbitrage. *Journal of Finance*, **52**, 35-55.

Tibshirani, R., Walther. G. and Hastie, T. (2001). Estimating the Number of Clusters in a Data Set via the Gap Statistic. *Journal of the Royal Statistical Society B,* **63**, 411-423.

U.S. Securities and Exchange Commission. (2003). *Implications of the Growth of Hedge Funds.* SEC Special Studies, 29 September.

Wang, K. (2005). Multifactor Evaluation of Style Rotation. *Journal of Financial and Quantitative Analysis*, **40**, 349-372.

In: The Recent Trend of Hedge Fund Strategies ISBN: 978-1-61668-338-2
Editor: Yasuaki Watanabe, pp. 133-155 

*Chapter 4*

# STYLE ANALYSIS FOR HEDGE FUNDS: THE ESTIMATION FOR THE ABILITY OF GENERATING ALPHA OF FUND OF HEDGE FUNDS BY APPLICATION OF MARKOV-SWITCHING MODEL

***Junichiro Goto*** [1]
Product Management
AllianceBernstein Japan Ltd.

## Abstract

Although hedge fund managers are considered capable of generating positive returns regardless of market conditions, they are actually affected by the market to some extent. However, it is difficult to isolate the market effect, or beta, because hedge fund managers' beta has not been clearly defined yet. In addition, traditional methods, such as multi-regression analysis, are also not satisfactory due to hedge funds' dynamic strategy changes.

In this analysis, I attempt to apply a seven-factor Markov-Switching Model to the Fung and Hsieh approach (2004) to enhance the coefficient of determination by taking into consideration the unique characteristics of hedge fund managers—specifically their tendencies to switch their allocations to different strategies.

---

[1] E-mail address: junichiro.goto@alliancebernstein.com. Tel: 81-3-3240-8553 Fax: 81-3-3240-8545.

# 1. Introduction

## 1.1. Disappointment of Hedge Fund Investors

By 2003, many Japanese pension funds had begun investing in hedge funds, expecting stable and high absolute returns. In 2004, however, hedge funds produced mediocre returns as major financial markets, such as bonds, equities and currencies, traded in relatively narrow ranges and their volatility dwindled. Furthermore, although oil and other commodity markets boomed, Japanese pension funds missed out on this opportunity as the hedge funds in which they had invested were mostly an extension of the traditional long-only equity strategy, such as long/short equities or market-neutral equities, which do not have much exposure to commodities.

In an equity long/short strategy, hedge fund managers buy stocks that are cheap relative to their fair value and sell stocks that are expensive on a relative basis, whereas a traditional long-only manger focuses on buying cheap stocks. Long/short strategies prevailed in Japan because they looked familiar to pension funds—their return sources and investment processes are similar to those of long-only managers who rely on fundamental and quantitative research to estimate the fair value of each stock.

In these hedge fund strategies, the managers were supposed to be able to generate positive absolute returns even if the market as a whole declined. They were supposed to capture the dispersion between cheaper securities and the more expensive ones in the market. However, the valuation gap had gradually diminished as a very result of the proliferation of such strategies because they had made the market more efficient. Consequently, the dispersion level in both U.S. and Japanese equity markets in 2004 declined to the lowest levels since the late 1990s. Hedge fund managers at the time found it difficult to earn steady absolute returns over risk-free interest rates not just because of the low volatility in market returns but also because of the narrower valuation dispersion.

Put bluntly, the disappointing returns of hedge funds were not necessarily because of events like the 9/11 incident or accounting frauds by Enron and WorldCom. They were because of narrower dispersion within each market and a dearth of market trends due, ironically, to an absence of game-changing events. The returns of major strategies in Hedge Fund Research indices are shown in Table 1. Most strategies have seen their performance worsen in recent years. Since 2003, the strategies which have an exposure to equity markets have done well, but market-neutral equity strategies have not done as well as they did in the late 1990s, presumably due to the smaller valuation dispersion in equity markets.

**Table 1. Annual Returns of Each Strategy**

| | Weighted Composite | Fund of Funds | Equity Hedge (Total) | Quantitative Directional | Equity Market Neutral | Short Bias | Relative Value (Total) |
|---|---|---|---|---|---|---|---|
| 1994 | 4.10% | -3.48% | 2.61% | 5.10% | 2.65% | 18.53% | 4.00% |
| 1995 | 21.50% | 11.10% | 31.04% | 34.80% | 16.33% | -17.14% | 15.66% |
| 1996 | 21.10% | 14.39% | 21.75% | 25.52% | 14.20% | -4.00% | 14.49% |
| 1997 | 16.79% | 16.20% | 23.41% | 17.56% | 13.62% | 3.86% | 15.93% |
| 1998 | 2.62% | -5.11% | 15.98% | 9.80% | 8.30% | -0.54% | 2.81% |
| 1999 | 31.29% | 26.47% | 44.22% | 41.82% | 7.09% | -24.40% | 14.73% |
| 2000 | 4.98% | 4.07% | 9.09% | -9.04% | 14.56% | 34.63% | 13.41% |
| 2001 | 4.62% | 2.80% | 0.40% | 1.36% | 6.71% | 8.99% | 8.92% |
| 2002 | -1.44% | 1.01% | -4.71% | -8.49% | 0.98% | 29.16% | 5.43% |
| 2003 | 19.55% | 11.62% | 20.53% | 37.55% | 2.46% | -21.77% | 9.73% |
| 2004 | 9.05% | 6.87% | 7.69% | 13.31% | 4.15% | -3.84% | 5.58% |
| 2005 | 9.27% | 7.50% | 10.61% | 9.93% | 6.23% | 7.26% | 6.03% |
| 2006 | 12.89% | 10.39% | 11.71% | 15.95% | 7.32% | -2.65% | 12.36% |
| 2007 | 9.95% | 10.27% | 10.50% | 12.36% | 5.29% | 4.73% | 8.94% |
| Average | 11.54% | 7.86% | 13.99% | 13.83% | 7.74% | 0.99% | 9.77% |

| | Fixed Income-Convertible Arbitrage | Multi-Strategy | Event-Driven (Total) | Merger Arbitrage | Distressed/Restructuring | Macro (Total) |
|---|---|---|---|---|---|---|
| 1994 | -3.73% | 7.56% | 6.00% | 8.88% | 3.84% | -4.30% |
| 1995 | 19.85% | 12.43% | 25.11% | 17.86% | 19.73% | 29.32% |
| 1996 | 14.56% | 14.83% | 24.84% | 16.61% | 20.77% | 9.32% |
| 1997 | 12.72% | 11.86% | 21.23% | 16.44% | 15.40% | 18.82% |
| 1998 | 7.77% | -2.04% | 1.70% | 7.23% | -4.23% | 6.19% |
| 1999 | 14.41% | 10.98% | 24.33% | 14.34% | 16.94% | 17.62% |
| 2000 | 14.50% | 3.42% | 6.74% | 18.02% | 2.78% | 1.97% |
| 2001 | 13.37% | 10.36% | 12.18% | 2.76% | 13.28% | 6.87% |
| 2002 | 9.07% | 6.48% | -4.30% | -0.86% | 5.28% | 7.42% |
| 2003 | 9.93% | 11.54% | 25.33% | 7.48% | 29.58% | 21.44% |
| 2004 | 1.18% | 8.22% | 15.02% | 4.08% | 18.89% | 4.64% |
| 2005 | -1.86% | 5.68% | 7.30% | 6.26% | 8.25% | 6.81% |
| 2006 | 12.17% | 9.00% | 15.34% | 14.24% | 15.95% | 8.17% |
| 2007 | 5.33% | 1.81% | 6.60% | 7.05% | 5.07% | 11.11% |
| Average | 9.03% | 7.91% | 13.00% | 9.87% | 11.91% | 10.08% |

*Source: Hedge Fund Research

** Shaded cells mean negative return

We can say from Table 1 that hedge fund managers, who seek to generate positive returns regardless of what the general market does, are in fact not fully independent of the market. Although the factors affecting their performance, such as trend, volatility and dispersion, are different from those affecting traditional long-only managers, hedge funds are not immune to market conditions. That is to say, they do have a beta of sorts and are not the pure active investment as they are sometimes advertised.

## 1.2. Appropriate Evaluation for Hedge Funds

In general, although hedge fund managers are considered capable of generating positive returns regardless of market conditions, they are actually affected by the market to some extent, as described in section 1-1.

Therefore, to evaluate their ability to generate alpha, returns that are attributable to the market must be separated from performance, in the same way they are in evaluating traditional assets.

Since the late 1990s, W. Fung and D. Hsieh have continued a series of style analyses that can appropriately reflect the characteristics of hedge fund managers. They have found some factors that can be substitutional variables for characteristics of hedge-fund performance and have succeeded in enhancing the coefficient of determination, which is a power of explanation, by using the factors as explained variables.

However, even those factors do not fully reflect hedge-fund characteristics, and the coefficient of determination is not at a sufficiently high level yet.

Therefore, in this research, I attempt to improve the coefficient of determination by constructing a style-analysis framework which explicitly reflects the dynamic changes that hedge fund managers make in their exposures to various factors. Specifically, I try to apply the Markov-Switching Model to a seven-factor multi-regression model established by Fung and Hsieh (2004) in order to estimate hedge-fund managers' true alpha-generation capability by calculating style-adjusted alpha.

This article consists of seven chapters. I touch upon various issues surrounding hedge fund analyses in Chapter 2 and briefly describe return sources of hedge fund managers in Chapter 3. Then, I attempt to analyze the performance of hedge funds using the Fung-and-Hsieh method (2004) in Chapter 4 and apply the Markov-Switching Model to the Fund-and-Hsieh model (2004) in Chapter 5. In Chapter 6, I try to estimate the true alpha-generating capability of hedge funds by observing the outcome of this analysis. Finally, I provide my conclusion in Chapter 7.

# 2. Issues Concerning Hedge Fund Analyses

## 2.1. Biases in Hedge Fund Indices

When performance of hedge fund managers is analyzed, indices are used in the same way they are in measuring the performance of traditional managers. Hedge Fund Research (HFR), TASS, MSCI Barra and SandP are typical indices used by many researchers today. According to Fung (2005), the number of hedge fund managers included in each of these representative indices is about 800 to 1,000. He notes that because only about 300 managers are common components across the indices, there is a considerable performance disparity. Still, the tendency of the indices' performance is largely similar, and I believe it is not a big issue which indices we select in our analysis. On the other hand, all of these indices have common biases, and we must pay close attention to potential distortions that they could cause to the results of the analysis. Major biases in hedge fund indices include: the selection bias, which is a result of hedge fund managers reporting only the performance of funds with good records; the survivorship bias, which is caused by the deletion of funds that have failed; and the instant-history bias, which occurs when hedge fund managers start reporting performance of funds with good past performance after a number of years since inception.

## 2.2. Using FOHF Indices

When we analyze hedge funds using the common hedge fund indices, the aforementioned biases are inevitable. However, it is difficult for the academic society to isolate these biases on its own as it requires assembling data from real-world investors. Yet, using the indices without eliminating their biases would undermine the credibility of an analysis, and we must find some measures to alleviate the problem.

Therefore, in applying the Markov-Switching Model in this research, I will draw from observations by Fung and Hsieh (2000) by using the performance of major fund of hedge funds (FOHFs) as a substitute for the performance of actual investors' portfolios. This is a very simple method based on the idea that the best way to analyze a hedge fund investor's performance is to look at how people actually investing in hedge funds have fared. From this standpoint, FOHFs' results generally reflect the experience of a typical investor who invests in investible hedge funds with long track records. I believe they can be used as a proxy to investments by hedge fund investors as a whole.

Let me explain the reasons in more detail. Track records of FOHFs include the performance of hedge funds which have failed due to their poor returns and those that have ceased to report their results to index providers. Therefore, performance of FOHFs is not subject to the survivorship bias that hedge fund indices are. Likewise, the selection bias would not be a factor either.

Furthermore, because FOHFs' historical returns are a result of their actual investment, they are not affected by past performance of hedge funds that are newly added to their portfolios. Therefore, there is no instant-history bias.

Weighted-average performance of FOHFs based on their assets under management (AUM) would be a good approximation of the experience of a hedge fund investor, but it is difficult for us to obtain precise historical AUM information of FOHF managers. Therefore, I shall use an equal-weighted performance of FOHFs, i.e. FOHF indices, as a proxy when I apply the Markov Switching Model in Chapter 5.

# 3. Return Sources for Hedge Funds

## 3.1. Selection of Appropriate Factors for Each Strategy

It is difficult to find common factors affecting the entire hedge fund universe through a top-down approach because asset classes and investment processes of hedge funds vary from strategy to strategy. Therefore, Fung and Hsieh (2004) identified seven common factors for the main strategies through a bottom-up approach based on the profit-and-loss diagram of each strategy.

To be more specific, they identified: U.S. equity market returns and the return spread between small-cap equities and large-cap equities as the two equity-related factors, based on their observation of equity long/short managers and merger-arbitrage managers; the change in the 10-year Treasury note yield and the change in the yield spread between 10-year T-notes and high-yield bonds as the two fixed income-related factors, based on their analysis of fixed income arbitrage managers; portfolios of look-back straddles on bonds, currencies, and on commodities as the three option-related factors, based on their scrutiny of global macro managers. Please refer to the thesis by Fung and Hsieh (2004) for more detailed rationale for these seven factors.

## 3.2. Factors in Tested This Research

In their research, Fung and Hsieh (2004) conducted a multi-regression analysis by using seven factors. Their formulation is as follows:

$$R_t - r_t = \alpha + \beta_1 F_{1t} + \cdots + \beta_7 F_{7t} + e_t$$
$$e_t \sim N(0, \sigma^2)$$

where $R_t$: monthly returns of hedge fund managers, $r_t$: U.S. interest rate, $F_{1t}$: monthly return of U.S. equity market, $F_{2t}$: spread between returns of small-cap and large-cap equities, $F_{3t}$: change in 10-year Treasury yields, $F_{4t}$: change in yield spread between 10-year T-notes and high-yield bonds, $F_{5t}$: return on a portfolio of look-back straddles on bonds, $F_{6t}$: return on a portfolio of look-back straddles on currencies, and $F_{7t}$: return on a portfolio of look-back straddles on commodities.

In the first phase of this analysis, I conduct the same analysis as Fung and Hsieh (2004), although I use the following data due to availability issues.

1) U.S. equity market: total return of SandP500*
2) Spread between small-cap and large-cap equity returns: total return of small-cap equity, based on Dimensional Fund Advisors (DFA) data, minus total return of SandP500*
3) Change in 10-year Treasury yields: yield on 10-year Treasury notes minus that of previous month*
4) Change in yield spread between 10-year T-notes and high-yield bonds: difference between yield of CSFB high-yield index and yield on 10-year T-notes minus that of the previous month*
5) The portfolio of look-back straddles on bonds: data from David A. Hsieh's website
6) The portfolio of look-back straddles on currencies: data from David A. Hsieh's website
7) The portfolio of look-back straddles on commodities: data from David A. Hsieh's website

*(1) through (4) were obtained from Ibbotson's database. Data from 01/1994 to 09/2007 were used.

# 4. Style Analysis by Multi-Regression Model

## 4.1.Outcome of Analysis for Hedge Fund Indices

First, I conducted a multi-regression analysis of 13 representative strategies in HFR indices from 01/1994 to 09/2007 that I described in the previous chapter, using seven factors identified by Fung and Hsieh (2004). The results are shown in Table 2 and Figure 1.

From these results, we can confirm that coefficients of determination for the all-strategy composite, equity hedge (total), quantitative directional, short bias and event-driven (total) are relatively high, while those for other strategies are not so high. There are three probable reasons for this. First, equity-hedge (aka equity-long/short) and quantitative-directional managers tend to have net long exposures to the equity market. Second, short-bias managers, by definition, sell stocks to maintain net short positions, which is basically the opposite of equity-hedge managers. Third, equity-hedge managers account for a large portion of the composite of all strategies.

**Table 2. Result of Multi-Regression Model Analysis**

| | Weighted Composite | Fund of Funds | Equity Hedge (Total) | Quantitative Directional | Equity Market Neutral | Short Bias | Relative Value (Total) |
|---|---|---|---|---|---|---|---|
| Intercept (alpha) | 0.002 | 0.000 | 0.003 | (0.000) | 0.002 | 0.012 | 0.004 |
| U.S. equity market | 0.134 | 0.049 | 0.167 | 0.345 | 0.017 | (0.444) | 0.022 |
| Spread between small-cap and large-cap | 0.228 | 0.171 | 0.324 | 0.467 | 0.031 | (0.729) | 0.055 |
| Change in 10-year yields | (0.307) | (0.740) | 0.246 | 0.197 | (0.234) | (1.027) | (0.602) |
| Change in yield spread | (0.222) | (0.319) | 0.668 | (0.090) | 0.237 | (1.976) | (0.559) |
| Lookback straddle on bonds | (0.006) | (0.014) | (0.000) | 0.004 | (0.007) | (0.009) | (0.011) |
| Lookback straddle on currencies | 0.004 | 0.007 | 0.002 | 0.006 | 0.008 | 0.015 | (0.002) |
| Lookback straddle on commodities | 0.010 | 0.016 | 0.014 | 0.013 | 0.004 | (0.012) | 0.001 |
| Coefficient of determination | 0.811 | 0.568 | 0.790 | 0.918 | 0.113 | 0.761 | 0.444 |

| | Fixed Income-Convertible Arbitrage | Multi-Strategy | Event-Driven (Total) | Merger Arbitrage | Distressed/Restructuring | Macro (Total) |
|---|---|---|---|---|---|---|
| Intercept (alpha) | 0.004 | 0.003 | 0.004 | 0.003 | 0.005 | 0.002 |
| U.S. equity market | (0.008) | (0.011) | 0.088 | 0.056 | (0.008) | 0.065 |
| Spread between small-cap and large-cap | 0.038 | 0.050 | 0.176 | 0.066 | 0.127 | 0.155 |
| Change in 10-year yields | (1.110) | (1.046) | (0.752) | (0.149) | (1.138) | (2.559) |
| Change in yield spread | (0.999) | (1.081) | (1.022) | (0.240) | (1.328) | (0.221) |
| Lookback straddle on bonds | (0.008) | (0.004) | (0.011) | (0.006) | (0.026) | (0.005) |
| Lookback straddle on currencies | 0.001 | 0.001 | 0.002 | 0.004 | 0.002 | 0.017 |
| Lookback straddle on commodities | 0.004 | 0.004 | 0.004 | (0.004) | 0.007 | 0.027 |
| Coefficient of determination | 0.295 | 0.493 | 0.757 | 0.398 | 0.398 | 0.409 |

*Shaded cells show significance level of 95%.

On the other hand, I believe the reason why coefficients of other strategies are not high is that the characteristics of these strategies cannot be explained by these seven factors. We cannot capture the quick, tactical moves in their capital from one position to another. Also, the intercepts of all strategies are positive except for quantitative directional strategy. This result shows that almost all strategies had the ability to generate positive style-adjusted alpha, which suggests that the seven factors were generating some effect that should be considered beta. This should be removed from managers' performance in our analysis.

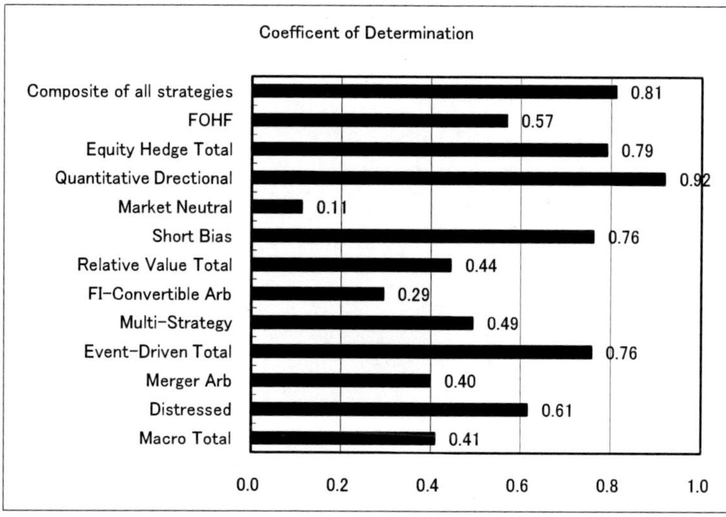


Figure 1. Coefficient of Determination for Each Strategy.

However, I have to point out that the credibility of these results is not very high because these coefficients of determination for most strategies are not particularly high.

# 5. Style Analysis by Markov-Switching Model

## 5.1. Markov-Switching Model

When current conditions dramatically shift from one state to another, a regression model tends to become unstable and unreliable in general. We can judge whether there are any structural changes by the F-test, a test on variance, if we already know in advance that a different condition exists. However, in many cases we cannot tell structural changes in advance. Therefore, we have to estimate the timing of a change as well as the values of the parameters. The Markov-Switching Model helps us estimate the timing and the value of the parameters. In the Markov-Switching Model, the probability that a certain state happens at a certain time depends only on the previous state. The estimation method for the model is described in detail by Kim and Nelson (1990), and in this research I estimated the timing, the parameters and probabilities by using this method.

Let me briefly describe the estimation method deployed as an example of a two-state, first-order Markov-Switching Model below.

First, given $y_t$ as observations, $x_t$ as factors, $S_t$ as a state variable int =1,...,T, $y_t$ is expressed by an equation of $x_t$ below:

$$y_t = x_t\beta_{S_t} + e_t$$

$$e_t \sim N(0,\sigma_{S_t}^2)$$

$$\beta_{S_t} = \begin{cases} \beta_0 & (S_t = 0) \\ \beta_1 & (S_t = 1) \end{cases}$$

$$\sigma_{S_t}^2 = \begin{cases} \sigma_0^2 & (S_t = 0) \\ \sigma_1^2 & (S_t = 1) \end{cases}$$

$$\Pr[S_t = 1 \mid S_{t-1} = 1] = p, \Pr[S_t = 0 \mid S_{t-1} = 0] = q$$

where $\beta_0$, $\beta_1$, $\sigma_0$, $\sigma_1$ are dependent on the state variable; $p$, $q$ are transition probabilities of a shift from one state to another.

Now, as we set $\psi_t = [y_1 \quad y_2 \quad \cdots \quad y_t]$ as a set of observations and $f(\cdot)$ as a probability density function, a likelihood function, L, is expressed as follows:

$$L = \prod_{t=1}^{T} \{f(y_t \mid S_t, \psi_{t-1})\Pr[S_t = 0 \mid \psi_{t-1}] + f(y_t \mid S_t, \psi_{t-1})\Pr[S_t = 1 \mid \psi_{t-1}]\}$$

$$= \prod_{t=1}^{T}\sum_{j=0}^{1} f(y_t \mid S_t, \psi_{t-1})\Pr[S_t = j \mid \psi_{t-1}]$$

Then we have a log likelihood function.

$$\ln L = \sum_{i=1}^{T} \ln \sum_{j=0}^{1} f(y_t \mid S_t, \psi_{t-1})\Pr[S_t = j \mid \psi_{t-1}]$$

However, we cannot maximize the log likelihood function above as you do not know $\Pr[S_t = j \mid \psi_{t-1}]$, j=0,1. Before maximizing it, we must calculate $\Pr[S_t = j \mid \psi_{t-1}]$, j=0,1 separately. We can calculate it by following process.

Step 1:

Given $\Pr[S_{t-1} = i \mid \psi_{t-1}]$, i=0,1, $\Pr[S_t = j \mid \psi_{t-1}]$, j=0,1 is calculated as follows:

$$\Pr[S_t = j \mid \psi_{t-1}] = \sum_{i=0}^{1} \Pr[S_t = j, S_{t-1} = i \mid \psi_{t-1}]$$
$$= \sum_{i=0}^{1} \Pr[S_t = j \mid S_{t-1} = i] \Pr[S_{t-1} = i \mid \psi_{t-1}]$$

Step 2:

Then $y_t$ is observed at the end of t, and the probability, $\Pr[S_t = j \mid \psi_t]$, is updated according to the process below.

$$\Pr[S_t = j \mid \psi_t] = \Pr[S_t = j \mid \psi_{t-1}, y_t] = \frac{f(S_t = j, y_t \mid \psi_{t-1})}{f(y_t \mid \psi_{t-1})}$$
$$= \frac{f(y_t \mid S_t = j, \psi_{t-1}) \Pr[S_t = j \mid \psi_{t-1}]}{\sum_{j=0}^{1} f(y_t \mid S_t = j, \psi_{t-1}) \Pr[S_t = j \mid \psi_{t-1}]}$$

By iteration of the two steps above, we arrive at $\Pr[S_t = j \mid \psi_{t-1}]$, t=1,2,...,T. However, we need an initial probability, $\Pr[S_0 \mid \psi_0]$, to calculate the probability at t=1. The initial probability, $\Pr[S_0 \mid \psi_0]$, is called the steady-state probability and is calculated by the equations below:

$$\pi_0 = \Pr[S_0 = 0 \mid \psi_0] = \frac{1-p}{2-p-q}$$
$$\pi_1 = \Pr[S_0 = 1 \mid \psi_0] = \frac{1-q}{2-p-q}$$

By using $\Pr[S_t = j \mid \psi_{t-1}]$ calculated in this step, the log likelihood function is expressed by parameters $\theta = [\beta_0 \;\; \beta_1 \;\; \sigma_0 \;\; \sigma_1 \;\; p \;\; q]$. We can estimate the parameters by maximization of the log likelihood function. Figure 2 expresses this process where $l(\theta)$ is the log likelihood function.

## 5.2. Formulation of Markov-Switching Model in Analysis

In this article, I applied the Markov-Switching Model to Fung-and-Hsieh model (2004). That is, I applied a two-state, first-order Markov-Switching Model to each factor one by one—U.S. equities, the small-cap/large-cap spread, the change in 10-year yields, the change in the credit spread and the look-back straddles. Exposure to other factors were not changed.

The formulation I explained above is as follows. $S_t$ in the formulation stands for state variable.

$$l(\theta) = 0$$

$$\Pr[S_0 = 0] = \pi_0, \Pr[S_0 = 1] = \pi_1 \text{ (Steady-State probability)}$$

$$\Pr[S_t = j, S_{t-1} = i \mid \psi_{t-1}] = \Pr[S_t = j \mid S_{t-1} = i]\Pr[S_{t-1} = i \mid \psi_{t-1}]$$

$$\Pr[S_t = j \mid \psi_{t-1}] = \sum_{i=0}^{1} \Pr[S_t = j \mid S_{t-1} = i]\Pr[S_{t-1} = i \mid \psi_{t-1}]$$

$$f(y_t \mid \psi_{t-1}) = \sum_{j=0}^{1} f(y_t \mid S_t = j, \psi_{t-1})\Pr[S_t = j \mid \psi_{t-1}]$$

$$l(\theta) = l(\theta) + \ln(f(y_t \mid \psi_{t-1}))$$

$$\Pr[S_t = j \mid \psi_t] = \frac{f(y_t \mid S_t = j, \psi_{t-1})\Pr[S_t = j \mid \psi_{t-1}]}{\sum_{j=0}^{1} f(y_t \mid S_t = j, \psi_{t-1})\Pr[S_t = j \mid \psi_{t-1}]}$$

$$l(\theta) = \sum_{t=1}^{T} \ln(f(y_t \mid \psi_{t-1})$$

where $\Pr[S_t = j \mid \psi_t]$ is calculated as a byproduct. It is called filtered probability, which express as the state probability estimated by using information from 0 to t.

Figure 2. The Process for Calculating a Log Likelihood Function.

$$R_t - r_t = B_{S_t} X_{1t} + B X_{2t} + e_t$$

$$e_t \sim N(0, \sigma_{S_t}^2)$$

$$B_{S_t} = \begin{cases} (\alpha_0 \quad \beta_{10}) & (S_t = 0) \\ (\alpha_1 \quad \beta_{11}) & (S_t = 1) \end{cases}$$

$$\sigma_{S_t}^2 = \begin{cases} \sigma_0^2 & (S_t = 0) \\ \sigma_1^2 & (S_t = 1) \end{cases}$$

$$\Pr[S_t = 1 \mid S_{t-1} = 1] = p$$

$$\Pr[S_t = 0 \mid S_{t-1} = 0] = q$$

where $X_{1t} = (1 \quad F_{1t})'$, $X_{2t} = (F_{2t} \quad F_{3t} \quad F_{4t} \quad F_{5t} \quad F_{6t} \quad F_{7t})'$, $B = (\beta_2 \quad \beta_3 \quad \beta_4 \quad \beta_5 \quad \beta_6 \quad \beta_7)$ and $S_t$ is a state variable which takes 0 or 1. That is to say, the parameters we have to estimate are $\alpha_0$, $\alpha_1$, $\beta_{10}$, $\beta_{11}$, $\sigma_0$, $\sigma_1$, which depend on the state variable, transition probabilities $p$, $q$ and $\beta_2$, $\beta_3$, $\beta_4$, $\beta_5$, $\beta_6$, $\beta_7$, which are constant variables.

## 5.3. The Result of Applying Markov-Switching Model to Fung and Hsieh (2004)

In accordance to the formulation in the previous section, I switched the state variable in each of the seven factors and estimated the parameters.

**Table 3. The Result of Switching The State Variable in The Change in 10-year Treasury Yields**

**Transition Probability Matrix**

| | | t | |
|---|---|---|---|
| | | **State 0** | **State 1** |
| **t-1** | **State 0** | 0.973 | 0.027 |
| | **State 1** | 0.091 | 0.909 |

**Parameters Dependent on State**

| | **State 0** | **State 1** |
|---|---|---|
| $\beta_3$ | (1.273) | 4.922 |
| $\alpha$ | 0.093 | (0.026) |
| $\sigma^2$ | 0.566 | 2.427 |

**Table 3. Continued**

**Parameters Independent of State**

| $\beta_1$ | $\beta_2$ | $\beta_4$ | $\beta_5$ | $\beta_6$ | $\beta_7$ |
|---|---|---|---|---|---|
| 0.053 | 0.155 | (0.176) | (0.009) | 0.008 | 0.021 |

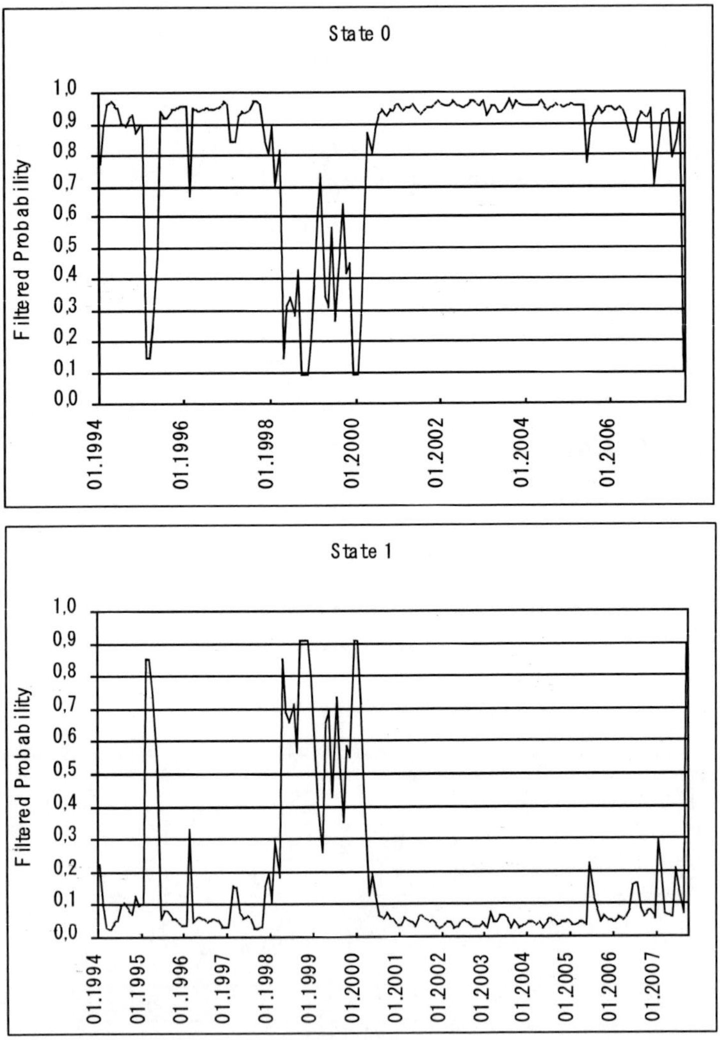


Figure 3. Filtered Probability: Switching State Variable in Treasury Yield Changes.

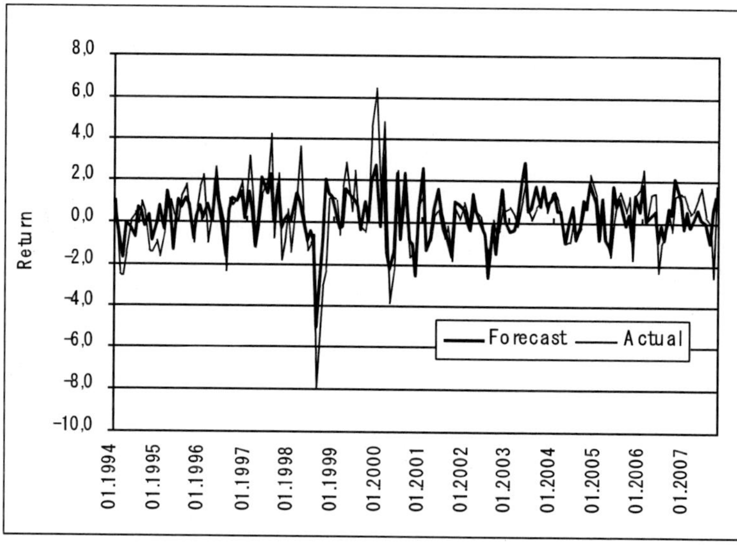


Figure 4. Forecast and Actual Return: Switching State Variable in Treasury Yield Changes.

The results showed that switching the state variable in the yield change and the credit-spread change produced the most remarkable changes in the coefficient of determination. Estimated parameters and filtered probability are shown in Table 3-4 and Figure 3-6.

**Table 4. Result of Switching St in Change in Yield Spread between 10-year T-notes and High-yield Bonds**

**Transition Probability Matrix**

| | | **t** | |
|---|---|---|---|
| | | **State 0** | **State 1** |
| **t-1** | **State 0** | 0.959 | 0.041 |
| | **State 1** | 0.079 | 0.921 |

**Parameters Dependent on State**

| | **State 0** | **State 1** |
|---|---|---|
| $\beta_4$ | (0.001) | (2.227) |
| $\alpha$ | 0.117 | 0.145 |
| $\sigma^2$ | 0.494 | 2.084 |

**Table 4. Continued**

**Parameters Independent of State**

| $\beta_1$ | $\beta_2$ | $\beta_3$ | $\beta_5$ | $\beta_6$ | $\beta_7$ |
|---|---|---|---|---|---|
| 0.048 | 0.154 | (0.985) | (0.008) | 0.009 | 0.019 |

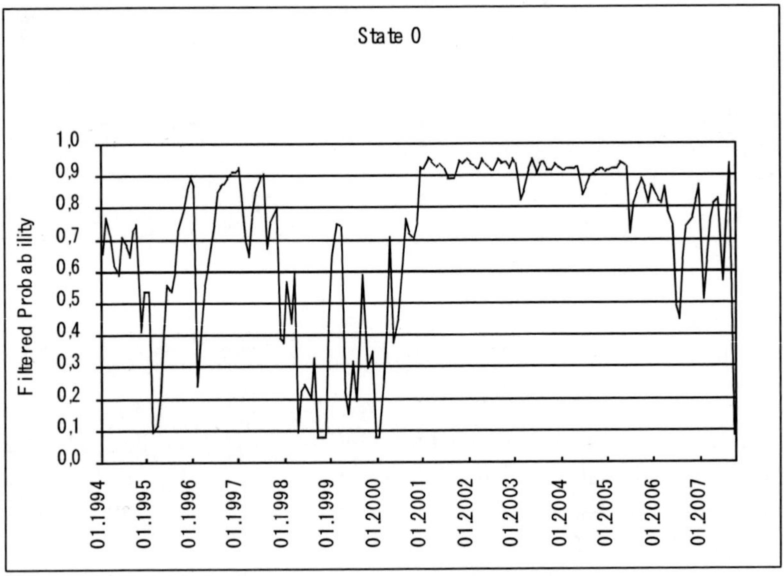


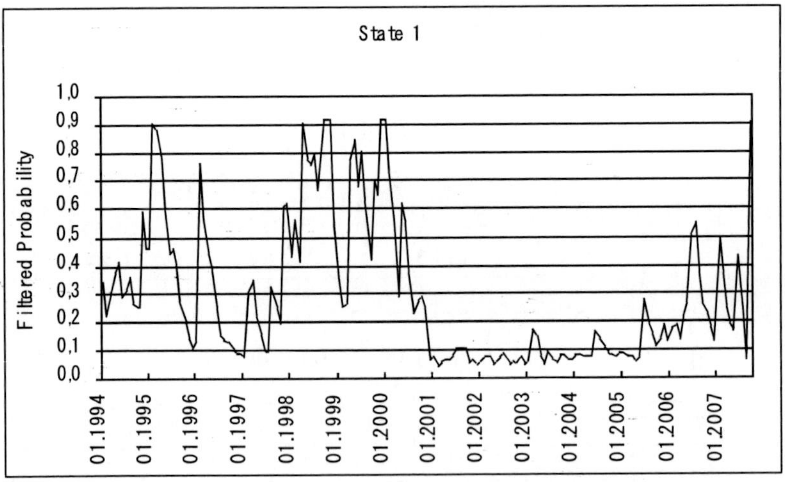


Figure 5. Filtered Probability: Switching State Variable in Credit Spreads.

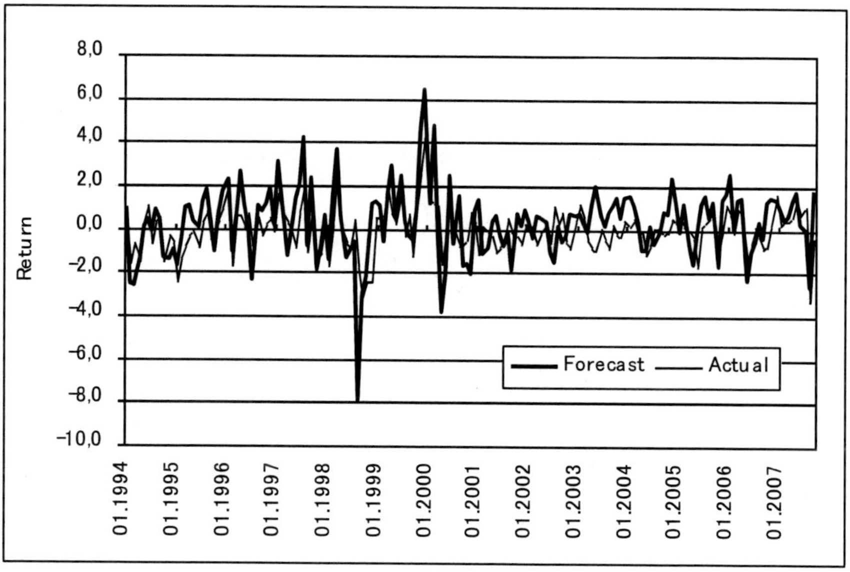


Figure 6. Forecast and Actual Return: Switching State Variable in Credit Spreads.

We can see that the state shifted in late 2000 and shifted back again in mid-2007 in both 10-year yield changes and credit spreads. I am under the impression that this is because the market condition shifted to another state, such as that of low volatility and small dispersion in after the collapse of dotcom bubble in 2000 or that of high volatility and wider credit spreads following the subprime-loan crisis triggered by high-profile hedge-fund failures in August 2007.

Let me analyze the results in more detail. The late 1990s, marked by numerous financial crises—including the Asian currency crisis, the Russian default and the LTCM debacle—was a period of State 1. The beta of Treasuries at that time was 4.922 in the switching model for 10-year bond yield changes. FOHF managers were taking long positions for the change in 10-year bond yield. This means they were taking short position in Treasuries in late 1990's.

At the same time, beta of credit spreads at the time was -2.227 in the switching model for credit-spread changes. FOHF managers were taking short position for the credit -spread changes, that is, they were taking long positions in credit back then.

The early 2000s was a period of State 0 in both yields and credit spreads. FOHF managers were taking long positions in Treasuries (beta=-1.273) and neutral positions in credit spreads (beta=-0.001).

Then, in mid-2007 a shift in the opposite direction took place.

From this analysis, it is reasonable to state that FOHF managers made dynamic shifts in their strategies during huge crises.

## 5.3. Summary of Analysis by Markov-Switching Model

I estimated the parameters for a state-variable switching in each of the seven factors. The coefficients of determination are as follows:

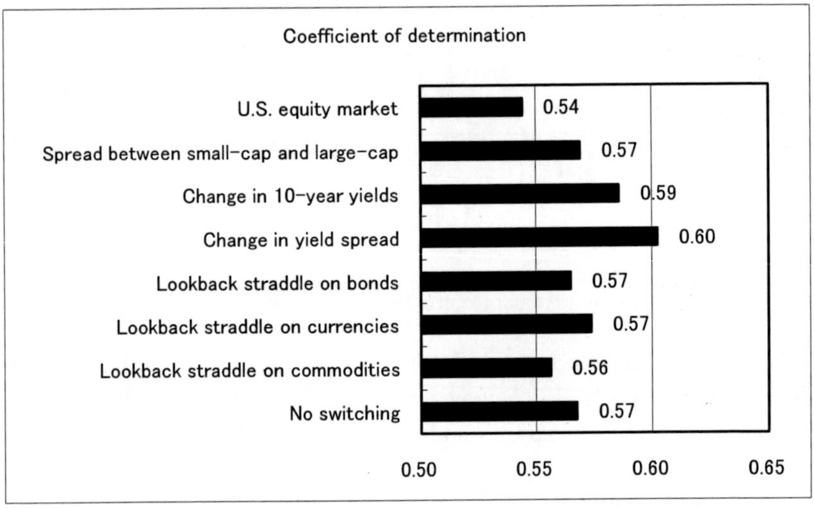


Figure 7. Coefficients of Determination by Markov-Switching Model.

Figure 7 shows that the coefficients of determination for state-variable switching in yield changes and credit spread changes were higher in this analysis than those in the multi-regression model explained in Chapter 4. Still, the coefficients of other factors did not improve. It is probable that FOHF managers did not shift their exposures to these factors during this period. We cannot tell the reason from this analysis, but I can make two statements based on this analysis.

First, FOHF managers have been taking exposures to 10-year Treasury yields and credit spreads and they have been fairly flexible in changing those exposures. Second, by applying the Markov Switching Model to FOHF managers, we can capture the quick movements by the managers and explain their performance more accurately.

# 6. FOHF Managers' Ability to Generate Alpha

## 6.1. FOHF Managers' Ability to Select Managers

In this section, I interpret the intercept of each model, alpha, as an ability of FOHF managers in selecting good individual hedge fund managers.

I compare the intercept of multi-regression model with that of the Markov-Switching Model to review their ability to select hedge fund managers. The intercepts I estimated are as follows:

**Table 5. FOHF Managers' Ability to Select Managers**

| Switching factor | State: 0 | | State: 1 | | Average Alpha (%) |
|---|---|---|---|---|---|
| | Average Probability | Alpha(%) | Average Probability | Alpha(%) | |
| U.S. equity market | 0.905 | 0.113 | 0.095 | (0.619) | 0.043 |
| Spread between small-cap and large-cap | 0.882 | 0.128 | 0.118 | (0.586) | 0.044 |
| Change in 10-year yields | 0.820 | 0.093 | 0.180 | (0.026) | 0.071 |
| Change in yield spread | 0.703 | 0.117 | 0.297 | 0.145 | 0.125 |
| Lookback straddle on bonds | 0.896 | 0.109 | 0.104 | (0.019) | 0.095 |
| Lookback straddle on currencies | 0.919 | 0.106 | 0.081 | (0.288) | 0.074 |
| Lookback straddle on commodities | 0.815 | 0.060 | 0.185 | 0.276 | 0.100 |
| No switching (Multi-regression) | - | - | - | - | 0.047 |

In the results of multi-regression, or no-switching model, the ability of selecting managers is just 0.047%. Also, the ability of selecting managers in some Markov-Switching Models is positive, too, and larger than that of multi-regression. The alpha of yield changes, whose coefficient of determination is the highest of all models, is a positive 0.125%. It is the highest alpha among all models as well.

FOHF managers typically set an absolute return target of more than 5%, even in low-risk strategies. However, the results of this analysis show that, even in switching the state variable for yield changes, where alpha is the greatest, the monthly alpha is only 0.125% (1.502% annually). It appears that FOHF managers' collective style-adjusted alpha does not come close to reaching their original targets.

## 6.2. FOHF Managers' Strategy-Allocation Capabilities

In this section, I define FOHF managers' strategy-allocation ("SA") capabilities using switching models for the seven factors and formulate it as follows:

$$SA = \{\beta_{S_t} F_{1t} + (\beta_2 F_{2t} + \cdots + \beta_7 F_{7t})\} - \{\beta_1 F_{1t} + \cdots + \beta_7 F_{7t}\}$$

This means that SA is defined as the factor return of the Markov-Switching Model minus that of the multi-regression model.

In Table 6 below, I show the SA figures in all Markov-Switching Models.

**Table 6. FOHF Managers' Strategy-Allocation Capability**

| Switching factor | Return from Beta | SA |
|---|---|---|
| U.S. equity market | 3.81% | -0.02% |
| Spread between small-cap and large- | 4.05% | 0.22% |
| Change in 10-year yields | 3.63% | -0.21% |
| Change in yield spread | 4.01% | 0.17% |
| Lookback straddle on bonds | 4.17% | 0.34% |
| Lookback straddle on currencies | 3.90% | 0.06% |
| Lookback straddle on commodities | 3.97% | 0.14% |
| No switching (Multi-regression) | 3.83% | — |

We can see that almost all SA values are positive. Especially, SA in the model of switching the state variable in look-back straddle on bonds is the largest (monthly 0.34%, annually 4.08%). However, the coefficient of determination of the model is not so high (0.57), so we can say that the confidence level of the SA is not reliable. On the other hand, SA in the model of switching the state variable in yield changes, whose coefficient of determination is the largest, is not so large (monthly 0.17%, annually 2.06%).

From the result, we can observe that FOHF managers probably switched their allocations to various strategies dynamically and generated positive, albeit small, alpha in doing so.

Based on these results, it is probable that FOHF managers have been effective in producing alpha from both selecting managers and switching allocation to strategies.

However, as I said before, the analysis merely covers FOHF indices, so I would like to clarify that I am not referring to the capability of FOHF managers itself in this article. Still, I recommend that investors and consultants considering hiring FOHF managers obtain performance data of each FOHF manager and run this type of analysis.

## 7. Conclusion

Fung and Hsieh (2004) conducted a style analysis for hedge fund managers, using seven factors—U.S. equity market returns; the spread between small-cap and large-cap equity returns; the change in 10-year Treasury yields; the change in the yield spread between 10-year T-notes and high-yield bonds; and portfolios of look-back straddles on bonds, currencies, and commodities—which were qualitatively selected from the viewpoint of profit-and-loss characteristics. However, the coefficient of determination of their model was not high enough.

Therefore, I attempted to apply a seven-factor Markov-Switching Model to the Fung and Hsieh approach (2004) to enhance the coefficient of determination by taking into consideration the unique characteristics of hedge fund managers—specifically their tendencies to switch their allocations to different strategies. But the analysis was based only on FOHF indices due to inherent biases in data on hedge-fund returns, such as the survivorship bias, the selection bias and the instant-history bias.

As a result of this, I was able to enhance the coefficient of determination in some switching models—the change in 10-year T-note yields and the change in the yield spread between 10-year T-notes and high yield bonds. From this outcome, I observed that FOHF managers have a tendency to make switches in these two factors with significant flexibility. The Markov-Switching Model is capable of capturing such shifts in strategies.

Disappointingly, the results of this analysis showed that FOHF managers' ability to select individual hedge fund managers and strategies may be falling short of their ambitious return targets.

Still, because the coefficient of determination after applying the Markov-Switching Model to FOHF managers' performance was also not satisfactory, more advanced research is required to improve the accuracy of style analysis for FOHF managers. For example, introducing additional factors to express the characteristics of hedge fund managers needs to be explored. Likewise, switching not only one factor but more than two factors in the model or applying a three-phase Markov-Switching Model might be areas of additional research.

Such efforts will be the building blocks for a systematic approach to evaluating the performance of a wide range of hedge fund managers. An increasing number of investors realize that conventional tools, such as hedge fund indices, are not enough and await an appropriate, effective means to measure their hedge fund managers' style-adjusted performance.

## References

Brown, Goetzmann, and Ibbotson. (1999). Offshore Hedge Funds: Survival and Performance Studies. *Review of Financial Studies,* 5, 91-118.

Brown, Goetzmann, and Park. (1997). Conditions for Survival: Changing Risk and the Performance of Hedge Fund Managers and CTAs. *Working Paper, NYU stern School of Business, Yale School of Management, and Long Island University.*

Ibbotson and Chen. (2005). Source of Hedge Fund Returns: Alpha, Beta, and Costs. *Working Paper, Yale School of Business.*

James D. Hamilton. (1989). A New Approach to the Economic Analysis of Nonstationary Time Series and the Business Cycle. *Econometrica,* vol. 57, no.2 (March), 357-384.

Kim, Chang-Jin, and Charles Nelson. (1999). *State-Space Models with Regime Switching: Classical and Gibbs-Sampling Approaches with Applications.* London, England: The MIT Press.

Masahiro Oda. (2001). Estimation of manager's alpha by Bayesian approach. *Securities analysts Journal*, vol.39, no.11.

Masahiro Oda. (2001). Estimation of manager's alpha. *Investigation report for The Research Institute for Policies on Pension and Aging (RIPPA), 03/2001.*

Mitchell, Mark, and Todd Pulvino. (2001). Characteristics of Risk Arbitrage. *Journal of Finance,* vol.56, no.6,(December), 2135-2176.

William F. Sharpe. (1992). Asset Allocation: Management Style and Performance Measurement. *Journal of Portfolio Management,* vol.18, no.2(Winter), 7-19.

William K. H. Fung and David A. Hsieh. (2000). Performance Characteristics of Hedge Funds and Commodity Funds: Natural Versus Spurious Biases. *Journal of Financial and Quantitative Analysis*, vol.35, no.3(September), 291-307.

William K. H. Fung and David A. Hsieh. (2001). The Risk in Hedge Fund Strategies: Theory and Evidence From Trend Followers. *Review of Financial Studies,* vol.14, no.2(Summer), 313-341.

William K. H. Fung and David A. Hsieh. (2004). Hedge Fund Benchmarks: A Risk Based Approach. *Financial Analyst Journal,* 14, 313-341.

William K. H. Fung. (2005). Theory of Alternative Investments. *17th SAAJ-CFA Institute/CFAJ Joint Seminar.*

In: The Recent Trend of Hedge Fund Strategies ISBN: 978-1-61668-338-2
Editor: Yasuaki Watanabe, pp. 157-180 

*Chapter 5*

# HEDGE FUNDS: ATTRITION, BIASES AND THE SURVIVOR PREMIUM

***Robert J. Bianchi*[*] *and Michael E. Drew***
Department of Accounting, Finance and Economics, Griffith University
Brisbane, Queensland, Australia

## Abstract

This paper examines the Lipper/TASS hedge fund database for the period 1994-2006 and we calculate hedge fund attrition, biases and the survivor premium. We estimate an attrition rate of between 9 to 10.5 per cent per year which is twice the rate reported in mutual fund studies. We measure the various hedge fund biases and we find that database returns in this sample are inflated by as much as 38 per cent. We find that the common characteristic of non-survival is chronic poor performance. Finally, we estimate the survivor premium which is the return investors receive if they are skilled or lucky enough to invest exclusively in surviving hedge funds only. After controlling for data biases, we calculate a hedge fund survivor premium of nearly 600 basis points per year, which is twice the size of those reported in mutual fund studies. Finally, we reveal that the survivor premium increases to 821, 728 and 621 basis points per year when

[*] E-mail address: r.bianchi@griffith.edu.au (Corresponding author); Tel: +61-7-3735 7078; Fax: +61-7-3735 3719; Postal address: Griffith Business School, Department of Accounting, Finance and Economics, Nathan campus, Griffith University, 170 Kessels Road, Nathan, Brisbane, Queensland, 4111, Australia. The authors would like to acknowledge and thank Hedge Fund Research (HFR), Lehman Brothers, Lipper/TASS and Morgan Stanley Commodity Index (MSCI) for the data. We also thank Martin Gruber, Madhu Veeraraghavan and Peter Whelan for helpful comments. Any remaining errors are our own.

examining funds in the Managed Futures, Global Macro and Long/Short Equity Hedge investment categories, respectively.

**Keywords**: Hedge Funds, Data Biases, Attrition, Survivorship, Investment Style

**JEL Classification**: *G11, G20, G23, G29*

# 1. Introduction

In the past, the hedge fund debate has raised the contentious issue of whether these fund managers truly provide investors with return and diversification benefits. Whilst supporters advocate that hedge funds deliver alternative investment strategies, critics argue that hedge funds provide little benefit for the high fees that they charge. One of the reasons for these polarised opinions is the large variation in the returns that are reported in global hedge fund indexes and individual hedge funds. More recently, researchers including Brown, Goetzmann and Ibbotson (1999), Edwards and Caglayan (2001), Fung and Hsieh (2000), Liang (2000, 2001) and Malkiel and Saha (2005) have identified numerous data biases that are associated in calculating accurate estimates of individual hedge funds and hedge find index returns. This paper contributes to the hedge fund debate by exploring these various data biases and their effects on estimating fund attrition, survivorship bias, backfilling and multiperiod sampling bias.

This study examines a sample of individual hedge funds from Lipper/TASS for the period 1994 to 2006 and distills important information for investors who wish to analyse and potentially invest in hedge funds. This study provides two new contributions to the hedge fund literature. First, we comprehensively examine the full range of data biases and we reveal that multiperiod sampling bias is very important when analyzing individual hedge fund returns. Multiperiod sampling bias (MSB) occurs when the researcher conditions hedge funds to exhibit a minimum amount of historical performance prior to their inclusion in an analysis. This study reveals that researchers that condition funds to exhibit a minimum performance history contaminate hedge fund returns by inducing a severe upward bias in returns which is caused by MSB. The second contribution of this study is the estimation of the hedge fund survivor premium. The survivor premium is the premium garnered by investors who are skilled or lucky enough to invest exclusively in survivors only whilst avoiding non-survivors. We reveal that the survivor premium in the global hedge fund industry is very high and has important implications for investors who engage in the activity of hedge fund manager selection.

The study provides five main findings which are of interest to hedge fund investors and researchers. First, we reveal that hedge fund data biases understate the mortality rate in the global hedge fund industry. The hedge fund mortality rate in this sample is estimated at between 9.0 to 10.5 per cent per year which is twice the size of those reported in mutual fund studies. We find that only 31 per cent of hedge funds at the start of the sample survive throughout the full sample period. Second, we find that non-survivors are strongly associated with short life-spans (i.e. mean and median of 4.25 and 3.58 years, respectively) and chronic poor performance.

Third, this study estimates survivorship bias at 271 basis points per year which is twice the size reported in mutual fund studies, and backfilling (or instant history) bias at 123 basis points per year. Fourth, we provide an incremental contribution by estimating multiperiod sampling bias across various minimum survival time periods. Multiperiod sampling bias is estimated in this sample at 18, 55 and 87 basis points per year across 12, 24 and 36 months, respectively. The biases estimated in this paper show that survivor-only database returns of 14.30 per cent per year are over-inflated by as much as 38 per cent as the reliable estimate of global hedge fund performance is estimated at 10.36 per cent per year over the 1994-2006 period.

Finally, we examine the information content of non-survivors by calculating the hedge fund survivor premium. The overall hedge fund survivor premium is estimated at 590 basis points per year and this statistically and economically significant premium is even more pronounced for investors engaged in fund manager selection in the Managed Futures, Global Macro and Long/Short Equity investment categories. We can conclude from this evidence that active manager selection in the global hedge fund industry is an important economic function for investors. The following section summarizes the body of literature that relates to hedge fund attrition, biases and the survivor premium.

## 2. Related Literature

The analysis of hedge fund attrition and biases originate from earlier works in the mutual fund literature. The first studies of mutual fund data biases and survivorship stem from Grinblatt and Titman (1989, 1992), Brown, Goetzmann, Ibbotson and Ross (1992) and Malkiel (1995). These studies demonstrated that mutual fund returns were inflated due to the exclusion of non-surviving funds in performance estimates. Subsequent studies such as Elton, Gruber and Blake (1996) demonstrated that attrition rates and survivorship in mutual funds are closely linked to poor performance, while Carpenter and Lynch (1999) showed that survivorship not only affects returns but may also affect performance persistence estimations.

Although data biases, attrition and survivorship have been considered in mutual fund studies since Grinblatt and Titman (1989), it is a relatively new area in the hedge fund literature. While some of the bias and survivorship methods can be borrowed from mutual fund studies, some unique characteristics exist in hedge fund databases which make them difficult to analyze.[1] Survivorship was one of the first hedge fund biases considered in Brown, Goetzmann and Ibbotson (1999), Fung and Hsieh (2000) and Liang (2000, 2001). Consistent with mutual fund research, hedge fund studies have revealed that survivorship bias inflates industry-wide hedge fund return estimates.[2]

The second source of bias in hedge fund database returns is backfilling (or instant history) bias which was explored in Edwards and Caglayan (2001), Edwards and Park (1996) and Fung and Hsieh (2000). This unique data bias is caused by the voluntary reporting regime in the global hedge fund industry. The voluntary nature of hedge fund reporting encourages funds to develop a performance track record in their first few months of operation prior to disclosing their performance to database vendors. If the hedge fund generates favourable returns since its inception, it will have a propensity to report its performance to database vendors in the hope of raising capital for their fund. The database vendor obtains the historical fund performance and inserts or backfills their database with these monthly returns thereby creating an instant history in the database. Alternately, a new hedge fund with poor performance will have a lower tendency to report their performance to database vendors as they have a lower probability of raising capital with poor returns. The literature informs us that this strategic behaviour in the hedge fund industry tends to create a bias in the overall estimation of hedge fund returns.

---

[1] A possible end-of-life reporting bias may exist in hedge fund returns, however, there is no data or valid methodology to comprehensively measure this form of bias.

[2] Ackermann, McEnally and Ravenscraft (1999) documents another bias which exists whereby successful funds cease reporting their results to database vendors when they have raised the capital they require and have no need to continue to report their results to anyone other than their investors. These funds that do not report imply that current disclosed returns may be partially downward biased as they do not include these successfully managed funds. Numerous examples of this include the renowned Renaissance Technologies Medallion Fund and the Global Asset Management GAMUT Fund managed by Caxton Corp who have been closed to investors and are not captured by many hedge fund database vendors.

The third type of bias in hedge fund returns is multiperiod sampling bias (MSB). While this data bias has been explored in the mutual fund literature by Carhart, Carpenter, Lynch and Musto (2002) and Carpenter and Lynch (1999), it has also been considered in hedge fund studies by Edwards and Caglayan (2001) and Fung and Hsieh (2000). MSB is a contamination caused by the researcher who imposes a minimum survival criteria (e.g. the requirement of at least 36 months of performance history) for a fund to be included in an analysis. The mutual and hedge fund literature demonstrates that this simple but subtle conditioning of the data by the researcher tends to cause survival requirements on the data which induces upward biases in mutual fund and hedge fund performance estimates.

Whilst much research attention has focused on data biases and survivorship, the recent introduction of non-survivors to empirical studies provides the researcher with new information content. One of the most recent types of information that can be extracted from the availability of defunct or non-surviving funds is the concept known as the 'survivor premium'. Blake and Timmermann (1998) coined this term to describe the difference in mean returns between an equal-weighted portfolio of survivors-only less the equal-weighted portfolio of non-survivors over the same sample period. Blake and Timmermann (1998) described the economic significance of the survivor premium as the premium that can be earned by those skilled or lucky enough to have invested in a portfolio that is exclusively composed of surviving funds only versus the performance drag of a portfolio that is exclusively composed of non-survivors.[3] This research contributes to the literature as it examines the hedge fund survivor premium for the first time.

This study proceeds to estimate fund attrition, survivorship bias, backfilling (or instant history) bias, multiperiod sampling bias (MSB) and the survivor premium. The remainder of the study is structured as follows. Section 3 introduces the data, section 4 presents the analysis of attrition, survivorship bias, instant history bias, multiperiod sampling bias and the survivor premium, while section 5 provides some concluding remarks.

## 3. Data

The database employed in the analysis was sourced from Lipper/TASS which consists of one hundred and fifty six (156) monthly return observations of both surviving and non-surviving hedge funds for the period January 1994 to December 2006. As there is no central global repository for hedge fund data, the Lipper/TASS dataset represents a sample of the global hedge fund industry. A total of 7,330 hedge funds were available for analysis, which was composed of 4,157 survivors and 3,173 non-survivors. The funds in the dataset are divided into 11 distinct investment styles as defined by Lipper/TASS.[4] The descriptive statistics of the hedge funds in the sample are presented in Table 1.

Table 1 reveals that whilst global hedge fund returns are not as strong as global stockmarkets, the volatility of the global hedge fund industry is, on average, lower than world stock returns. This translates to superior sharpe ratios for the global hedge fund industry with the exception of the Dedicated Short Bias investment category. The Jarque-Bera statistic in nearly all hedge fund investment categories rejects the null hypothesis of normality which supports the empirical fact that hedge fund returns do not exhibit normally distributed returns. The descriptive statistics in this study are consistent with similar results reported in Ackermann, McEnally and Ravenscraft (1999), Asness, Krail and Liew (2001), Brown *et. al.*, (1999) and Malkiel and Saha (2005).

---

[3] It is important to recognize that the survivor premium and survivorship bias are different calculations.

[4] These investment style categories were: Convertible Arbitrage, Dedicated Short Bias, Emerging Markets, Equity Market Neutral, Event-Driven, Fixed Income Arbitrage, Fund of Funds, Global Macro, Long/Short Equity Hedge, Managed Futures and Multistrategy.

## Table 1. Descriptive Statistics

This table presents the descriptive statistics of the sample of hedge funds. To account for survivorship bias and backfilling bias, the sample contains both survivors and non-survivors and the first twelve months of return history of each fund was removed prior to the analysis. For comparative purposes, the descriptive statistics for proxies representing world stocks, global bonds and the global hedge fund industry are also reported.. * denotes statistical significance at the 1% level.

| | Annual | | Monthly | | | | | | | |
|---|---|---|---|---|---|---|---|---|---|---|
| **Categories** | **Return** | **StdDev** | **Return** | **StdDev** | **Max** | **Min.** | **Skew.** | **Kurtosis** | **Sharpe** | **JB Stat** |
| All Funds (inc FOFs) | 9.63 | 5.48 | 0.80 | 1.58 | 6.24 | -5.32 | 0.11 | 4.44 | 0.30 | 17.10* |
| All Funds (ex FOFs) | 10.36 | 5.66 | 0.86 | 1.63 | 6.34 | -5.48 | 0.06 | 4.29 | 0.33 | 14.65* |
| Convertible Arb. | 8.50 | 4.30 | 0.71 | 1.22 | 4.05 | -4.61 | -0.71 | 4.90 | 0.32 | 16.84* |
| Dedicated Short Bias | 1.42 | 18.13 | 0.12 | 5.23 | 21.74 | -14.56 | 0.55 | 4.39 | -0.04 | 20.02* |
| Emerging Markets | 12.23 | 15.25 | 1.02 | 4.40 | 12.84 | -23.65 | -1.24 | 8.76 | 0.16 | 172.38* |
| Equity Market Neutral | 9.24 | 2.59 | 0.77 | 0.75 | 3.10 | -1.09 | 0.53 | 3.34 | 0.60 | 11.88* |
| Event Driven | 11.28 | 4.43 | 0.94 | 1.28 | 3.72 | -6.79 | -1.56 | 10.88 | 0.49 | 583.01* |
| Fixed Income Arb. | 7.13 | 3.53 | 0.59 | 1.02 | 2.83 | -5.54 | -2.30 | 13.44 | 0.27 | 2151.63* |
| Fund of Funds (FOFs) | 7.25 | 5.13 | 0.60 | 1.48 | 5.85 | -4.68 | 0.29 | 4.77 | 0.19 | 18.10* |
| Global Macro | 7.19 | 6.05 | 0.60 | 1.75 | 7.48 | -4.25 | 0.89 | 5.41 | 0.16 | 36.23* |
| Long/Short Eq. Hedge | 13.19 | 8.95 | 1.10 | 2.59 | 9.99 | -9.11 | 0.04 | 4.99 | 0.30 | 35.78* |
| Managed Futures | 8.12 | 9.54 | 0.68 | 2.76 | 7.92 | -6.19 | 0.13 | 2.74 | 0.13 | 1.31 |
| Multistrategy | 10.77 | 4.94 | 0.90 | 1.43 | 4.41 | -6.28 | -1.09 | 7.88 | 0.41 | 45.28* |
| MSCI World Eq. Idx | 9.83 | 13.45 | 0.82 | 3.88 | 9.06 | -13.32 | -0.66 | 3.84 | 0.13 | 15.13* |
| Lehman Glob.Agg. Bnd | 6.23 | 3.10 | 0.52 | 0.89 | 3.49 | -2.06 | -0.30 | 3.53 | 0.22 | 3.741 |
| HFR FOF Index | 7.58 | 5.73 | 0.63 | 1.66 | 6.85 | -7.47 | -0.25 | 7.12 | 0.19 | 107.09* |

# 4. Results

## 4.A. Attrition Rates

To fully understand the impact of non-survivors in the hedge fund industry, we must first examine the level of fund mortality. The birth and death statistics of the hedge funds in this sample are presented in Table 2. Attrition rates prior to 1994 were not analyzed as the literature informs us that database vendors commenced the archiving of hedge fund non-survivors from January 1994 onwards.[1] Any attempt to include pre-1994 data would contaminate the analysis with survivorship bias. To fully understand hedge fund data biases and their impact on attrition, Table 2 reports two sets of statistics. Panel A reports the birth and death statistics of the original dataset whilst Panel B reports identical statistics on the dataset adjusted for twelve months of backfilling bias. We adjust the birth and attrition statistics to account for backfilling bias as Malkiel and Saha (2005) have found that this data bias affects various forms of hedge fund statistics. This backfilling bias adjustment causes the commencement of each fund to be delayed which results in differing birth and death rates in each year. Panel A of Table 2 reports the mean annual attrition rate on the original dataset at 9.0 per cent per year with attrition peaking at 13.1 percent in 2006. The high levels of fund attrition is accentuated in this sample by the fact that only 248 funds (or 31 per cent) of the 802 funds reporting in January 1994 survived the full sample period.

Table 2 reports strong rate birth rates in hedge funds in the mid-1990s with the birth rate being relatively stable over time. In contrast, the attrition rates were relatively small in 1994 and have progressively increased each year. The total number of defunct funds in this sample is 43.3 per cent which equates to more than one-third of all hedge funds available in this dataset. The estimates in this study are consistent with similar results found in Fung and Hsieh (1997b), Brown *et. al.,* (1999), Liang (2000), Liang (2001) and Brown, Goetzmann and Park (2001) who calculate hedge fund attrition rates in a range from 4.3 per cent to 15 per cent per year. The different empirical results in hedge fund attrition rates can be attributed to various researchers studying different databases over various time periods.

[1] Refer to Fung and Hsieh (2000), Brown, Goetzmann and Park (2001) and Liang (2001) for literature which defines and clarifies the inherent survivorship bias problems associated with estimating pre-1994 hedge fund returns from individual hedge fund datasets.

**Table 2. Hedge Fund Birth and Death Rates**

Birth and death rates were calculated as the number of funds that were born or died during a particular calendar year divided by the number of funds in existence at the end of the previous year. The attrition rates were calculated as the number of funds that died in a particular year divided by the funds alive at the end of the previous year. NA denotes not available.

| Year | Funds born during year | Birth rate (%) | Funds dying during year | Death rate (%) | Funds alive at end of year |
|---|---|---|---|---|---|
| *Panel A: Original Data* | | | | | |
| < 1994 | NA | NA | NA | NA | 802 |
| 1994 | 267 | 33.3 | 20 | 2.5 | 1049 |
| 1995 | 312 | 29.7 | 67 | 6.4 | 1294 |
| 1996 | 355 | 27.4 | 124 | 9.6 | 1525 |
| 1997 | 379 | 24.9 | 109 | 7.1 | 1795 |
| 1998 | 381 | 21.2 | 171 | 9.5 | 2005 |
| 1999 | 470 | 23.4 | 191 | 9.5 | 2284 |
| 2000 | 484 | 21.2 | 229 | 10.0 | 2539 |
| 2001 | 637 | 25.1 | 247 | 9.7 | 2929 |
| 2002 | 663 | 22.6 | 281 | 9.6 | 3311 |
| 2003 | 788 | 23.8 | 269 | 8.1 | 3830 |
| 2004 | 889 | 23.2 | 349 | 9.1 | 4370 |
| 2005 | 638 | 14.6 | 531 | 12.2 | 4477 |
| 2006 | 265 | 5.9 | 585 | 13.1 | 4157 |
| Mean | | 22.8% | | 9.0% | |
| *Panel B: Original data adjusted for backfilling bias* | | | | | |
| < 1994 | NA | NA | NA | NA | 544 |
| 1994 | 254 | 46.7 | 16 | 2.9 | 782 |
| 1995 | 260 | 33.2 | 59 | 7.5 | 983 |
| 1996 | 306 | 31.1 | 115 | 11.7 | 1174 |
| 1997 | 344 | 29.3 | 97 | 8.3 | 1421 |
| 1998 | 367 | 25.8 | 156 | 11.0 | 1632 |
| 1999 | 363 | 22.2 | 176 | 10.8 | 1819 |
| 2000 | 458 | 25.2 | 216 | 11.9 | 2061 |
| 2001 | 464 | 22.5 | 229 | 11.1 | 2296 |
| 2002 | 619 | 27.0 | 260 | 11.3 | 2655 |
| 2003 | 650 | 24.5 | 254 | 9.6 | 3051 |
| 2004 | 765 | 25.1 | 324 | 10.6 | 3492 |
| 2005 | 857 | 24.5 | 493 | 14.1 | 3856 |
| 2006 | 584 | 15.1 | 568 | 14.7 | 3872 |
| Mean | | 27.1% | | 10.4% | |

Panel B of Table 2 reports attrition rates adjusted for backfilling bias. Panel B reveals that the attrition rate rises to 10.4 per cent per year. As stated in Malkiel and Saha (2005), backfilling bias may affect various forms of hedge fund statistics and this analysis indicates that attrition rates in previous studies may be understated if backfilling bias has not been accounted for.

A closer examination of the 3,173 non-surviving funds in the sample shows that their mean and median life spans are, on average, 51 months ( ie. 4.3 years) and 43 months (ie. 3.6 years), respectively. When survivors are included with non-survivors, the average and median life span of all hedge funds in the sample increases to 57 months (i.e. 4.8 years) and 46 months (i.e. 3.8 years), respectively. These estimates of very short life-spans of hedge funds are consistent with earlier studies by Edwards and Caglayan (2001a) and Brown *et. al.*, (2001).

In order to appreciate hedge fund attrition rates, a comparison can be made with the mutual fund industry. The Lunde, Timmermann and Blake (1999) study finds that 70 per cent of UK mutual funds die within 3 to 15 years and the annual attrition rate is 4.56 per cent per annum. In another study, Carhart, Carpenter, Lynch and Musto (2002) estimate US mutual fund attrition at no more than 3.6 per cent per year. In this hedge fund study, we find that 70 per cent of hedge funds die within 63 months (i.e. 5.3 years) and the annual attrition rate is between 9.0 and 10.4 per cent per annum. The evidence suggests that hedge funds have relatively short life-spans and hedge fund attrition rates are more than twice the levels of those reported in mutual fund studies.

A feature of the hedge fund industry is its voluntary reporting regime which tends to produce varying estimates of hedge fund attrition rates from various hedge fund databases. By construction, hedge fund attrition rates are a function of the proportion of non-survivors included in the database. For example, Liang (2000) researched two hedge fund databases and reported that 9.5 per cent of the HFR dataset were non-survivors, while the TASS dataset contained 26.2 per cent of non-survivors. In this study, 43.3 per cent of all funds in the Lipper/TASS dataset are non-survivors.

The high attrition rates in this sample reflect the high proportion of defunct funds that are included in this study. It is clear that non-survivors have a significant effect on the level of data biases in this sample. The significant number of non-survivors terminating over the full 1994-2006 period suggests that hedge fund research that excludes non-survivors will lead to empirical results that are spurious and misleading. The inclusion of non-survivors leads us to consider survivorship bias in hedge fund returns.

## 4.B. Survivorship Bias

The survivorship bias calculation in this study is identical to Malkiel (1995), Brown *et. al.*, (1999), Fung and Hsieh (2000) and Liang (2000, 2001) and is expressed as:

$$\frac{1}{T}\sum_{t}(r_{s,t}-r_{b,t})=\frac{1}{T}\sum_{t}\left[\left(r_{s,t}-\frac{n_{n,t}r_{n,t}+n_{s,t}r_{s,t}}{n_{n,t}+n_{s,t}}\right)\right] \tag{1}$$

where

$r_{s,t}$ = the return in period $t$ on the equal-weighted portfolio of surviving funds;

$r_{n,t}$ = the return in period $t$ on the equal-weighted portfolio of non-surviving funds;

$r_{b,t}$ = the return in period $t$ of the equal-weighted portfolio of both the surviving funds and non-surviving funds;

$n_{s,t}$ = the number of funds at time $t$ that survived before the end of the sample period, respectively; and,

$n_{n,t}$ =the number of funds at time $t$ that died before the end of the sample period.

Survivorship bias in hedge fund returns has been extensively recognized in Brown, Goetzmann and Ibbotson (1999), Fung and Hsieh (2000) and Liang (2000, 2001) and they follow the Malkiel (1995) methodology in defining this bias. Table 3 presents the survivorship bias estimates on this hedge fund sample and summarizes the return and volatility estimates of the full sample and across investment styles.[2] For the moment we shall focus on the category in Table 3 known as "All Funds (ex FOFs)" which excludes fund of funds as they invest their funds in individual hedge funds. The results presented in Table 3 show that

[2] It is important to recognise that the TASS classification categories are specific to TASS themselves. Other hedge fund data vendors categorise the hedge fund industry using other categories and classifications. For example, HFR Research divides the hedge fund industry into:- Convertible Arbitrage, Distressed Securities, Emerging Markets, Equity Hedge, Event Driven, Fixed Income, Fund of Funds, Macro, Merger Arbitrage, Relative Value Arbitrage, and Sector. As a second example, the VAN Hedge Fund Advisors classify funds into: Aggressive Growth, Distressed Securities, Emerging Markets, Fund of Funds, Income, Macro, Market Neutral – Arbitrage, Market Neutral – Securities Hedging, Market Timing Opportunistic, Several Strategies, Short Selling, Special Situations, and Value. We can see that each hedge fund data vendor has their own investment style classification system.

survivors-only generated an annual rate of return of 14.30 per cent while the dataset containing both survivors and non-survivors generated an annual return of 11.59 per cent. These calculations produce an estimated survivorship bias in this sample of 271 basis points per year. This estimate of survivorship bias is consistent with the findings in Brown *et. al.,* (1999), Fung and Hsieh (2000) and Liang (2001) who estimated survivorship bias in the global hedge fund industry at 300, 300 and 243 basis points per year, respectively.

**Table 3. Survivorship Bias Estimates**

The table presents the return and volatility estimates of the sample of all funds versus the same sample consisting of survivors only. Survivorship bias is calculated as the portfolio return of survivors only minus the portfolio return of all funds. The sample period is from January 1994 to December 2006. Ann. ROR denotes annualized rate of return. Ann. S.D. denotes annualized standard deviation. Survivor Bias denotes the bias between survivors only and the full sample of all funds. Bias S.E. denotes the standard error mean of the survivorship bias.

| | **All Funds** | | **Survivors** | | **Survivorship Bias** | |
|---|---|---|---|---|---|---|
| | **Ann. ROR (%)** | **Ann. S.D. (%)** | **Ann. ROR (%)** | **Ann. S.D. (%)** | **Ann. Bias (%)** | **Ann. S.E. (%)** |
| All Funds (inc FOFs) | 10.66 | 5.40 | 12.86 | 5.20 | 2.19 | 0.91 |
| All Funds (ex FOFs) | 11.59 | 5.59 | 14.30 | 5.41 | 2.71 | 1.05 |
| Convertible Arb. | 10.67 | 5.40 | 11.04 | 4.37 | 0.37 | 4.32 |
| Dedicated Short Bias | 2.01 | 17.90 | 3.36 | 21.43 | 3.05 | 12.74 |
| Emerging Markets | 13.69 | 14.65 | 17.90 | 16.94 | 4.21 | 3.93 |
| Equity Market Neutral | 10.42 | 2.53 | 12.19 | 2.76 | 1.78 | 1.49 |
| Event Driven | 12.07 | 4.41 | 12.92 | 4.14 | 0.85 | 0.99 |
| Fixed Income Arb. | 8.56 | 3.35 | 10.97 | 3.52 | 4.61 | 2.63 |
| Fund of Funds(FOFs) | 7.59 | 4.98 | 8.83 | 4.85 | 1.25 | 1.21 |
| Global Macro | 7.92 | 5.65 | 12.02 | 5.25 | 4.09 | 2.90 |
| Long/Short Eq. Hedge | 14.99 | 8.89 | 16.81 | 8.14 | 1.82 | 1.68 |
| Managed Futures | 8.54 | 9.33 | 12.76 | 12.20 | 4.22 | 4.02 |
| Multistrategy | 11.70 | 4.45 | 12.57 | 3.94 | 0.87 | 2.14 |

In order to appreciate the magnitude of survivorship bias in hedge fund returns, a comparison can be made with the traditional mutual fund industry. Brown and Goetzmann (1995), Malkiel (1995), Elton, Gruber and Blake (1996) and Carhart, Carpenter, Lynch and Musto (2002) estimate survivorship bias in mutual funds at 20 to 140 basis points per year. When one considers that the hedge fund literature has estimated survivorship bias in a range between 16 to 301 basis points per year, the evidence suggests that hedge fund survivorship bias is twice the size than those reported in mutual fund studies.[3] These results demonstrate that excluding non-survivors in a hedge fund analysis will result in inflated industry-wide hedge fund return estimates.

## 4.C. Backfilling (or Instant History Bias) Bias

The second bias calculated on this dataset is backfilling bias which employs the same methodology in Edwards and Caglayan (2001) and Fung and Hsieh (2000) which is expressed as:

$$\frac{1}{T}\sum_{t}(r_{b,t}-r_{b,t|t>12})=\frac{1}{T}\sum_{t}\left[\left(\frac{n_{n,t}r_{n,t}+n_{s,t}r_{s,t}}{n_{n,t}+n_{s,t}}\right)-\left(\frac{n_{n,t|t>12}r_{n,t|t>12}+n_{s,t|t>12}r_{s,t|t>12}}{n_{n,t|t>12}+n_{s,t|t>12}}\right)\right] \quad (2)$$

where

$r_{b,t|t>12}=$ the return in period $t$ of the equal weighted portfolio of both the surviving funds and non-surviving funds excluding the first twelve months of every fund's performance history.

$r_{s,t|t>12}=$ the return in period $t$ on the equal-weighted portfolio of surviving funds excluding the first twelve months of every fund's performance history;

$r_{n,t|t>12}=$ the return in period $t$ on the equal-weighted portfolio of non-surviving funds excluding the first twelve months of every fund's performance history;

$n_{s,t|t>12}=$ the number of funds at time $t$ that survived before the end of the sample period excluding the first twelve months of every fund's performance history; and,

$n_{n,t|t>12}=$ the number of funds at time $t$ that died before the end of the sample period excluding the first twelve months of every fund's performance history.

---

[3] While Brown et. al., (1999), Fung and Hsieh (2000) and Liang (2001) reported annual hedge fund survivorship bias estimates of 3.00, 3.00 and 2.43 per cent, respectively, the work of Ackermann et al., (1999) reported an unusually low annual hedge fund survivorship bias at 0.16 per cent, however, their research methodology has been extensively critiqued in the subsequent hedge fund literature.

### Table 4. Backfilling (or Instant History) Bias Estimates

The table presents the return and volatility estimates of the sample of all funds adjusted for backfilling bias versus the original sample of all funds. Backfilling bias has been adjusted in the sample by excluding the first twelve months of performance history from every fund. Backfilling bias is therefore the difference between these two portfolio returns. The sample period is from January 1994 to December 2006. Ann. ROR denotes annualized rate of return. Ann. S.D. denotes annualized standard deviation. Backfilling Bias denotes the bias between a sample of all funds with the first twelve months of performance history excluded and the original full sample of all funds. Ann. S.E. denotes the standard error of the backfilling bias.

| | All Funds – Backfill Adj. Survivors and Non-survivors | | All Funds – Original Data Survivors and Non-survivors | | Backfilling Bias | |
|---|---|---|---|---|---|---|
| | Ann. ROR (%) | Ann. S.D. (%) | Ann. ROR (%) | Ann. S.D. (%) | Ann. Bias (%) | Ann. S.E. (%) |
| All Funds (inc FOFs) | 9.63 | 5.48 | 10.66 | 5.40 | 1.03 | 0.40 |
| All Funds (ex FOFs) | 10.36 | 5.66 | 11.59 | 5.59 | 1.23 | 0.43 |
| Convertible Arb. | 8.50 | 4.30 | 10.67 | 5.40 | 2.17 | 4.03 |
| Dedicated Short Bias | 1.42 | 18.10 | 2.01 | 17.90 | 0.59 | 1.51 |
| Emerging Markets | 12.23 | 15.30 | 13.69 | 14.65 | 1.46 | 1.45 |
| Equity Market Neutral | 9.24 | 2.59 | 10.42 | 2.53 | 1.18 | 1.16 |
| Event Driven | 11.28 | 4.43 | 12.07 | 4.41 | 0.79 | 0.44 |
| Fixed Income Arb. | 7.13 | 3.53 | 8.56 | 3.35 | 1.43 | 0.87 |
| Fund of Funds (FOFs) | 7.25 | 5.13 | 7.59 | 4.98 | 0.34 | 0.38 |
| Global Macro | 7.19 | 6.05 | 7.92 | 5.65 | 0.73 | 1.13 |
| Long/Short Eq. Hedge | 13.19 | 8.95 | 14.99 | 8.89 | 1.80 | 0.67 |
| Managed Futures | 8.12 | 9.54 | 8.54 | 9.33 | 0.42 | 0.70 |
| Multistrategy | 10.77 | 4.94 | 11.70 | 4.45 | 0.93 | 1.44 |

Similar to Edwards and Caglayan (2001), Fung and Hsieh (2000) and Kosowski, Naik and Teo (2007), this study adjusts for backfilling bias by excluding the first twelve months of performance history from every fund.[4] The effects of backfilling bias in this study are reported in Table 4. This study contributes to the literature by providing the hedge fund performance histories on the full sample, survivors and non-survivors across their relevant investment styles.

[4] Fung and Hsieh (2000) and Brown, Goetzmann and Park (2001) estimate a fund incubation period of 15 months prior to funds appearing on hedge fund databases. Given this finding, Fung and Hsieh (2000) remove the first twelve months of performance history in order to estimate backfilling bias.

The results in Table 4 estimate the backfilling bias on the full sample at 123 basis points per year (i.e. 11.59 per cent minus 10.36 per cent in Table 4) from 1994 to 2006. This estimate is consistent with previous backfilling bias estimates from Edwards and Caglayan (2001) and Fung and Hsieh (2000) of 117 and 140 basis points per year, respectively. The results in Table 4 show that backfilling bias occurs on the full sample and across all investment styles. The estimates of backfilling bias in Table 4 in comparison to Table 3 are significant as they show that across all investment styles, the backfilling bias adjustment reduces the annual rates of return for all funds and investment styles.

The results of Table 4 support the fact that hedge fund returns, on average, permeate an upward bias due to the inclusion of the first twelve months of a hedge fund's performance record. This is further evidence of the importance of the data collection process when conducting hedge fund research, as backfilling bias inflates hedge fund returns due to the voluntary reporting regime inherent in the global hedge fund industry.

## 4.D. Multiperiod Sampling Bias

The third bias estimated in this study is multiperiod sampling bias (MSB). As there are no generally accepted methods to calculate MSB, this study employs the same methodology as Edwards and Caglayan (2001) and Fung and Hsieh (2000) which is expressed as:

$$\frac{1}{T}\sum_t (r_{b,t|t>12+i} - r_{b,t|t>12}) = \frac{1}{T}\sum_t \left[\left(\frac{n_{n,t|t>12+i} r_{n,t|t>12+i} + n_{s,t|t>12+i} r_{s,t|t>12+i}}{n_{n,t|t>12+i} + n_{s,t|t>12+i}}\right) - \left(\frac{n_{n,t|t>12} r_{n,t|t>12} + n_{s,t|t>12} r_{s,t|t>12}}{n_{n,t|t>12} + n_{s,t|t>12}}\right)\right] \quad (3)$$

where

$r_{b,t|t>12+i}$ = the return in period $t$ of the equal-weighted portfolio of both the surviving funds and non-surviving funds excluding the first twelve plus $i$ months of every fund's performance history, $i$ equals twelve, twenty-four or thirty-six months;

$r_{s,t|t>12+i}$ = the return in period $t$ on the equal-weighted portfolio of surviving funds excluding the first $i$ months of every fund's performance history;

$r_{n,t|t>12+i}$ = the return in period $t$ on the equal-weighted portfolio of non-surviving funds excluding the first $i$ months of every fund's performance history;

$n_{s,t|t>12+i}$ = the number of funds at time $t$ that survived before the end of the sample period excluding the first $i$ months of every fund's performance history; and,

$n_{n,t|t>12+i}$ = the number of funds at time $t$ that died before the end of the sample period excluding the first $i$ months of every fund's performance history.

MSB is an important issue in empirical research, yet it receives little attention. This study contributes to the literature by estimating the impact of various MSB on both returns, volatility and across investment styles. The measurement of MSB compares the results of the adjusted dataset against the same data conditional upon funds requiring at least 12, 24 and 36 months of performance history, respectively. The estimates of MSB are presented in Table 5.

The results in Panel A of Table 5 show the return and volatility estimates that are adjusted for survivorship and backfilling bias. To estimate MSB, the returns in Panel A are re-calculated with the condition that each hedge fund must exhibit a minimum performance history of 12, 24 and 36 months which are presented in Panels B, C and D, respectively.

Table 5 shows that MSB inflates industry-wide hedge fund returns when funds are conditioned to exhibit longer performance history. That is, as $i$ increases in Equation (3), MSB increases also. In Panel B of Table 5, MSB is estimated at 0.18 per cent per annum (i.e. 10.36 per cent in Panel A versus 10.54 per cent in Panel B). This upward bias is caused by the conditioning of funds to exhibit at least 12 months of performance history. When the minimum performance history requirement is increased from 12 to 24 months, the results presented in Panel C of Table 5 estimate the 24 month MSB on the full sample at 0.55 per cent per annum (i.e. 10.36 per cent in Panel A versus 10.91 per cent in Panel C). This result is slightly higher than the Edwards and Caglayan (2001) estimate of 0.32 percent per annum. Finally, the 36 month MSB estimate in Panel D is calculated at 0.87 per cent per annum (i.e. 10.36 per cent in Panel A versus 11.23 per cent in Panel D). The 36 month MSB reports an upward bias on the full sample and across all investment styles. The evidence of MSB is present in the entire sample and in all investment styles. This result is consistent with Fung and Hsieh (2000) who estimated a 36 month MSB of 0.60 per cent per annum.

Table 5 reveals new findings on the effects of MSB on survivors and non-survivors. The survivors in the sample from Panels A to D are unaffected by MSB as the requirement for a performance history lengthens. Conversely, MSB causes non-survivor returns to be markedly different. As the required performance history lengthens, the non-survivor portfolio returns increase from 7.22 to 8.31 per cent per year. Put simply, MSB causes an upward bias in non-survivor returns.

### Table 5. Multiperiod Sampling Bias Estimates

This table reports multiperiod sampling bias (MSB) on annual returns and standard deviation estimates on the full sample and across investment styles. Ann. ROR denotes annualized rate of return. Ann. S.D. denotes annualized standard deviation. Ratio denotes annualized rate of return divided by annualized standard deviation. MB Bias denotes the multiperiod sampling bias. Panel A reports survivors and non-survivors adjusted for survivorship and backfilling bias. Panel B presents the Panel A data conditioned with funds that exhibit at least 12 months of performance history. Panel C reports Panel A data conditioned with funds that exhibit at least 24 months of performance history. Panel D presents Panel A data conditioned with funds that exhibit at least 36 months of performance history.

| Categories | *Panel A:* | | | | *Panel B:* | | | |
|---|---|---|---|---|---|---|---|---|
| | **Ann. ROR (%)** | **Ann. S.D. (%)** | **Ratio** | **MS Bias (%)** | **Ann. ROR (%)** | **Ann. S.D. (%)** | **Ratio** | **MS Bias (%)** |
| All Funds (inc FOFs) | 9.63 | 5.48 | 1.76 | --- | 9.77 | 5.48 | 1.78 | 0.14 |
| All Funds (ex FOFs) | 10.36 | 5.66 | 1.83 | --- | 10.54 | 5.66 | 1.86 | 0.18 |
| Convertible Arb. | 8.50 | 4.30 | 1.98 | --- | 8.53 | 4.31 | 1.98 | 0.03 |
| Dedicated Short Bias | 1.42 | 18.13 | 0.08 | --- | 1.46 | 28.32 | 0.05 | 0.04 |
| Emerging Markets | 12.23 | 15.25 | 0.80 | --- | 12.25 | 15.25 | 0.80 | 0.02 |
| Equity Market Neutral | 9.24 | 2.59 | 3.57 | --- | 9.38 | 2.60 | 3.61 | 0.14 |
| Event Driven | 11.28 | 4.43 | 2.55 | --- | 11.32 | 4.42 | 2.56 | 0.04 |
| Fixed Income Arb. | 7.13 | 3.53 | 2.02 | -- | 7.21 | 3.57 | 2.02 | 0.08 |
| Fund of Funds (FOFs) | 7.25 | 5.13 | 1.41 | --- | 7.31 | 5.13 | 1.42 | 0.06 |
| Global Macro | 7.19 | 6.05 | 1.19 | --- | 7.46 | 6.10 | 1.22 | 0.27 |
| Long/Short Eq. Hedge | 13.19 | 8.95 | 1.47 | --- | 13.32 | 8.93 | 1.49 | 0.13 |
| Managed Futures | 8.12 | 9.54 | 0.85 | --- | 8.47 | 9.62 | 0.88 | 0.35 |
| Multistrategy | 10.77 | 4.94 | 2.18 | --- | 10.89 | 4.84 | 2.25 | 0.12 |
| | | | | | | | | |
| Survivors (inc FOF) | 11.99 | 5.29 | 2.27 | --- | 11.99 | 5.29 | 2.27 | 0.00 |
| Non-survivors (inc FOF) | 6.72 | 5.80 | 1.16 | --- | 6.99 | 5.78 | 1.21 | 0.27 |
| | | | | | | | | |
| Survivors (ex FOF) | 13.12 | 5.47 | 2.40 | --- | 13.12 | 5.48 | 2.39 | 0.00 |
| Non-survivors (ex FOF) | 7.22 | 6.00 | 1.20 | --- | 7.54 | 5.99 | 1.26 | 0.32 |

**Table 5. Continued**

| Categories | Panel C: Ann. ROR (%) | Ann. S.D. (%) | Ratio | MS Bias (%) | Panel D: Ann. ROR (%) | Ann. S.D. (%) | Ratio | MS Bias (%) |
|---|---|---|---|---|---|---|---|---|
| All Funds (inc FOFs) | 10.10 | 5.49 | 1.84 | 0.47 | 10.39 | 5.55 | 1.87 | 0.76 |
| All Funds (ex FOFs) | 10.91 | 5.69 | 1.92 | 0.55 | 11.23 | 5.70 | 1.97 | 0.87 |
| Convertible Arb. | 8.82 | 4.35 | 2.03 | 0.32 | 8.72 | 4.32 | 2.02 | 0.22 |
| Dedicated Short Bias | 1.53 | 18.31 | 0.08 | 0.11 | 1.62 | 18.35 | 0.09 | 0.20 |
| Emerging Markets | 12.25 | 15.25 | 0.80 | 0.02 | 12.77 | 15.17 | 0.84 | 0.54 |
| Equity Market Neutral | 9.60 | 2.63 | 3.65 | 0.36 | 9.67 | 2.63 | 3.68 | 0.43 |
| Event Driven | 11.38 | 4.38 | 2.60 | 0.10 | 11.49 | 4.39 | 2.62 | 0.21 |
| Fixed Income Arb. | 7.37 | 3.60 | 2.05 | 0.24 | 7.48 | 3.69 | 2.03 | 0.35 |
| Fund of Funds (FOFs) | 7.48 | 5.11 | 1.46 | 0.23 | 7.68 | 5.09 | 1.51 | 0.43 |
| Global Macro | 8.11 | 6.09 | 1.33 | 0.92 | 8.60 | 6.31 | 1.36 | 1.41 |
| Long/Short Eq. Hedge | 13.69 | 8.88 | 1.54 | 0.50 | 14.14 | 8.93 | 1.58 | 0.95 |
| Managed Futures | 8.65 | 9.81 | 0.88 | 0.53 | 9.03 | 10.15 | 0.89 | 0.91 |
| Multistrategy | 11.29 | 4.75 | 2.38 | 0.52 | 12.06 | 4.50 | 2.68 | 1.29 |
| | | | | | | | | |
| Survivors (inc FOF) | 11.99 | 5.30 | 2.26 | 0.00 | 12.00 | 5.31 | 2.26 | 0.01 |
| Non-survivors (inc FOF) | 7.35 | 5.83 | 1.26 | 0.63 | 7.72 | 5.88 | 1.31 | 1.00 |
| | | | | | | | | |
| Survivors (ex FOF) | 13.12 | 5.48 | 2.39 | 0.00 | 13.12 | 5.51 | 2.38 | 0.00 |
| Non-survivors (ex FOF) | 7.93 | 6.04 | 1.31 | 0.71 | 8.31 | 6.11 | 1.36 | 1.09 |

The findings in Table 5 present new insights on the survival conditioning of hedge fund returns. As the minimum performance history requirement lengthens, the MSB effect provides a small but favourable impact on the return/standard deviation ratio in all categories. However, the estimates suggest that MSB effects are smaller than survivorship and backfilling biases. The results in Table 5 also demonstrate that researchers who impose a minimum performance history on hedge fund track records are inadvertently creating an upward bias in hedge fund return estimates.

The short life spans and chronic poor performance of non-survivors can explain the MSB effects on non-survivor returns. Hedge fund non-survivors exhibit high attrition rates which are reflected in their short life-spans. MSB imposes minimum performance history on funds which unintentionally excludes many non-survivors in the analysis which re-contaminates survivorship bias in the data. The return estimates of non-survivors in Table 3 clearly show that non-survivors exhibit chronic poor performance. By conditioning on a minimum performance history, non-survivors that exhibit short life spans and poor performance are excluded in the analysis.

## Table 6. Hedge Fund Survivor Premium

The table presents the Hedge Fund Survivor Premium which equates to the difference in returns between an equal weighted portfolio of survivors only versus non-survivors only. The data presented in this table has already been adjusted for backfilling bias with the exclusion of the first twelve of performance history for every fund. The results are for the period January 1994 to December 2006. Ann. ROR denotes annualized rate of return. Ann. S.D. denotes annualized standard deviation. Ann. S.E. denotes the standard error of the survivor premium. The T-test presents the parametric two-tailed test for equality of means. The Wilcoxon is the nonparametric Wilcoxon Signed Ranks two-tailed test for equality of medians. The F-test represents the two-tailed test for equality of variances. * and ** denote statistical significance at the 5% and 1% levels, respectively.

| | Backfill Adj. Survivors only | | Backfill Adj. Non-survivors only | | Survivor Premium | | Equality Tests | | |
|---|---|---|---|---|---|---|---|---|---|
| | Ann. ROR (%) | Ann. S.D. (%) | Ann. ROR (%) | Ann. S.D. (%) | Ann. Premium (%) | Ann. S.E. (%) | T-test | Wilcoxon | F-test |
| All Funds (inc FOFs) | 11.99 | 5.29 | 6.72 | 5.80 | 5.27 | 1.76 | 2.42* | 2.55* | 1.20 |
| All Funds (ex FOFs) | 13.12 | 5.47 | 7.22 | 6.00 | 5.90 | 2.00 | 2.62** | 2.74** | 1.20 |
| Convertible Arb. | 10.23 | 4.72 | 6.54 | 4.23 | 3.69 | 2.78 | 2.10* | 2.04* | 1.24 |
| Dedicated Short Bias | 2.95 | 22.56 | 0.47 | 16.16 | 2.52 | 15.00 | 0.43 | 0.44 | 2.05** |
| Emerging Markets | 14.76 | 17.18 | 10.46 | 15.10 | 4.37 | 6.32 | 0.65 | 0.93 | 1.30 |
| Equity Market Neutral | 11.11 | 2.66 | 7.38 | 3.37 | 3.75 | 3.03 | 3.13** | 3.37** | 1.59** |
| Event Driven | 12.15 | 4.15 | 9.75 | 5.09 | 2.41 | 2.43 | 1.32 | 1.68 | 1.50** |
| Fixed Income Arb. | 9.36 | 3.32 | 4.92 | 4.07 | 4.43 | 3.17 | 3.05** | 3.71** | 1.51** |
| Fund of Funds (i.e. FOFs) | 8.84 | 5.03 | 4.96 | 5.41 | 3.87 | 2.36 | 1.89 | 2.22* | 1.16 |
| Global Macro | 11.44 | 5.40 | 4.16 | 6.64 | 7.28 | 4.25 | 3.07** | 3.50** | 1.51** |
| Long/Short Eq. Hedge | 15.21 | 8.21 | 10.00 | 9.82 | 5.22 | 3.33 | 1.47 | 1.64 | 1.43* |
| Managed Futures | 12.61 | 12.41 | 4.40 | 7.81 | 8.21 | 6.11 | 2.02* | 1.62 | 2.53** |
| Multistrategy | 11.93 | 4.20 | 8.94 | 7.72 | 2.99 | 6.21 | 1.23 | 1.42 | 3.39** |

This suggests that MSB can be avoided by engaging in hedge fund analysis with analytical techniques that do not condition on survival. Studies such as Kowoski, Naik and Teo (2007) suggest Bayesian statistics suit hedge fund studies that are inherently constrained by limited data. The MSB in this study suggests that hedge fund research which conditions on survival may be over-estimating industry-wide returns by 18 to 87 basis points per annum.

## 4e. Survivor Premium

The final analysis of this study examines the global hedge fund survivor premium. The estimation of the survivor premium highlights the difference in returns between survivors versus non-survivors. The survivor premium can be defined as the premium garnered by exclusively investing in survivors-only versus avoiding non-survivors. The calculation of the survivor premium follows Blake and Timmermann (1998) and can be expressed as:

$$\text{survivor premium} \equiv \text{survivor bias} + \text{nonsurvivor bias}$$

or

$$\frac{1}{T}\sum_t (r_{s,t} - r_{n,t}) = \frac{1}{T}\sum_t \left[ \left( r_{s,t} - \frac{n_{n,t}r_{n,t} + n_{s,t}r_{s,t}}{n_{n,t} + n_{s,t}} \right) + \left( \frac{n_{n,t}r_{n,t} + n_{s,t}r_{s,t}}{n_{n,t} + n_{s,t}} - r_{n,t} \right) \right] \tag{4}$$

where

$r_{s,t}$ = the return in period $t$ on the equal-weighted portfolio of surviving funds;

$r_{n,t}$ = the return in period $t$ on the equal-weighted portfolio of non-surviving funds;

$n_{s,t}$ = the number of funds at time $t$ that survived before the end of the sample period; and,

$n_{n,t}$ = the number of funds at time $t$ that died before the end of the sample period.

Table 6 presents the information required to estimate the hedge fund survivor premium. Table 6 reveals that an equal-weighted portfolio of survivors-only generated a return of 13.12 per cent per year while an equal-weighted portfolio of non-survivors generated a return of 7.22 per cent per year, resulting in a survivor premium of 590 basis points per year. It is clear that the difference in mean returns between these two portfolios is an economically significant benefit to be garnered by investors. The equality tests in Table 6 for All Funds suggest that the differences in mean and median returns between survivor and non-survivor portfolios are statistically significant. Conversely, the equality tests for variance indicate that the volatility of returns between these two groups are similar. These findings on the full sample are supported by identical results reported in the Fund of Funds investment category which is regarded in the literature as a realistic proxy for global hedge fund returns.

Table 6 also reveals significant economic benefits to be garnered when selecting fund managers within investment styles. Table 6 reports significant survivor premiums of 821, 728 and 522 basis points per year in the Managed Futures, Global Macro and Long/Short Equity Hedge investment categories, respectively. Whilst these survivor premiums are large and economically significant, the equality tests in Table 6 indicate that some of these are not statistically significant.

The estimation of the survivor premium contributes to the literature as it is the first study to explicitly calculate the survivor premium and its significance in the global hedge fund industry. In short, there is economic and statistical evidence to justify the investment activity of active manager selection when constructing a diversified portfolio of hedge funds. There is significant economic benefits to be gained by seeking out funds that are likely to survive whilst avoiding the selection of non-survivors in a diversified hedge fund portfolio.

To understand the nature of the survivor premium, Figure 1 presents the monthly time series for the 'All Funds (ex FOF)' category for the 1994-2006 period. Whilst Table 6 implies a mean monthly survivor premium of 49 basis points per month, Figure 1 illustrates the variation in the returns of the survivor premium over time. The largest positive monthly survivor premium occurred in February 2001 when a premium of 235 basis points was garnered. Conversely, the largest negative monthly survivor premium was recorded in February 2000 with a loss of -107 basis points. It is clear that the greatest variation in the hedge fund survivor premium occurred in 2000 and 2001 where luck or skill in selecting exclusively survivors would have resulted in substantial benefits to investors.

In order to appreciate the magnitude of the hedge fund survivor premium, we can compare it directly with three mutual fund studies. Blake and Timmerman (1998) estimate the survivor premium on the UK mutual fund industry at 240 basis points per year, while Drew and Stanford (2001) estimate a survivor premium of 281 basis points per year on the Australian pension fund industry. In a US study, Carhart, Carpenter, Lynch and Musto (2002) estimate an implied survivor premium of 4 per cent per year.

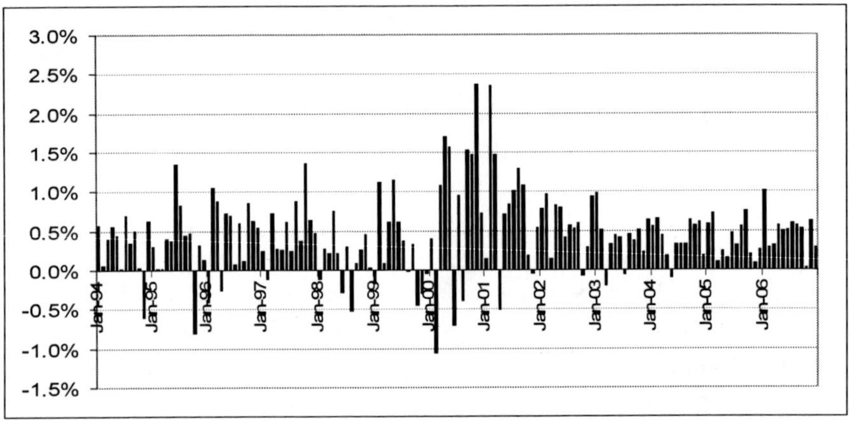


Figure 1. Hedge Fund Survivor Premium (All Funds (ex FOFs)) for the period 1994-2006.

The hedge fund survivor premium of 590 basis points per year in this study is of the magnitude of 1.4 to 2 times the size of the survivor premiums reported in the mutual fund industry. The survivor premium is an important concept which suggests that significant investment return can be garnered by selecting surviving funds and avoiding non-survivors when making hedge fund investment decisions.

## 5. Conclusion

The evidence presented in this study suggests that data biases can be significant and problematic if appropriate methods are not properly considered in hedge fund research. The empirical findings in this study demonstrate that hedge funds have high attrition rates which are nearly twice the rates reported in mutual fund studies. This high level of attrition causes the average life-span of hedge funds to be shorter than those of mutual funds. This study shows that the key characteristic of non-survivors is chronic poor performance. These characteristics raise the profile of non-survivors as important contributors to any rigourous hedge fund analysis.

The importance of non-survivors is further supported by the survivorship bias estimated at 271 basis points per year. This level of survivorship bias is twice as high as those reported in mutual fund studies. This paper also estimated the backfilling bias at 123 basis points per year and the various impacts of multiperiod sampling bias at 18 to 87 basis points per year. The evidence shows that hedge fund returns become inflated when they are conditioned to exhibit a performance history. When hedge fund returns are adjusted for these biases, we find that survivor-only returns are inflated by as much as 38 per cent.

Finally, the evidence informs us that investors with the ability to exclusively invest in survivors whilst avoiding non-survivors are likely to garner a significant hedge fund survivor premium. This finding is pivotal to investors wishing to construct hedge fund investment portfolios. It is evident from this study that chronic poor performance is a key characteristic of non-survivors. The avenues for future research should concentrate on the identification of conditioning variables to assist in predicting hedge fund survival.

## References


Ackermann, C., McEnally, R. and Ravenscraft, D. (1999). The Performance of hedge Funds: Risk, Return, and Incentives. *Journal of Finance.* **54**, 833-874.

Asness, C., Krail, R. and Liew. J. (2001). Do Hedge Funds Hedge?. *Journal of Portfolio Management.* **28**, 6-19.

Blake, D. and Timmermann, A. (1998). Mutual Fund Performance: Evidence from the UK. *European Finance Review.* **2**, 57-77.

Brown, S. and Goetzmann, W. (1995). Performance persistence. *Journal of Finance.* **50**, 679-698.

Brown, S., Goetzmann, W. and Ibbotson, R. (1999). Offshore Hedge Funds: Survival and Performance, 1989-95. *Journal of Business.* **72**, 91-117.

Brown, S., Goetzmann, W., Ibbotson, R. and Ross, S. (1992). Survivorship Bias in Performance Studies. *Review of Financial Studies.* **5**, 553-580.

Brown, S., Goetzmann, W. and Park, J. (2001). Careers and Survival: Competition and Risk in the Hedge Fund and CTA industry. *Journal of Finance.* **56**, 1869-1886.

Carhart, M., Carpenter, J., Lynch, A. and Musto, D. (2002). Mutual fund survivorship. *Review of Financial Studies.* **15**, 1439-1463.

Carpenter, J. and Lynch, A. (1999). Survivorship bias and attrition effects in measures of performance persistence. *Journal of Financial Economics.* **54**, 337-374.

Drew, M. and Stanford, J. (2001). The impact of fund attrition on superannuation returns. *Economic Analysis and Policy.* **31**, 25-32.

Edwards, F. and Caglayan, M. (2001). Hedge Fund Performance and Manager Skill. *Journal of Futures Markets.* **21**, 1003-1028.

Edwards, F. and Park, J. (1996). Do Managed Futures Make Good Investments?. *Journal of Futures Markets.* **16**, 475-517.

Elton, E., Gruber, M. and Blake, D. (1996). Survivorship bias and mutual fund performance. *Review of Financial Studies.* **9**, 1097-1120.

Fung, W. and Hsieh, D. (1997). Survivorship bias and investment style in the returns of CTAs. *Journal of Portfolio Management.* **24**, 30-41.

Fung, W. and Hsieh, D. (2000). Performance characteristics of hedge funds and commodity funds: natural vs. Spurious Biases. *Journal of Financial and Quantitative Analysis.* **35**, 291-307.

Grinblatt, M. and Titman, S. (1989). Mutual fund performance: an analysis of quarterly portfolio holdings. *Journal of Business.* **62**, 393-416.

Grinblatt, M. and Titman, S. (1992). The persistence of mutual fund performance. *Journal of Finance.* **47**, 1977-1984.

Kosowski, R., Naik, N. and Teo, M. (2007). Do hedge funds deliver alpha? A Bayesian and Bootstrap analysis. J*ournal of Financial Economics.* **84**, 229-264.

Liang, B. (2000). Hedge funds: the living and the dead. *Journal of Financial and Quantitative Analysis.* **35**, 309-326.

Liang, B., (2001). Hedge fund performance: 1990-1999. *Financial Analysts Journal.* **57**, 11-18.

Lunde, A., Timmermann, A. and Blake, D. (1999). The hazards of mutual fund underperformance: a cox regression analysis. *Journal of Empirical Finance.* **6**, 121-152.

Malkiel, B. (1995). Returns from investing in equity mutual funds: 1971 to 1991. *Journal of Finance.* **50**, 549-572.

Malkiel, B. and Saha A. (2005). Hedge Funds: Return and Risk. *Financial Analysts Journal.* **61**, 80-88.

In: The Recent Trend of Hedge Fund Strategies ISBN: 978-1-61668-338-2
Editor: Yasuaki Watanabe, pp. 181-199 

*Chapter 6*

# STYLE ANALYSES OF DESIRABLE HEDGE FUND STRATEGIES FOR ACTUAL INVESTORS

***Yasuaki Watanabe***[1]
Kochi University of Technology, Management Department,
Massachusetts Institute of Technology, Economics Department,

## Abstract

We select the top four hedge fund strategies as desirable ones based on the Prospect Ratio in this paper, and we examine the risk factors of each hedge fund strategy to specify the source of return in the past ten years. We use multifactor models based on GMM analysis. And we use AIC (Akaike Information Criterion) and SIC (Schwarz Information Criterion) to resolve the problem to specify the valid exogenous variables in each strategy. The result shows that the selected model contains only significant exogenous variables in each strategy.

**JEL Classification** : *C-4, C-5, G-1, G-2*

**Keywords** : Prospect Ratio, GMM, AIC, SIC

[1] E-mail address: watanabe.yasuaki@kochi-tech.ac.jp. Home Phone No. :+81-887-57-2776, Fax Number : +81-887-57-2811. Mailing Address : 185 Miyanokuchi, Tosayamada-cho, Kami City, Kochi Prefecture 782-8502, Japan.

Hedge funds were used to "hedge" or protect against loss due to market uncertainties. The roots of hedge funds seem to be in the 1930s, but they formally broke ground with A.W. Jones in the late 1940s. The growth of hedge funds industry was slow, but steadily going well through the 1950s. The business of hedge funds began to bear fruits in the mid-1960s. Although they encountered some troubles with treacherous markets in the late 1960s and early 1970s, the business of hedge funds again enjoyed real growth and development in the 1980s. Recently, hedge funds encompass almost every financial product and tangible asset and follow both conservative and aggressive investing approaches. One of the measures to examine the exposure to risk in hedge funds is style analysis.

We can identify the factor exposures of hedge fund strategies through multifactor analysis. Fung and Hsieh (1997,2001,2004) and Schneeweis and Spurgin (1998) are among the initiators of style analysis in hedge fund strategies. In a recent paper, Jaeger and Wagner (2005) identify the risk exposures in each hedge fund strategy from Jan.1994 to Dec.2004. Gehin and Vaissie (2006) examine the exposure to risk factors by hedge fund strategy using data from Jan.1997 to Dec.2004. The results of these studies reveal that the measured exposures vary according to the historical data period and vendor's selection. Our main point in this paper is to single out the valid exogenous variables based on AIC (Akaike Information Criterion) and SIC (Schwarz Information Criterion) in selected four hedge fund strategies through a new ratio named Prospect Ratio developed by the author. Concerning exogenous variables, we mainly use the data in both U.S. and Japan. Because we have a strong concern to check how hedge fund strategies in U.S. had involved in Japanese market. And Pochon and Teiletche (2006) use both AIC and SIC for estimating a mixture of normal distribution for core assets in hedge funds.

In addition, although many articles on hedge fund strategies use the Sharpe Ratio such as Lo (2002) to measure each performance of hedge fund strategy, we propose to use the Prospect Ratio instead of Sharpe Ratio. The reason is explained in the selection criterion part of this paper.

## Model

Sharpe (1992) introduced a multiple-factor model for the general mutual fund. Here, we apply this multiple-factor model to hedge fund style analysis. The multiple-factor model is

$$R_t = \alpha + \sum_k \beta_k F_{kt} + u_t \tag{1}$$

where, $R_t$: Hedge Fund Return, $\beta_k$: Coefficient of Factor $k$, $F_{kt}$: Return of Factor $k$, $u_t$: Error Terms

If we decompose the equation (1), $\sum_k \beta_k F_{kt}$ is referred to as style and $\alpha$ as skill.

In Sharpe's case, $\beta_k$ is assumed to be non-negative and the sum of $\beta_k$ is assumed to be equal 1, because a mutual fund is used. However, we can omit these constraints in the hedge fund case in order to allow for short sales and leverage. In addition, Ordinary Least Squares (OLS) is used for the style analysis of Sharpe's mutual fund. Here, we use the Generalized Method of Moments (GMM) to obtain $\beta_k$. GMM is based on $L$ population moments for $k$ parameters, $\theta_0$:

$$E_0 m(Y_t, \theta_0) = 0 \text{ or } E_0 \begin{bmatrix} m_1(Y_t, \theta_0) \\ m_2(Y_t, \theta_0) \\ \vdots \\ m_L(Y_t, \theta_0) \end{bmatrix} = \begin{bmatrix} 0 \\ 0 \\ \vdots \\ 0 \end{bmatrix} \tag{2}$$

To compute (2), we replace population moments with the sample analogs $m(y,\theta)$ and minimize $Q_T(\theta) = m(y,\theta)' W_T m(y,\theta)$ for some $LxL$ weighting matrix $W_T$.

## Selection Criterion

In this analysis, we select four hedge fund strategies. The selection criterion is based on the results shown in Table 1[2].

[2] We examine thirteen out of thirty three hedge fund strategies from HedgeFund.Net. The criterion of selection is based on the numbers of funds exceeding one hundred as of Dec. 30th, 2005. Other publicly available sources of hedge fund data are Altvest, HFR, MSCI, TASS, CTI, SPHF, and ZCAP/MAR,etc.
We take the data of monthly return and multiply them by 12 to annualize them.

**Table 1. Prospect Ratio and Skewness/Kurtosis Ratio (Jan. 1996 –Dec.2005: US$)**

| Hedge Fund Strategy | Prospect Ratio (a) | Skewness/Kurtosis Ratio (b) | (a)+(b) |
|---|---|---|---|
| ***Hedge Fund Aggregate*** | 2.9665 | -0.0474 | 2.9191 |
| Market Neutral Equity | 4.5035 | -0.0043 | 4.4992 |
| Macro | 2.6861 | -0.0081 | 2.6780 |
| Multi-Strategy | 2.5637 | -0.0061 | 2.5576 |
| Fixed Income (non-arbitrage) | 1.6018 | -0.0628 | 1.5390 |
| Long/Short Equity | 1.5445 | -0.0448 | 1.4996 |
| Fund of Funds - Multi-Strategy | 1.3540 | -0.0514 | 1.3027 |
| Convertible Arbitrage | 1.1726 | -0.0968 | 1.0758 |
| Fixed Income Arbitrage | 0.9230 | -0.0434 | 0.8796 |
| Event Driven | 0.8966 | -0.0616 | 0.8350 |
| Distressed | 0.7857 | -0.0508 | 0.7349 |
| Fund of Funds - Single-Strategy | 0.4979 | -0.0453 | 0.4526 |
| Emerging Markets | -0.0070 | -0.0674 | -0.0744 |
| CTA/Managed Futures | -0.2704 | -0.0713 | -0.3417 |

Namely, the strategies having the top four highest values of (a)+(b) are selected as desirable hedge fund strategies for actual investors. Multi-Strategy is omitted due to high correlation with Long/Short Equity (see Table 2).

**Table 2. Correlation Coefficient among Hedge Fund Strategies (Jan. 1996 – Dec. 2005:US$)**

| Hedge Fund Strategy | HFA | MNE | MS | M | LSE | CA | FI(NA) | ED | FOFMS | D | FIA | EM | FOFSS | CMF |
|---|---|---|---|---|---|---|---|---|---|---|---|---|---|---|
| *Hedge Fund Aggregate* | 1.0000 | | | | | | | | | | | | | |
| Market Neutral Equity | 0.9468 | 1.0000 | | | | | | | | | | | | |
| Multi-Strategy | 0.9094 | 0.4256 | 1.0000 | | | | | | | | | | | |
| Macro | 0.3254 | 0.3779 | 0.7363 | 1.0000 | | | | | | | | | | |
| Long/Short Equity | 0.9487 | 0.4601 | 0.8507 | 0.6852 | 1.0000 | | | | | | | | | |
| Convertible Arbitrage | 0.4255 | 0.3233 | 0.5682 | 0.3790 | 0.4748 | 1.0000 | | | | | | | | |
| Fixed Income (non-arbitrage) | 0.8979 | 0.3020 | 0.7038 | 0.6839 | 0.6386 | 0.5365 | 1.0000 | | | | | | | |
| Event Driven | 0.8269 | 0.3193 | 0.7459 | 0.5851 | 0.8401 | 0.5579 | 0.7515 | 1.0000 | | | | | | |
| Fund of Funds - Multi-Strategy | 0.8594 | 0.4851 | 0.8800 | 0.8204 | 0.8721 | 0.5965 | 0.7454 | 0.8357 | 1.0000 | | | | | |
| Distressed | 0.2299 | 0.2154 | 0.6407 | 0.4749 | 0.6863 | 0.5306 | 0.7201 | 0.8611 | 0.7417 | 1.0000 | | | | |
| Fixed Income Arbitrage | 0.7897 | 0.1192 | 0.1793 | 0.2233 | 0.1542 | 0.4191 | 0.3188 | 0.2565 | 0.3567 | 0.2794 | 1.0000 | | | |
| Emerging Markets | 0.5484 | 0.2224 | 0.7387 | 0.5969 | 0.7021 | 0.4547 | 0.6883 | 0.7242 | 0.7595 | 0.7445 | 0.2476 | 1.0000 | | |
| Fund of Funds - Single-Strategy | 0.7705 | 0.4520 | 0.8890 | 0.8248 | 0.9199 | 0.4996 | 0.7132 | 0.8247 | 0.9684 | 0.7143 | 0.2852 | 0.7683 | 1.0000 | |
| CTA/Managed Futures | 0.7265 | 0.1176 | 0.2058 | 0.5497 | 0.0497 | 0.0290 | 0.1801 | 0.0084 | 0.2783 | -0.1326 | 0.0145 | -0.0123 | 0.2342 | 1.0000 |

The Prospect Ratio, developed by the author, uses Tversky and Kahneman (1992)'s value function in the numerator and downside risk in the denominator.

That is to say, Prospect Ratio

$$= \frac{\frac{1}{T}\sum_{t=1}^{T}\left(Max(r_t,0) \; - \delta(-Min(r_t,0)) \;\right) - r_{Target}}{\sigma_D} \tag{3}$$

where, $T = 120, \delta = 2.25, r_{Target} = 0.41$ percent[3].

The advantage of using the Prospect Ratio is that it fully accounts for investors' behavior under prospect theory. The idea behind prospect theory differs from the standard assumptions about investor behavior made by Markowitz and Sharpe regarding the utility function within a loss domain[4]. Prospect theory holds true not only to the hedge fund strategies but also to the traditional investment strategies (e.g., long only) from the behavioral finance view point. We can show the difference of utility functions between rational (in other words: traditional) investors and actual investors in Figure 1.

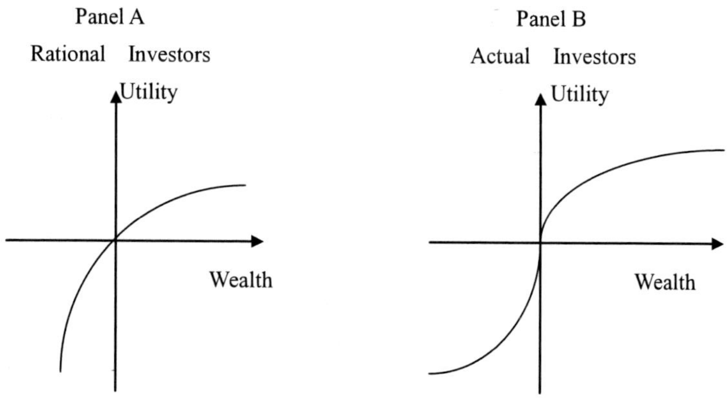


Figure 1.

The utility curve at left side shows that an investor's utility slowly rises as wealth increases. This is a typical risk-averse investor. In Panel B, however, the investor, when facing a loss, becomes risk-seeking but, when facing a profit, the investor becomes a risk-averse in the conventional sense.

So, we do not use Sharpe Ratio or Sortino Ratio as a performance measurement here. Since these measures are only valid when the return distribution is normal. For example, the paper written by Lo (2002) shows the improvement of Sharpe Ratio in terms of serially correlated return. But, he does not refer to higher order moments in this case. A skewness/kurtosis ratio has also been used by the author to supplement the Prospect Ratio. Evidence shows that

[3]The value of $\delta$ depends on the samples selected. So, we choose the value of Tversky and Kahneman's value for convenience. This risk free rate is based on the data from HedgeFund.Net.

[4] The utility function of prospect theory is convex, not concave within a loss domain.

the distributions of hedge fund strategies are not normally distributed in many cases. This means that consideration of higher moments such as skewness and kurtosis may be important. In this Table, a skewness/kurtosis ratio is calculated using downside risk and these ratios are negative for each strategy. The reason for this is that the weight of the negative value function is heavier than positive value function in equation (3). Given all of this, the sum of Prospect Ratio and skewness/kurtosis ratio will give us a more precise performance measurement[5].

# Data Analysis

## Market Neutral Equity

Market neutral equity is a class of hedge funds that follow strategies to exploit factors unique to particular stocks, but remain neutral on factors that reflect broader conditions in the sector, industry, level of market capitalization, country, or region.

The results for market neutral equity given by Generalized Method of Moments (GMM) are shown in Table 3. The risk factors that are used are the SandP 500, Transaction Volumes of New York Stock Exchange (TNY), Transaction Volumes of Tokyo Stock Exchange (TTKO), and CBOE Volatility Index (VIX). The reason we take these risk factors is to check the sensitivity to the market. The adjusted $R^2$ is the lowest (approximately 5.5%) among all the strategies. This implies that the net exposure to the market is negligible. Judging from the transition of the five years movement, the adjusted $R^2$ is decreasing over time. S&P 500 is the only risk factor that has a positive correlation with market neutral equity. There is a tendency for t-values associated with the S&P 500 to be significant during the period of positive adjusted $R^2$.

During the each period from Jan.99-Dec.03, Jan.00-Dec.04, and Jan.01-Dec.05, the adjusted $R^2$ is negative[6]. We can infer that the other risk factors have no affect on the return of market neutral equity. However, it is necessary to see which exogenous variables are important as a reference. So, we single out the

5 Suppose that there exist Fund A and Fund B. Concerning mean, variance, skewness and kurtosis, each fund have the only one value, respectively. Thus, we can simply sum up Prospect Ratio and skewness/kurtosis ratio.

6 Suppose that the number of sample is n and parameter is k respectively. $AdjR^2 = 1-(1-R^2)\dfrac{n-1}{n-k}$. Thus, $AdjR^2$ becomes negative when $R^2 < \dfrac{k-1}{n-k}$.

valid exogenous variables by using AIC and SIC. Here, we propose three equations as follows:

$$R_{t|MNE} = \alpha + \beta_1 F_{1t|S\&P500} + \beta_2 F_{2t|TNY} + \beta_3 F_{3t|TTKO} + \beta_4 F_{4t|VIX} + u_t \tag{4}$$

$$R_{t|MNE} = \alpha + \beta_1 F_{1t|S\&P500} + u_t \tag{5}$$

$$R_{t|MNE} = \alpha + \beta_1 F_{1t|TNY} + \beta_2 F_{2t|TTKO} + \beta_3 F_{3t|VIX} + u_t \tag{6}$$

**Table 3. Market Neutral Equity**

| | Jan96-Dec05 | Jan96-Dec00 | Jan97-Dec01 | Jan98-Dec02 | Jan99-Dec03 | Jan00-Dec04 | Jan01-Dec05 |
|---|---|---|---|---|---|---|---|
| Intercept | 0.007592 | 0.010139 | 0.008987 | 0.008539 | 0.006918 | 0.005876 | 0.004755 |
| | (9.374934)** | (9.032856)** | (8.326748)** | (7.391433)** | (6.364749)** | (5.983457)** | (7.528034)** |
| S&P 500 | 0.064988 | 0.090309 | 0.084047 | 0.072584 | 0.010056 | -0.004283 | -0.012298 |
| | (2.968616)** | (2.893604)** | (3.145451)** | (2.209922)* | (0.453104) | (-0.196228) | (-0.682537) |
| TNY | 0.006280 | 0.012088 | 0.007605 | 0.004561 | 0.001272 | -0.001352 | -0.001140 |
| | (1.454229) | (1.543286) | (1.078033) | (0.601239) | (0.267535) | (-0.307986) | (-0.284410) |
| TTKO | 0.001728 | 0.001935 | 0.008058 | 0.007498 | 0.004399 | 0.004673 | 0.002448 |
| | (0.559519) | (0.349248) | (1.299599) | (1.346073) | (1.235114) | (1.109934) | (1.047526) |
| VIX | 0.000511 | -0.004590 | -0.000643 | 0.003208 | -0.000550 | -0.003828 | -0.001624 |
| | (0.128118) | (-0.872782) | (-0.119449) | (0.513894) | (-0.094856) | (-0.664841) | (-0.390598) |
| Adjusted $R^2$ | 0.054647 | 0.113335 | 0.103753 | 0.046750 | -0.047667 | -0.045289 | -0.056889 |

* Significant with 95% confidence (t-values in parentheses)

** Significant with 99% confidence

**Table 4.**

(a) The Result of AIC's Equation selection (Market Neutral Equity)

| Order by AIC | AIC | Equation | k | Sum of squared residuals |
|---|---|---|---|---|
| 1 | -6.977790 | (5) | 2 | 0.006336 |
| 2 | -6.949004 | (4) | 5 | 0.006203 |
| 3 | -6.898195 | (6) | 4 | 0.006636 |

(b) The Result of SIC's Equation selection (Market Neutral Equity)

| Order by SIC | SIC | Equation | k | Sum of squared residuals |
|---|---|---|---|---|
| 1 | -6.931332 | (5) | 2 | 0.006336 |
| 2 | -6.832859 | (4) | 5 | 0.006203 |
| 3 | -6.805278 | (6) | 4 | 0.006636 |

Judging from the Table 4, Equation (5) is selected. So, the SandP 500 is the only exogenous variable that affects the return of market neutral equity.

## Macro

Macro trading and investment strategies developed historically as directional strategies. Several macroeconomic variables and indicators lead to macroeconomic views favorable to a particular asset.

**Table 5.**

| | Macro | | | | | | |
|---|---|---|---|---|---|---|---|
| | Jan.96-Dec.05 | Jan.96-Dec.00 | Jan.97-Dec.01 | Jan.98-Dec.02 | Jan.99-Dec.03 | Jan.00-Dec.04 | Jan.01-Dec.05 |
| Intercept | 0.010280 | 0.013090 | 0.013289 | 0.012795 | 0.010229 | 0.005392 | 0.005772 |
| | (8.526005)** | (6.192225)** | (8.595825)** | (7.481418)** | (5.563518)** | (3.943220)** | (5.181139)** |
| Short Rate | -0.014630 | 0.005781 | 0.102725 | 0.049661 | 0.020907 | -0.038406 | -0.025345 |
| | (-0.609873) | (0.074035) | (3.004596)** | (2.498590)* | (1.106937) | (-2.065057)* | (-1.849220) |
| CI (AAA) | -0.013165 | -0.041571 | -0.060105 | -0.039030 | -0.017692 | -0.006588 | 0.039495 |
| | (-0.509012) | (-1.793250) | (-4.324741)** | (-1.523154) | (-0.675425) | (-0.286080) | (2.335058)* |
| CI (AA) | -0.040679 | -0.124284 | -0.073797 | 0.035800 | 0.060270 | 0.041779 | -0.011248 |
| | (-1.199188) | (-2.681207)** | (-2.179050)* | (0.826048) | (1.748905) | (0.953137) | (-0.518437) |
| CI (A) | 0.013852 | 0.244270 | 0.215998 | 0.015138 | -0.023193 | -0.040340 | -0.039548 |
| | (0.380611) | (3.178469)** | (3.702347)** | (0.336501) | (-0.735140) | (-1.763017) | (-2.367070)* |
| CI (BAA) | 0.014115 | -0.105486 | -0.127801 | -0.068341 | -0.048117 | -0.001087 | 0.007259 |
| | (0.720775) | (-1.484848) | (-2.432418)* | (-1.724074) | (-1.277126) | (-0.033784) | (0.438528) |
| VIX | 0.019936 | 0.014298 | 0.022581 | 0.041662 | 0.034345 | -0.006897 | 0.001144 |
| | (1.720070) | (0.997698) | (1.712920) | (2.155202)* | (1.835099) | (-0.442629) | (0.118802) |
| FX(US/JP) | 0.155568 | 0.247693 | 0.171926 | 0.113325 | 0.031954 | 0.116925 | 0.075264 |
| | (3.036067)** | (4.964071)** | (3.488800)** | (2.318072)* | (0.443892) | (2.860431)** | (1.807972) |
| FX(US/BP) | 0.209711 | 0.085537 | 0.162933 | 0.023284 | 0.045051 | 0.039753 | -0.002647 |
| | (1.538509) | (0.553101) | (1.067009) | (0.138000) | (0.297442) | (0.408768) | (-0.033303) |
| FX(US/EU) | -0.169361 | -0.233303 | -0.229570 | -0.094736 | -0.135935 | 0.075401 | 0.144439 |
| | (-1.481815) | (-1.632194) | (-1.904141) | (-0.623559) | (-0.907391) | (0.705637) | (2.281126)* |
| MSCI World | 0.182916 | 0.566356 | 0.633499 | 0.512442 | 0.998530 | 1.710811 | 0.248518 |
| | (0.317829) | (1.104532) | (1.199212) | (0.551484) | (0.791383) | (1.685856) | (0.420463) |
| MSCI G7 | -0.086673 | -0.374971 | -0.521189 | -0.439029 | -0.983330 | -1.669745 | -0.298091 |
| | (-0.158432) | (-0.788749) | (-1.022063) | (-0.503580) | (-0.814984) | (-1.741933) | (-0.536408) |
| MSCI EM | 0.103731 | 0.121513 | 0.118959 | 0.100311 | 0.140161 | -0.016491 | 0.089546 |
| | (2.487220)* | (1.842969) | (3.229534)** | (1.857447) | (2.458883)* | (-0.243236) | (1.526502) |
| USB | -0.054768 | -0.090132 | -0.121463 | -0.092611 | -0.103194 | -0.080247 | -0.063707 |
| | (-2.176308)* | (-2.121821)* | (-2.839602)** | (-2.097756)* | (2.468446)* | (-2.131541)* | (-3.196255)* |
| JGB | -0.001029 | -0.010383 | -0.001906 | 0.013772 | 0.004767 | 0.018200 | 0.010268 |
| | (-0.122985) | (-1.160710) | (-0.254727) | (1.459224) | (0.418479) | (1.629405) | (1.574068) |
| TOCOM | -0.067256 | -0.016022 | -0.052769 | -0.080335 | -0.064804 | -0.027849 | -0.058607 |
| | (-2.008120)* | (-0.278888) | (-1.039736) | (-1.493512) | (-1.136569) | (-0.712236) | (-1.303374) |
| S&P COM | 0.059671 | -0.050052 | -0.073444 | 0.041801 | 0.080845 | 0.078338 | 0.063360 |
| | (2.052111)* | (-1.181481) | (-2.337900)* | (0.950891) | (1.659298) | (2.458330)* | (1.626681) |
| Adjusted $R^2$ | 0.311746 | 0.524041 | 0.531123 | 0.321092 | 0.281744 | 0.333632 | 0.424544 |

* Significant with 95% confidence (t-values in parentheses)

** Significant with 99% confidence

The results for macro given by the Generalized Method of Moments (GMM) estimation are shown in Table 5. Risk factors that we use are the Federal funds effective rate (Short Rate), Lehman Brothers Credit Indices (CI(AAA), CI(AA), CI(A), CI(BAA)), CBOE Volatility Index (VIX), Foreign Exchange between USA and Japan (FX(US/JP)), FX(US/BP), FX(US/EU), Morgan Stanley Capital International World (MSCI World), MSCI G7, MSCI Emerging Markets (MSCI EM), the 10 year Japanese government bond (JGB), 10 year U.S. government bond (USB), The Tokyo Commodity Exchange Index(TOCOM), and S&P Commodity Index(S&P COM). The reason we take these risk factors is that we want to check the effects of the interest rate, credit risk, volatility, currencies, stocks, bonds, and commodities for the macro strategy. However, in practice it is rather difficult for us to specify the risk factors in the macro strategy, because there are many transaction patterns in macro trading based on mispricings and arbitrage. The coefficient of determination of adjusted $R^2$ is approximately 31.2% during the period from Jan.96-Dec.05. As we can see in the macro, there is a tendency for the adjusted $R^2$ to be decreasing in the middle, but increasing in the latter periods.

**Table 6.**

(a) The Result of AIC's Equation selection (Macro)

| Order by AIC | AIC | Equation | k | Sum of squared residuals |
|---|---|---|---|---|
| 1 | -5.452905 | (9) | 6 | 0.027234 |
| 2 | -5.384549 | (7) | 17 | 0.024276 |
| 3 | -5.369547 | (10) | 8 | 0.028631 |
| 4 | -5.252808 | (8) | 5 | 0.033826 |

(b) The Result of SIC's Equation selection (Macro)

| Order by SIC | SIC | Equation | k | Sum of squared residuals |
|---|---|---|---|---|
| 1 | -5.313530 | (9) | 6 | 0.027234 |
| 2 | -5.183715 | (10) | 8 | 0.028631 |
| 3 | -5.136662 | (8) | 5 | 0.033826 |
| 4 | -4.989655 | (7) | 17 | 0.024276 |

FX(US/JP), MSCI EM , and S&P COM have a positive correlation with macro, while, USB and TOCOM has a negative correlation with macro. There are all significant at the 95% confidence level except for FX(US/JP). Judging from movements of credit indices, macro strategies have shifted from risk seeking to risk averse until the middle of the whole sub-periods. It seems that Asian crisis which triggered the global financial crisis in 1998 may have affected this tendency to avoid the risk. Namely, the shift from CI(BAA) to Short Rate is apparent during the period from Jan.97-Dec.01 to Jan.98-Dec.02. With respect to FX(US/JP), it has a positive correlation with macro except for Jan.99-Dec.03, and Jan.01-Dec.05.

There are no noteworthy relations in both FX(US/BP) and FX(US/EU) about macro except for Jan.01-Dec.05 of FX(US/EU). MSCI EM and S&P COM have a positive correlation, while, USB and TOCOM have a negative correlation with macro during the period of Jan.96-Dec.05. MSCI EM is important from Jan.99-Dec.03, because of its significance with 95% confidence. The reason perhaps lies in the recovery of emerging markets from their crises in 1998. USB shows a negative correlation with macro during the whole sub-periods. This may imply that macro transactions are related with USB. We also single out the valid exogenous variables by using AIC and SIC, and propose four equations as follows:

$$R_{t|MACRO} = \alpha + \beta_1 F_{1t|SR} + \beta_2 F_{2t|CIAAA} + \beta_3 F_{3t|CIAA} + \beta_4 F_{4t|CIA} + \beta_5 F_{5t|CIBAA} + \beta_6 F_{6t|VIX} + \beta_7 F_{7t|FUJ} + \beta_8 F_{8t|FUG} + \beta_9 F_{9t|FUE} + \beta_{10} F_{10t|MSW} + \beta_{11} F_{11t|MS7} + \beta_{12} F_{12t|MSE} + \beta_{13} F_{13t|USB} + \beta_{14} F_{14t|JGB} + \beta_{15} F_{15t|TOCOM} + \beta_{16} F_{16t|S\&PCOM} + u_t \quad (7)$$

$$R_{t|MACRO} = \alpha + \beta_1 F_{1t|SR} + \beta_2 F_{2t|CIAAA} + \beta_3 F_{3t|CIAA} + \beta_4 F_{4t|CIA} + u_t \quad (8)$$

$$R_{t|MACRO} = \alpha + \beta_1 F_{1t|FUJ} + \beta_2 F_{2t|MSE} + \beta_3 F_{3t|USB} + \beta_4 F_{4t|TOCOM} + \beta_5 F_{5t||S\&PCOM} + u_t \quad (9)$$

$$R_{t|MACRO} = \alpha + \beta_1 F_{1t|CIBAA} + \beta_2 F_{2t|VIX} + \beta_3 F_{3t|FUB} + \beta_4 F_{4t|FUE} + \beta_5 F_{5t|MSW} + \beta_6 F_{6t|MS7} + \beta_7 F_{7t|JGB} + u_t \quad (10)$$

Judging from the Table 6, Equation (9) is selected. So, we can confirm that FX(US/JP), MSCI EM, USB, TOCOM, and S&P COM are the exogenous variables that affect the return of macro.

## Fixed Income (Non-arbitrage)

Fixed income (non-arbitrage) is an investing strategy generally associated with hedge funds that are not based on the exploitation of inefficiencies in the pricing of bonds. The results for fixed income (non-arbitrage) given by the Generalized Method of Moments (GMM) estimates are shown in Table 7. The risk factors that we use are the 10 year Japanese government bond (JGB), 10 year

Japanese Swap (JPSWAP), 10 year U.S. government bond (USB) and 10 year U.S. Swap (USSWAP). The reason we use these former risk factors is to check the effect of the government bond and swap rates in both the U.S. and Japan on the funds. The coefficient of determination of adjusted $R^2$ is approximately 16.7% during the period from Jan.96-Dec.05. However, the values of the adjusted $R^2$ in each period of the past five years are higher than the whole period and are relatively stable. This implies that a large portion of funds' returns are determined by the factors in the last five years rather than in the past whole period.

**Table 7. Fixed income (non-arbitrage)**

| | Jan96-Dec.05 | Jan96-Dec.00 | Jan97-Dec.01 | Jan98-Dec.02 | Jan99-Dec.03 | Jan00-Dec.04 | Jan01-Dec.05 |
|---|---|---|---|---|---|---|---|
| Intercept | 0.007760 | 0.010124 | 0.009048 | 0.007945 | 0.008412 | 0.006973 | 0.006470 |
| | (7.792794)** | (9.240098)** | (8.376841)** | (6.666934)** | (10.71062)** | (16.26460)** | (15.99439)** |
| JGB | -0.000424 | -0.039354 | -0.035101 | -0.034044 | -0.001506 | 0.001628 | 0.003320 |
| | (-0.052621) | (-1.532444) | (-1.450923) | (-1.422561) | (-0.321779) | (0.671459) | (1.404873) |
| JPSWAP | 0.010266 | 0.105454 | 0.088044 | 0.091453 | -0.005469 | -0.004980 | -0.006701 |
| | (0.478134) | (1.733949) | (1.515588) | (1.532003) | (-0.968994) | (-1.696274) | (-2.437457)* |
| USB | 0.418846 | 0.588106 | 0.487191 | 0.443464 | 0.244578 | 0.185352 | 0.214904 |
| | (3.241465)** | (3.509249)** | (3.421801)** | (3.302527)** | (4.535963)** | (4.376658)** | (5.389494)** |
| USSWAP | -0.419271 | -0.575787 | -0.474712 | -0.448836 | -0.242442 | -0.195707 | -0.225491 |
| | (-3.139761)** | (-3.118225)** | (-3.208915)** | (-3.032586)** | (-4.507465)** | (-4.614687)** | (-5.895461)** |
| Adjusted $R^2$ | 0.166501 | 0.391409 | 0.328200 | 0.322076 | 0.251585 | 0.262998 | 0.330309 |

* Significant with 95% confidence (t-values in parentheses)

** Significant with 99% confidence

**Table 8.**

(a) The Result of AIC's Equation selection (Fixed Income (non-arbitrage))

| Order by AIC | AIC | Equation | k | Sum of squared residuals |
|---|---|---|---|---|
| 1 | -6.436380 | (12) | 3 | 0.010708 |
| 2 | -6.414033 | (11) | 5 | 0.010591 |
| 3 | -6.251152 | (13) | 3 | 0.012887 |

(b) The Result of SIC's Equation selection (Fixed Income (non-arbitrage))

| Order by SIC | SIC | Equation | k | Sum of squared residuals |
|---|---|---|---|---|
| 1 | -6.366692 | (12) | 3 | 0.010708 |
| 2 | -6.297887 | (11) | 5 | 0.010591 |
| 3 | -6.181464 | (13) | 3 | 0.012887 |

Concerning fixed income (non-arbitrage), it seems that only USB and USSWAP are relevant to the fixed income (non-arbitrage) except for JPSWAP during the period from Jan.01-Dec.05. It is noteworthy that both USB and USSWAP are significant at a 99% confidence level during the whole period of time. In addition, USB has a positive correlation with fixed income (non-arbitrage), while, USSWAP has a negative correlation with fixed income (non-arbitrage). The t-values of recent past five years in both USB and USSWAP are increasing. This may imply that the relevance of USB and USSWAP is increasing for fixed income (non-arbitrage). Once again, we single out the valid exogenous variables by using AIC and SIC. Here, we propose three equations as follows:

$$R_{t|FINA} = \alpha + \beta_1 F_{1t|JGB} + \beta_2 F_{2t|TJPSWAP} + \beta_3 F_{3t|USB} + \beta_4 F_{4t|USSWAP} + u_t \tag{11}$$

$$R_{t|FINA} = \alpha + \beta_1 F_{1t|USB} + \beta_2 F_{2t|USSWAP} + u_t \tag{12}$$

$$R_{t|FINA} = \alpha + \beta_1 F_{1t|JGB} + \beta_2 F_{2t|TJPSWAP} + u_t \tag{13}$$

Judging from the Table 8, Equation (12) is selected. So, we can confirm that USB and USSWAP are the exogenous variables that affect the return of fixed income (non-arbitrage).

## Long/Short Equity

Long/short equity is an investment strategy used by hedge funds, which earns its returns from stock picking, but isolates the risk as well as the return of a particular stock from the risk/return of the broader market or industry of which it is a part. The results of Long/Short Equity given by the Generalized Method of Moments (GMM) estimation are shown in Table 9. The risk factors that we employ are the S&P 500, TNY, TTKO, and VIX. The reason we use these risk factors is to check the effect of the S&P 500, TNY, TTKO, and VIX on the market. The coefficient of determination of adjusted $R^2$ is approximately 41.9% and is the highest among the selected four hedge fund strategies. It seems that the adjusted $R^2$ remains relatively constant except for the period from Jan.01-Dec.05. The adjusted $R^2$ during this period is approximately 65.3%, which is quite high and the reason for this may be that long/short equity followed the movement of the S&P 500 more closely. The t-values of both the S&P 500 and VIX are close to being significant during this particular period of time. The S&P 500 has a relatively strong correlation with long/short equity. While, the VIX has a negative correlation with long/short equity. The relationships with the S&P 500 and VIX are opposite, because option prices will become higher rapidly during the period of falling market price of equity rather than that of rising market price of equity, and the value of VIX is calculated based on the option price of S&P 500 Index. In other words, VIX is derived from S&P 500 options. For this class of hedge funds, we also single out the valid exogenous variables by using AIC and BIC. Here, we propose three equations as follows:

$$R_{t|L/S} = \alpha + \beta_1 F_{1t|S\&P500} + \beta_2 F_{2t|TNY} + \beta_3 F_{3t|TTKO} + \beta_4 F_{4t|VIX} + u_t \qquad (14)$$

$$R_{t|L/S} = \alpha + \beta_1 F_{1t|S\&P500} + \beta_2 F_{2t|VIX} + u_t \qquad (15)$$

$$R_{t|L/S} = \alpha + \beta_1 F_{1t|TNY} + \beta_2 F_{2t|TTKO} + \beta_3 F_{3t|VIX} + u_t \qquad (16)$$

Judging from the Table 10, Equation (14) is selected in AIC, but Equation (15) is selected in SIC. We usually choose the result of SIC only when the sample size is large enough. Thus, we choose Equation (15) instead of Equation (14). So, we can confirm that the S&P 500 and VIX are the exogenous variables that affect the return of long/short equity.

**Table 9. Long/Short Equity**

| | Jan.96-Dec.05 | Jan.96-Dec.00 | Jan.97-Dec.01 | Jan.98-Dec.02 | Jan.99-Dec.03 | Jan.00-Dec.04 | Jan.01-Dec.05 |
|---|---|---|---|---|---|---|---|
| Intercept | 0.011814 | 0.015963 | 0.013688 | 0.013973 | 0.013975 | 0.008238 | 0.006886 |
| | (5.291831)** | (3.428345)** | (3.616854)** | (3.897031)** | (3.816095)** | (4.291855)** | (5.079331)** |
| S&P 500 | 0.397995 | 0.463922 | 0.464770 | 0.410214 | 0.347274 | 0.153038 | 0.247005 |
| | (5.660899)** | (3.375651)** | (4.255846)** | (3.340713)** | (2.633565)** | (1.820897) | (6.536795)** |
| TNY | 0.019048 | 0.035831 | 0.054136 | 0.020580 | 0.012637 | 0.005668 | 0.000418 |
| | (1.780650) | (1.991754) | (3.395888)** | (1.029722) | (0.975361) | (0.466314) | (0.043423) |
| TIKO | 0.010929 | 0.013959 | 0.013658 | 0.022259 | 0.016906 | 0.022931 | 0.008983 |
| | (1.751813) | (1.072255) | (1.140102) | (1.741123) | (1.608957) | (1.696076) | (1.956487) |
| VIX | -0.044991 | -0.054954 | -0.047399 | -0.042513 | -0.041612 | -0.068324 | -0.045504 |
| | (-3.602518)** | (-3.321172)** | (-3.059811)** | (-2.011305)* | (-1.759632) | (-3.742624)** | (-4.714035)** |
| Adjusted $R^2$ | 0.419399 | 0.375618 | 0.435708 | 0.418951 | 0.310646 | 0.388495 | 0.652655 |

* Significant with 95% confidence (t-values in parentheses)

** Significant with 99% confidence

**Table 10.**

(a) The Result of AIC's Equationl selection (Long/Short Equity)

| Order by AIC | AIC | EQUATION | k | Sum of squared residuals |
|---|---|---|---|---|
| 1 | -4.936199 | (14) | 5 | 0.046425 |
| 2 | -4.929111 | (15) | 3 | 0.048340 |
| 3 | -4.652853 | (16) | 4 | 0.062668 |

(b) The Result of SIC's Equationl selection (Long/Short Equity)

| Order by SIC | SIC | EQUATION | k | Sum of squared residuals |
|---|---|---|---|---|
| 1 | -4.859424 | (15) | 3 | 0.048340 |
| 2 | -4.820054 | (14) | 5 | 0.046425 |
| 3 | -4.559937 | (16) | 4 | 0.062668 |

The SandP 500 Index moves in an upward direction sharply during the period from Jan.97-Dec.01 as seen from the Table 11. Thus, the t-value of TNY is significant at the 99% confidence level only during this period of time.

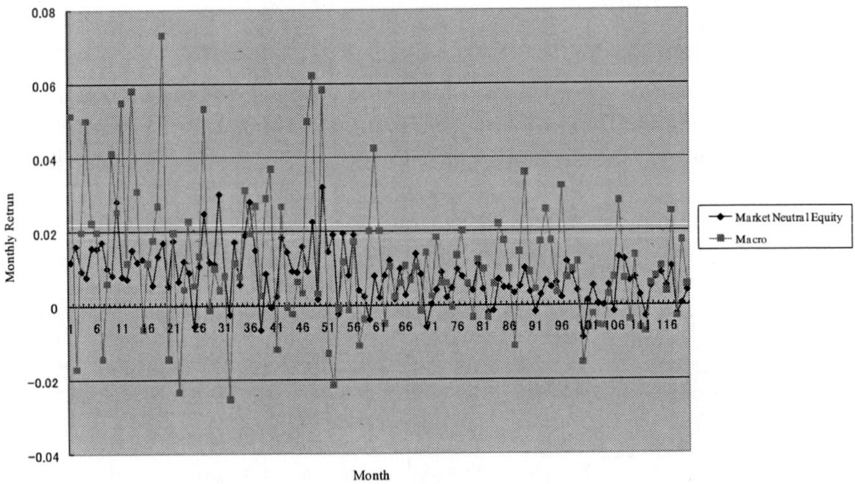


Figure 2.

## Concluding Remarks

In this paper, we can see that market neutral equity has little exposure to the market such as SandP 500, but long/short equity has a positive correlation with the S&P 500 with the highest adjusted $R^2$. This difference comes from the investment style.

Namely, the former strategy always balances the long and short positions, while the latter strategy doe not balance the long and short positions by changing the ratio of positions according to the perspective of the market. In macro, we find that FX(US/JP), MSCI EM, USB, TOCOM, and SandPCOM are significant with 95% confidence during the past ten years. The reason that only FX(US/JP) is significant in foreign exchange may be due to the historical low interest rates in Japan, so fund managers in macro can enjoy a lucrative opportunity by using the Yen to carry the transaction. Furthermore, the reason that only MSCI EM is significant in equity markets may be due to inefficient market characteristics checked by regulations. This means that arbitrage opportunities based on mispricing exist in MSCI EM. In addition, $\alpha$ is all positive and significant statistically in every strategy. So, we can confirm the existence of skills of hedge fund managers.

Finally, a difficult problem in style analysis is to determine the appropriate exogenous variables for each strategy. One of the main reasons may be in the insufficient information disclosure in hedge funds strategies. However, in the analysis of Jaeger and Wagner (2005), there exists a relatively high adjusted $R^2$ in each hedge fund strategy. The reason lies in the appropriate selection of risk factors. Thus, we can confirm that the selections of risk factors are very important in executing the style analysis in hedge funds strategies. In our case, we apply the AIC (Akaike Information Criterion) and SIC (Schwarz Information Criterion) to specify the valid exogenous variables in each strategy. The result shows that the selected equation contains only significant exogenous variables for each strategy.

# Appendix

1. Prospect Ratio

$$\text{Prospect Ratio} = \frac{\frac{1}{T}\sum_{t=1}^{T}\left(Max(r_t,0)-\delta(-Min(r_t,0))\right)-r_{Target}}{\sigma_D}$$

$$\left(=\frac{\left(\frac{1}{T}\sum_{t=1}^{T}(Max(r_t,0)-\delta(-Min(r_t,0)))-r_{Target}\right)}{\sigma_D^2}*\sigma_D\right)$$

Note that Prospect Ratio can be rewritten as first order moment over second order moment multiply downside risk.

2. Skewness/Kurtosis Ratio

$$\text{Skewness/Kurtosis Ratio} = \frac{1}{T}\sum_{t=1}^{T}\left(r_t - \bar{r}\right)^3 \Big/ \sigma_D{}^3 \Big/ \frac{1}{T}\sum_{t=1}^{T}\left(r_t - \bar{r}\right)^4 \Big/ \sigma_D{}^4$$

$$= \left(\frac{1}{T}\sum_{t=1}^{T}\left(r_t - \bar{r}\right)^3 \Big/ \frac{1}{T}\sum_{t=1}^{T}\left(r_t - \bar{r}\right)^4\right) * \sigma_D$$

where, $r_t$ is replaced by $\left(Max(r_t,0) \; - 2.25(-Min(r_t,0))\;\right)$ and $\bar{r}$ is replaced by $\frac{1}{T}\sum_{t=1}^{T}\left(Max(r_t,0) - 2.25(-Min(r_t,0))\;\right)$ in the case of Prospect Ratio. Note that skewness/kurtosis ratio can be rewritten as third order moment over fourth order moment multiply downside risk (=Prospect and Sortino Ratios). While, standard deviation is used in case of Sharpe Ratio.

3. Downside Risk

$$\sigma_D = \sqrt{\sum_{t=1}^{T}\frac{\min\left[\left(r_t - r_{Target}\right),0\right]^2}{T}}$$

where, $r_{Target}$ is minimum target return and equals risk free rate(0.41 percent) in this case.

4. AIC (Akaike Information Criterion)

$$AIC = -2l/T + 2k/T \left( \because l = -\frac{T}{2}\left(1 + \log(2\pi) + \log\left(\hat{e}'\hat{e}/T\right)\right)\right)$$

where, $l$ is the value of the log of the likelihood function with $k$ parameters estimated using $T$ observations. $\hat{e}'\hat{e}$ is sum of squared residuals. It is based on -2 times the average log likelihood function, adjusted by a penalty function.
In addition, smaller values of the AIC are preferred for model selection.

5. SIC (Schwarz Information Criterion)

$$SIC = -2l / T + (kLN(T)) / T$$

The SIC is an alternative to the AIC that imposes a larger penalty for additional coefficients. Generally, SIC is better than AIC only when sample size is large enough.


### Acknowledgement

The author would like to thank Paul Pfleiderer, Terry Marsh, Jeffrey Bohn and James Primbs for their helpful comments. The author is solely responsible for all errors in the article.


## References


Amenc, Noel and Veronique Le Sourd. 2003. *Portfolio theory and performance analysis*. John Wiley and Sons.

Asness, Clifford. 2004. "An Alternative Future: Part II." *The Journal of Portfolio Management Fall*: 8-23.

Bacon, Carl. 2004. *Practical Portfolio Performance measurement and attribution*. John Wiley and Sons.

Burstein, Gabriel. 1999. *Macro Trading and Investment Strategies*. John Wiley and Sons.

Crerend, J. Williams. 1998. *Fundamentals of Hedge Fund Investing*. McGraw-Hill.

Dubil, Robert. 2004. *An Arbitrage guide to financial markets*. John Wiley and Sons

Fung, William and David A. Hsieh. 1997. "Empirical Characteristics of Dynamic Trading Strategies: The Case of Hedge Funds," *The review of Financial Studies*, Vol.10, No.2: 275-302.

Fung, William and David A. Hsieh. 2001. "The Risk in Hedge Fund Strategies: Theory and Evidence from Trend Followers," *The review of Financial Studies*, Vol.14, No.2 : 313-341.

Fung, William and David A. Hsieh. 2004. "Hedge Fund Benchmarks : A Risk-Based Approach," *Financial Analyst Journal*, vol.60, no.5 (September/October) : 65-80.

Fung,William. 2005. "Theoretical Analysis of Alternative Investments." *Security Analysts Journal* Vol.43, No.6: 7-22.

Gehin Walter and Mathieu Vaissie. 2006. "The Right Place for Alternative Betas in Hedge Fund Performance," *The Journal of Alternative Investments*, Vol.9, No.1: 9-27.

Hall, R. Alastair. 2005. Generalized Method of Moments : Oxford University Press.

Jaeger, Lars and Christian Wagner. 2005. "Factor Modeling and Benchmarking of Hedge Funds: Can Passive Investments in Hedge Fund Strategies Deliver?," *The Journal of Alternative Investments*, Vol.8, No.3: 9-36.

Kraus, A. and R. H. Litzenberger. 1976. "Skewness Preference and the Valuation of Risk Assets." *Journal of Finance* Vol.38, No.4 (September) : 1085-1100.

Liew, Jimmy, and Craig French. 2005. "Quantitative Topics in Hedge Fund Investing.", *The Journal of Portfolio Management* (Summer) : 21-32.

Lo. W. Andrew. 2001. "Risk Management for Hedge Funds: Introduction and Overview." *Financial Analysts Journal*, Vol.57, No.6 (November/December): 16-33.

Lo. W. Andrew. 2002. "The Statistics of Sharpe Ratios." *Financial Analysts Journal*, Vol.58, No.4 (July/August): 36-52.

Malevergne, Yannick and Didier Sornette. 2005. "Higher-Moment Portfolio Theory." *The Journal of Portfolio Management* (Summer) : 49-55.

Markowitz, H. 1952. "Portfolio Selection." *Journal of Finance*, Vol.7, No.1 (March) : 77-91.

Mitusbishi Trust Bank Pension Investment Research Group. 2003. Seeking for$\alpha$: New Strategy of Asset Investment. Kinzai.

Nicholas, G. Joseph. 2000. Market-Neutral Investing. : Bloomberg L.P..

Pochon Florent and Jerome Teiletche. 2006. "A Conditional Approach to Hedge Fund Risk." *The Journal of Alternative Investments*, Vol.9, No.1: 64-77.

Schneeweis, Thomas and Richard Spurgin. 1998. "Multifactor Analysis of Hedge Fund, Managed Futures, and Mutual Fund Return and Risk Characteristics," *The Journal of Alternative Investments*, Vol.1, No.2 : 1-24.

Schneeweis, Thomas, George Martin, Hossein Kazemi, and Vassilis Karavas. 2005. "The Impact of Leverage on Hedge Fund Risk and Return," *The Journal of Alternative Investments*, Vol.7, No.4 : 10-21.

Sharpe, F. William. 1992. "Asset Allocation : Management Style and Performance Measurement," *The Journal of Portfolio Management*, (Winter): 7-19.

Tversky, Amos and Daniel Kahneman. 1992. "Advances in Prospect Theory : Cumulative Representation of Uncertainty." *Journal of Risk and Uncertainty*, **5** : 297-323.

Warwick, Ben. 2000. Searching for alpha ; The Quest For Exceptional Investment Performance. John Wiley and Sons.

# INDEX

## D



## E

## F



## G



## H



## I

## P



## Q



## R

## S



## T



## U



## V

## W